A Landscape of War

A Landscape of War

ECOLOGIES OF RESISTANCE AND
SURVIVAL IN SOUTH LEBANON

Munira Khayyat

UNIVERSITY OF CALIFORNIA PRESS

University of California Press
Oakland, California

All photographs are by Munira Khayyat. All illustrations are by Jala Makhzoumi.

Library of Congress Cataloging-in-Publication Data

Names: Khayyat, Munira, 1976– author.
Title: A landscape of war : ecologies of resistance and survival in South Lebanon / Munira Khayyat.
Description: Oakland, California : University of California Press, 2022. | Includes bibliographical references and index.
Identifiers: LCCN 2022013810 (print) | LCCN 2022013811 (ebook) | ISBN 9780520389984 (hardback) | ISBN 9780520389991 (paperback) | ISBN 9780520390003 (ebook)
Subjects: LCSH: Lebanon War, 2006—Environmental aspects. | Lebanon—Social conditions. | Lebanon—History—Civil War, 1975–1990—Environmental aspects.
Classification: LCC HN659.A8 K58 2022 (print) | LCC HN659.A8 (ebook) | DDC 306.095692—dc23/eng/20220629
LC record available at https://lccn.loc.gov/2022013810
LC ebook record available at https://lccn.loc.gov/2022013811

31 30 29 28 27 26 25 24 23 22
10 9 8 7 6 5 4 3 2 1

For Tata and Mama, light and love

I mean, you must take living so seriously
that even at seventy, for example, you'll plant olive trees—
and not for your children, either,
but because although you fear death you don't believe it,
because living, I mean, weighs heavier.

—Nazim Hikmet, *"On Living"*

Contents

Illustrations

Prelude

Warlight

I have lived with war in one way or another my entire life. During the Lebanese civil war (1975–90), which began the year before I was born, war materialized equally in the fear of death and in the warmth of kinship, love, and care. One cannot parse darkness and light into separate realms, for they belong to the same world. The questions that fire this book are sourced from my experiences of war, the childhood habitat that burst back into my life in 2006, first as experience and then as object of study. I did not set out to study war. To me, war was life, at once too intimate and too removed. I felt I could not hold it, behold it. But with the summer conflagration of 2006, war blasted back into my grasp. Still, the object handled in this book remains different from its better known forms: it is lit from within—the sun setting into the Mediterranean sea, the glowing coals of my grandmother's brazier on cold nights, the buzz and flicker of the neon tube in the kitchen, the reassuring whoosh of gas lanterns coming alive, the clean beams of flashlights slicing the dark, the fragile, flickering fire of candles, colorful tracer bullets arcing through the night sky, graceful flares floating to earth like incandescent jellyfish—glimmers of what I know and have lived of war.

This book sits in an ambiguous ethnographic space. It shows war, a condition dominated and defined by ideologies of hate and technologies of death and misery, as a place where life resolutely tumbles ahead, carries on nevertheless. Processes of care and pathways of destruction are always copresent in war. Any rendering that seeks to stay true to the experience of war as lived cannot reduce war to one or the other.

. . . . .

War narrated from afar, streamlined into standardized, recognizable forms (say as a militarized fight between friend and foe) cannot account for the lushness—and harshness—of lived detail, such as when my grandmother and her neighbors were forced out of their homes by the militia boys, including the younger sons of the shopkeeper from downstairs with whom we used to play among the olives and along the broken wall. My old grandmother, our neighbors, and their children were roughed up by the armed youths and thrown out into the street in the darkness of a terrible night. The building was ransacked—our beloved chatty cockatoo was never seen again—and my grandma and our neighbors from across the landing and the floor below were evacuated by the Red Cross and came to live with us for a spell. What a fun state of affairs! We kids played lots of Atari—*Space Invaders!* Months later, when the Israeli occupation of Saida, our hometown, ended and their militia partisans had been dealt an ugly retribution in that vicious cycle, we accompanied my grandmother back to her beloved home where she had vowed to die (and would die, years later), carrying her up the six floors in a chair because she was too overcome with emotion, and her poor old knees would not carry her (and the elevator was, as usual, broken). Excited, we children swarmed through the open front door: shrapnel and glass and rubble coating the gray marble floor, glittering and crunching underfoot, the dusty rose and olive velvet furniture overturned, a fascinating shell-hole in the balcony floor, a bullet through the gilt-framed portrait of my dead grandfather, a gentle, reserved smile on his lips, as in life. And the crystal chandeliers hanging from the ceiling in the salon presided impassively upon the scene of destruction, shedding giant frozen tears.

This is the world of my childhood. The destruction and disorder were nothing unusual—we often played in the blasted and picked-over ruins of homes—and we were only marginally concerned with the feelings of the adults (who in return thought nothing of our childish presence in war) as we tumbled through the wreckage collecting spent bullets and empty shells.

It wasn't a bad childhood. My childhood world, in many ways a lovely place awash with that magical Mediterranean light and filled with laughter, took place amidst waves of destruction, constantly shifting mortal danger, violence, and tragedy. Bullet-riddled walls, faded signs, long-abandoned businesses, flayed, disintegrating homes still embroidered with clingy shreds of care—a picture on the last standing wall, flowery curtains framing shattered windows, plants on balconies gone wild and then relentlessly scorched by the sun year after year, empty birdcages. Endless traffic jams at innumerable checkpoints manned by Lebanese militiamen, Israeli occupiers, US Marines, multinational peacekeepers, the Syrian Army. Kidnappings, assassinations, massacres. Sticky toffees wrapped in golden paper, mismatched felt *pantoufles,* the gluey darkness of nights with no electricity, boiling precious water for baths on the gas stove, rooms piled up to the ceiling with years of accumulated junk, the tightness and tenseness of families and neighbors living under one roof, flickering black-and-white TVs ensnaring Israeli or Cypriot airwaves to watch grainy reruns of American programs, the smell of diesel and kerosene, the shine of melted candles on cold terrazzo floors, tangerine peels on glowing embers, the rhythmic patter of shooting and the thud and boom of bombs willfully imagined away as thunder on stormy nights. Scenes of a childhood in war, a natural habitat of destruction—and of love. Still, the seasons predictably turned, the sun rose behind the gorgeous mountains every morning and then set into our beautiful sea. I was always fascinated by the seamless overlap of the calm cycles of days and seasons and the ragged rhythms of war.

.   .   .   .   .

In 2006, in the summer of my thirtieth year, war returned to life. I was living in Beirut, nurturing an infant and contemplating a (perhaps impossible) dissertation project. I was embroiled in the daily life of a city tangled up in the muted remains of many wars that silently and not so silently lived on. To think about war in such a setting required a move of simultaneous distance and immersion, and the insistent clamor of the everyday I ordinarily inhabited made that hard to do. But the summer war of 2006 brought submerged perceptions, orientations, and sensations back into the light and set me on the path of my dissertation and this book.

One July morning we woke up and there was this empty feeling in the air. The excitement of the 2006 World Cup football championships that had possessed us all for a month was just over, and our daily rhythms and emotional cadences were readjusting to an everyday lacking the anticipation and excitement of the games. It was a Wednesday, one of those mornings when the humid Lebanese summer had really started to boil. Short tempers, honks and shouts from the street, the ever-present drum of construction work near and far, the smell of frying onions and boiled lentils in stairwells, exhaust, street-cats squalling, neighbors on balconies, the persistent growl of generators, and the buzz and drip of AC: summer in Beirut.

Over breakfast, we heard some news blowing in fresh from the South and rippling through the city: Hizbullah had just kidnapped two Israeli soldiers in an ambush along the southern border. It was a newsworthy occurrence to be sure, but just another event in an ongoing story that had been unfolding already for decades with different twists and turns since before I was born, so nothing to worry about, we thought.

We thought wrong. All of us misjudged where this incident would take us—even Hizbullah, it appears. A little later, we watched the first press conference after the kidnapping, with Hassan Nasrallah, the secretary general, projected on a large screen to a roomful of media people. Nasrallah, a familiar personality to us all, displaying his usual charismatic mix of sweet smiles and angry defiance, appeared relaxed and unperturbed as he exchanged friendly banter with some of the journalists in the room. Nasrallah's message was reassuring: soon after the kidnapping that morning, Israel had retaliated forcefully with aerial bombing raids and a few botched incursions across the border, and Nasrallah seemed to think that after this show of force there would be no further military escalation. Instead, he reminded us, this morning's abduction was the first step in the realization of a "true promise," *al wa'ad al sadiq*, he had made to bring back Lebanese and Palestinian prisoners—including remains of fighters and prisoners—being held by Israel. Hizbullah was ready for war, Nasrallah said, but this ambush was not a declaration of war: the abducted Israeli soldiers were to be used as bargaining chips in a forthcoming prisoner exchange. And so it seemed to us all that this was indeed another twist in the ongoing struggle with Israel that defines the coarser and finer grain of life and politics and the parameters of our moral and political landscape in the Middle East. As neither side had played the military escalation card for some time—the last major encounter was the horrible "Operation Grapes of Wrath" in the spring of 1996 (and we barely counted the repeated Israeli aerial attacks against Lebanese infrastructure in 1998 and 1999)— we were easily assured that this event would play out in the sphere of negotiations and political quid pro quo, not war.

By the break of the following dawn, the bombardment that would not cease for thirty-four days had begun (I documented some of those days in a "war diary"; see Khayyat 2006). With the bombing of Beirut airport we were instantly trapped in another war. I speak for myself, but I sensed it all around: the barely closed containers of wartime—emotional, bodily, temporal, existential modes and orientations that stirred beneath the everyday textures of "postwar" life in Lebanon—burst open and took hold.

The war washed over us, reviving the war-beings in us, reminding us of its rhythms, readjusting our existential parameters, revitalizing our resistant networks of care and survival. And then it receded. But like any low tide, it left in its wake things usually concealed from view. The 2006 war brought back into the light the lived thickness war, the experience that defined my childhood, the object I sought to grasp in theory. War to me is an intimate object. The 2006 war provided the opening necessary to conduct ethnographic fieldwork in a fresh battlefield at a moment when my sensorium and social world had been immersed in an unexpected return to war. This book began in this opening, this moment of creative destruction. Warlight shone.

Acknowledgments

This is a book about resistant life in impossible worlds, so it is perhaps fitting that it finally came together in utterly impossible times: through the tragic decline of my parents, the bottomless pit of misery that is my homeland, and many other less reportable challenges, dramas, and unravelings. Despite its many shortcomings, it is a work that I am modestly content with as I feel it says what I have long wanted to say. Its many imperfections (utterly my own!) haunt me, yet it is time to let it go. I would have never completed this impossible task but for the kindness, care, support, and brilliance of so many beautiful people. To those of you named here, please accept my most loving gratitude and endless appreciation. To those of you unintentionally left out, please forgive me, for the road has indeed been long—in time as well as space.

At the University of Chicago, where this journey began, I encountered the poetry and passion of Michel-Rolph Trouillot, my first and most brilliant and exacting teacher who left us too soon; he is with me every time I ask a "burning question." At Chicago, Saba Mahmood, Elizabeth Povinelli, Arjun Appadurai, Jean Comaroff inspired and supported. To my "Systems" comrades, Rob Blunt, Santiago Giraldo, Joe Hankins, Laura Zoë Humphreys, Kelda Jamison, Rocio Magaña, Kabir Tambar, and the "non-aligned nations" gang; also, Toufoul Abou Hodeib, Lori Allen, Diana Bocarejo, Don Fette, Mark Geraghty, Sean Mitchell, Alejandro Paz and of course, the legendary Anne Chi'en.

At Columbia University in the city of New York, I am ever grateful to Brinkley Messick for his warm humanity and constant support through the long years; to Michael Taussig for illumination sacred and profane. Nadia Abu el-Haj, Lila Abu Lughod, and Yael Navaro remain luminous models and mentors. Rashid Khalidi, Mona Khalidi, Tim Mitchell, and especially the one and only Talal Asad: shukran! New York wayfarers: Fadi Bardawil, Anuj Bhuwania, Max Black, Jonathan Bogarín, Jon Carter, Yogesh Chandrani, Ayça Çubukçu, Bethlehem Dejene, Marie-Stéphanie Delamaire, Danielle DiNovelli-Lang, Narges Erami, Lilianne Fan, Felipe Gaitan-Ammann, Daniella Gandolfo, Adriana Garriga-Lopez, Asmara Ghebremichael, Seema Golestaneh, Nadia Guessous, Trisha Gupta, Thushara Hewage, Mythri Jegathesan, Katie Kilroy-Marac, Richard Kernaghan, Nadia Latif, Ashok Mathew, Sofian Merabet, Stuart McLean, Jun Mizukawa, Nada Moumtaz, Eleni Myrivili, Nauman Naqvi, Juan Obarrio, Sergei Oushakine, Sonali Pahwa, Poornima Paidipaty, Valeria Procupez, Angeliki Rouvatsu, Zainab Saleh, Antina von Schnitzler, Christina Sornito-Carter, Anand Vivek Taneja, Antonio Tomas. I am ever grateful to the formidable Joyce Monges and Marilyn Astwood, who always had my back, and to Ellen Cohen and Marcia Stark.

Fieldwork in South Lebanon would never have been as exciting and productive as it was without the companionship and guidance of fellow maquisards Jala Makhzoumi and Rabih Shibli: our southern adventures were truly unforgettable! Jala, you have always been a guiding light and inspiration and this book, which you have illuminated with your beautiful line drawings, is also yours. To my southern family and friends, especially the Awalis and the Issas, your generosity, homes, stories, and steadfast lives light up this book. As I embarked on this research I benefitted from the wisdom and guidance of Riad al-Asa'ad, Mustapha Bazzi, Ahmad Beydoun, Lara Deeb, Timur Göksel, Mona Harb, Howayda al-Harithy, Jaafar al-Husseini, Mona Fawaz, Abdelhalim Fadlallah, Munzir Jabir, Fawwaz Traboulsi, Rami Zurayk. Sami Hermez, Nikolas Kosmatopoulos, and Abed Zaazaa: you are comrades in the field and beyond. I could not have made it through the difficult fieldwork years that encompassed a war or two while caring for a toddler without the life-giving presence of my beloved jara Im Walid, her million cats and rooftop jungle; friends and neighbors in our Kantari habitat, Layla al-Zubaidi and Muzna al-Masri; and Rajaa el-Helou: thank you for your love and care.

In Berlin, I embrace Tucho, our precious squat and home (to many), and to the city (and yoga) that saved me; Khodor Mardini and Eriko Matsuo, Munir and Melina; Steffi and Calle Schultz, Muriel Amal Helow and kids; lovely Antje and formidable Arno Gentzmann; Rachel Volloch. Thank you to Katharina Lange and Juliane Schumacher at the ZMO.

In Beirut, at the American University of Beirut, I thank my dear professors Kamal Salibi, Tarif Khalidi, Abdulrahim Abu Husayn, and Samir Seikaly for inspiring me to scholarship early on. Thank you to Kirsten Scheid and Livia Wick, Sari Hanafi, Jad Melki, Patrick McGreevy, Vijay Prashad, Lisa Hajjar, Jasbir Puar, Omar al-Dewachi, Anaheed Hardan, Waleed Hazbun, Hibah Osman, Sylvain Perdigon, Nisreen Salti, Alan Shihadeh. My students and friends: Ahmad Abu Mohamad, Sara Aridi, Hadi Aridi, Monique Dabbous, Azza Hajjar, Laurel Harig, Emily Johansen, Dana Mazraani, Diana Rishani, May Tamim, Mac Skelton, Annabel Turner, Michael Oghia, Thurayya Zurayk.

In Cairo, at the American University in Cairo, I am ever grateful to my SOAN fam: Soraya Altorki, Ramy Aly, Hanan Sabea, Reem Saad, Helen Rizzo, Ian Morrison, Mona Abaza, Salima Ikram, Nicholas Hopkins, Dina Makram-Ebeid, Yasmine Moataz, Manuel Schwab, Hakem el-Rustom, Nadine Abdallah; and to Tahia Abdelnasser, Ehab Abdelrahman, Jason Beckett, Amina el-Bendary, Ahmad Dallal, Kate Ellis, Pascale Ghazaleh, Camilo Gomez, Parastou Hassouri, Dina Heshmat, Anne Justus, Hanan Kholoussy, Sean Lee, John Meloy, Martina Rieker, Matt Parnell, Mounira Soliman, Emmanuelle Salgues, Sherene Seikaly, Rob Switzer, Steve Urgola. The Maadi crowd: Justin Kolb and Kirsten Fryer, Allison Hodgkins and George Rizkallah, Mohamad al-Ississ and Nora Jarrah, Khaled Mattawa and Reem Gibriel, Mona Selim and Ahmad Kilani, Steve Double and Neena Hwaidak, Byron and Jennifer Skaggs, Irene Strasser and Martin Hege; Ivana Lawrence, Sumaya Holdijk, Inna Javakhadze, and the remarkable Maroun Obeid, life guru; my sweet sisters Jehan Agha, Susie Bilal, and Ericka Gallegher; and to the CAC "pool of salvation" and lifeguards, daily companions in the quest to stay the course. The most important part of my life here, who keep me going even when I sag under the weight of everything, my students, friends, and interlocutors: Lara Aasem, Jihad Abaza, Nayera Abdelrahman, Hagar Adam, Sarah Aly, Nourhan Attalah, Alia Ayman, Tia Aziz, Nader Andrawos, Ebrahim Bahaa-Eldin, Sohayla el-Fakahany, Fatma Fakhry, Zein Hassib, Hatem Hegab, Reem Hatem, Farida Hussein, Fayrouz Ibrahim, Salma Ihab, Doaa Kaddah, Omar Elkafrawy, Hana and Farah Khayry, Farida Lotayef, Amira Mahmoud, Soha Mohsen, Omar Morsy, Aya Sabry, Mostafa El Sadek, Noor Salama, Menna Salama, Alia Shaddad, Sara Shaltout, Laura Stauth, Farida Swelim, Ghosoun Tawfik, Nourine Taha, Walid Zarrad. I am always grateful to Dalia Edris, Lilian Roumy, and Shorouk el-Sayed.

In Princeton: merci to Didier Fassin for bringing me to the Institute for Advanced Study in Princeton, where this book finally took shape. And to the luminous people I met there: Hector Amaya, João Biehl, Marilyn Booth, Beshara Doumani, Ismat Atireh, Denise Brennan, John Borneman, Caroline Bynum, Robin Celikates, Rodrigo Cordero, Hae Yeon Choo, Daniel Aldana Cohen, Anne Claire Defossez, Andreas Eckert, Freeman Dyson, Julia Elyachar, Maggie Hennefeld, Axel Honneth, Murad Idris, Rahel Jaeggi, Mai al-Khamissi, Theresa Krüggler, Rima Majed, Aldo Marchesi, Clara Mattei, Anne McNevin, Dirk Moses, Linh Nguyen Vu, Jennifer Petersen, Sole Pinto, Carolyn Rouse, Joan Scott, Jessica Winegar. Thank you to Donne Petito, Greg Kaytus, Carol Zanca. Munirah Bishop, my one and only name-twin, you made it magic!

As writing progressed I was blessed with the friendship and kindness of Amira Mittermaier, who set me on this path; and Maria José de Abreu, Seda Altug, Can Açiksöz, Amro Ali, Hannah Baumann, Lucas Bessire, Alice von Bieberstein, Zerrin Özlem Biner, Khaldun Bshara, Michael Burawoy, Marisol de la Cadena, Irene Calis, Shannon Lee Dawdy, Danilyn Rutherford, Bridget Guarasci, Gastón Gordillo, Ghassan Hage, Frances Hasso, David Henig, Sintia Issa, Marianne Ferme, Eleana Kim, Laleh Khalili, Kristina Lyons, Kenneth MacLeish, Alia Musallam, Joanne Randa Nucho, Natalie Rothman, Sandra Rozental, Kali Rubaii, Juno Salazar Parreñas, Sophia Stamatopoulou-Robbins, Françoise Vergès, Joseph Viscomi, Zoë Wool, Rihan Yeh, Umut Yildirim. I am grateful to the three generous and insightful reviewers of this book for showing me its promise. To my wonderful editor Kate Marshall, and to Enrique Ochoa-Kaup,

David Sassian, Julie Van Pelt, and the University of California Press: thank you for making this dream real!

The research and writing of this book were supported by the Wenner-Gren Foundation, the Arab Council for the Social Sciences (ACSS), the Institute for Advanced Study in Princeton, the Rachel Carson Center (RCC) in Munich, and the American University in Cairo. At the ACSS, I am grateful to Seteney Shami, Moushira al-Geziri, Farah al-Souri, Hiba Hammoud, Rebecca Daher, Rola Kiladjian. At the RCC: Christof Mauch, Arielle Helmick, Young Rae Choi, Robert Gioelli, Rebecca Kariuki, Kirk Sides, Olesegun Titus, Huiying Ng, Sevgi Sirakova, Tracie Wilson.

And family comes last because they always come first. (Some of) my cats throughout the years and now: Ty, Tinsel, Yama, Zaatar, Bello, Pumpkin, Katyusha, Leo, Fyo, Stella, and Manga. And dogs: dear Shnoodles, Chippy, Leah, and Schwartz. Our crochety parrot Sakko. And our one and only mule, beloved Beauty. Thank you to my soul sisters Mariana Cavalcanti, Daniela Altmanninger, Aspa Plakatonaki, Nour el-Zouhairy. Students, sisters, scholars, and muses Alaa Attiah and Noha Fikry shining lights; and Yuichi Yokoyama, brother, first advisee, and future co-author of "War and Peace." Richard Pelgrim, from student to teacher in the arts of life. Vyjayanthi Rao, Satya Pemmaraju, and Sundar: thanks for all the jazz! My third sister, Julia Choucair Vizoso, and Mahmoud Choucair, for the love of the South. Ali Wick, Dahlia Gubara, Amalia and Shams: comrades in scholarship, life, and hilarity, always. Samar Kanafani, Walid Sadek, Dounya and Nadja, kinship from the source. Smriti Upadhyay, I am so glad you are my friend: nawwarti masr! My big sisters Ghada and Mona Awali; Dunya al-Souri, Ali Jaafar, Dennis and Ana Landicho, Betty Heran held down the fort; Hasnaa Gaber, I truly wouldn't have been able to do any of this without you, and I thank you, dear Zainab, Safwa, and Lou'ay from the bottom of my heart. Tala Ramzi Brack and Yvonne Stead Nasr my sister and my other mother and the entire Nasr clan: you have always been there for me. So much love! Nitzan Shoshan, my dearest brother and other always kept me afloat; Alejandra Leal, Camila and Noa; Efrat and David Shoshan, family across borders and wars. Aunty Bushra, feisty and fun-loving always, reminded me to finish the task at hand; uncle Tahseen, you have always been our rock. Danke liebe Brigitte Wimmen! My father Adnan Khayat, Sidonian and adventurer, taught me to love the South and to always do things differently. I am sorry you did not live to see this book Pop, although you fought so hard. My brothers: Amer, my first friend and competitor and Ghassan, rockstar. My sisters: Rola, inspired artist and adventurer, and Yasmine, who deserves a very special thank you. We proceeded along our academic paths (and motherhood and everything after) in lockstep; no one more than you knew what I was going through and I always turned to you to tell me to carry on. Despite having your own load to carry, you always took time to encourage and to read and comment. I am so very grateful to you for helping me believe in myself. And to my beautiful nieces, Darya, Qamar and Leony, my fierce and feminist daughters, my hope for tomorrow. Heiko Wimmen lived this journey from the very beginning: you know how grateful I am for your calming presence in my life. David Bond, I would not be here without you. This work and my life took on new meaning when I found you again. You read every word a million times, and you reminded me how to laugh and to shine. To our celestial river, this revolution, and the olive trees we will plant when we are seventy. Nessim and Qais, my beautiful boys, marked the passage of time by growing big and bigger than me as I worked on this book: my habibis, you are my joy, my light and my life. And to my beloved mama Fadia Basrawi: you gave me life and taught me love. You always believed in me and although now you are sadly no longer able to recognize it, this achievement is yours. You always said I could do it. Mama, I did it! It is to you, Mama, and to my beloved Tata Munira, Im Bashar, my namesake, first love, and eternal guiding light, that this book is dedicated.

Note on Language and the Text

In this book I use a simplified transliteration system that allows the reader a sense of spoken Lebanese Arabic. I have eliminated most diacritical markings and have tried to use more common/intuitive spellings of names and places. I have transliterated the Arabic to reflect the way it is spoken in Lebanon and South Lebanon, respecting the diversity of local dialect and expression, especially those of South Lebanon. Most translations, unless stated otherwise, are mine. I have changed the names and identifying features of most characters in this book.

Introduction

الشمس تشرق من الجنوب

Ash-shams tashriq min al-janub.
[The sun rises from the South.]

—A leftist call to arms and resistance during the bloody days of
war in the South in the 1970s and 1980s

"RAIN OR SHINE"

Dusk falls in hues of rust and mauve in a borderland hamlet in South
Lebanon, and the family, having completed the tasks of the day, gathers
after the sunset prayer in the cool stone courtyard of their home. The first
star appears overhead. Words, sweet hot tea, and cold grapes from the
vine, still sour, are shared. This July evening at the peak of tobacco season,
we are talking about what everyone talks about when anyone talks about
anything around here: war. Of course, war is never mentioned. Still, it is
present in the persistence of poverty, the absence of sons, the border that
snakes past nearby, the female labor of tobacco, the earth and sky, their
plenitude and limits, blessings and dangers, the sharp, swift rush of time,
its breathless pauses, the risks and pain of love and care, and the unrelent-
ing grip upon anything that proves viable, reliable, resistant, steadfast.
This is how war is lived here, most of the time.

Hajj Bou Sahel and his sweet-faced wife the hajji Im Sahel are the
elders of this household. They center this evening's gathering of daughters, neighbors, and anthropologist—another kind of daughter. Stocky
and strong, Bou Sahel's shock of white hair contrasts brightly with his

1

sun-weathered skin, and one of his eyes has a squint, giving him a perpetually mirthful look that can belie his weighty words. Bou Sahel was
born in this tiny village in 1931, during the French mandate, when the
border between the areas of French and British control freshly separated
the nascent states of Lebanon and Palestine. He was a teenager during the
Palestinian Nakba in May 1948, when thousands of Palestinians, forced
out of their villages by armed Zionists, fled over the hills of Galilee and
into Lebanon. Many Palestinians from neighboring Galilee took refuge
that first summer and fall, and through the winter rains, in the laurel and
olive orchards of the Lebanese border villages awaiting the right moment
to return to their hastily abandoned homes *just there* in Palestine, clutch-
ing their keys. Im Sahel remembers this vividly as the delight of a little girl
with new playmates her own age everywhere. But the Palestinians, too
close to home in South Lebanon, were soon rounded up and sent to refugee camps scattered across the Lebanese coastal cities. They continued to
await their return as wars erupted and raged. They waited through massacres. They waited as many took off to farther shores, refugees once
again. Still they wait.[1]

The hajj and hajji married in the 1960s, when Palestinian guerrillas
roamed the borderland; they had ten children (one died in childhood)
through the '60s and '70s, as the guerrilla war with Israel, with its many
conflagrations, intensified. The family, small children in tow, was displaced from their home during Israel's first land invasion of Lebanon in
1978. They lived in a Red Cross camp in the coastal city of Sur (Tyre) for
a spell and then moved to the outskirts of Beirut, where they, along with
other displaced southerners, built homes on squatted land near the capital's only public park, in the swelling "belt of misery" surrounding the city
(now its southern suburbs, *al-dahiyeh*). A few years later, soon after the
second Israeli invasion (1982), which would become its twenty-two-year
occupation of the borderland (and in the middle of the Lebanese civil
war),[2] Bou Sahel and his family returned to their village. "The first thing I
did when I returned here is to plant fruit trees in my garden," the old hajj
says, pointing to the ground with a hand that now trembles, but with a
defiant lift of his chin. "I planted myself here and never left again!" Like
many, Im and Bou Sahel sent their two older sons out of the occupation

zone well before they came of age to avoid their conscription into Israel's proxy militia, the South Lebanon Army (SLA), which pressed the young men of the 150 occupied Lebanese border villages into its ranks. Their youngest son eventually left for Brazil to work, sending home remittances. Their daughters one by one married and moved to their husbands' homes and villages nearby. Young women who did not marry, like my friends Khawla, Nawal, and Zahra, stayed at home with their aging parents and carried on. The women farmed tobacco, tended to their goats, their olives and vines, some grain, their fruit trees and kitchen gardens, unheroically, stoically resisting the vicissitudes of war by staying—like their fruit trees— rooted through rough seasonal war storms. Bou Sahel says to me:

> First Lebanon was under the Ottomans and then the French, and then when the French left Lebanon became a great place where MEA [the Lebanese national airline] brought passengers from all over the world. Then the Nakba happened and the Palestinians all came here. And Beirut and the South were swimming with money. Those were good days. And then the Palestinians left and Lahd (SLA) came, and again the area was swimming with money and income. But these days are gloomy. These days we are marginal, poor, and no one cares about us. There is no money, everything is expensive, and the municipality is split bickering between political factions who are so taken up with their petty disputes that the village has no water and no electricity and people have to buy water from a nearby Christian village at 30,000 LBP a delivery and in order to watch *Nur* [a popular Turkish soap opera] my daughters have hooked up our TV to a battery.

Bou Sahel is well loved and deeply respected in the village. He is known for being idiosyncratic in his views but always direct, honest, and fair. He shakes his head at my earnest questions and sighs. "*Ya binti*, my daughter," he says to me about the years and years of war, displacement, and occupation that he has lived in this place, "Some things were better and some things were worse." A murmur of muffled protest ruffles the gathering, some respectfully disagreeing with such a measured appraisal of desperate times. A more adversarial, militant stance is generally preferred. But Bou Sahel remains grounded, equanimous, stubborn, brutally honest. Fanning his fingers through the air and knowingly eyeing the heavens, the old hajj describes the ongoing play of life and war as "rain or shine."

RESISTANT ECOLOGIES, OR THE WORLDS
THAT GROW IN WAR

This book is about the worlds that grow in war. It explores the life that goes on in the midst of enduring conflict by examining what I call resistant ecologies: vitalizing, more-than-human relations that persist and make life amidst returning seasons of devastation. In this work, I source a theory of war from the South. Unfolding as a journey through landscape (theorized below), I ask how life is lived in a place of war. South Lebanon[3] is an agricultural borderland that since 1948 is also a battlefield. Life in these parts, for the most part, revolves around tobacco farming, olive cropping, goat herding, and other forms of agriculture that generate subsistence and income and make viable an ongoing presence in place. The southern borderland is also deeply entangled in an ongoing condition of war that cyclically erupts, disrupts, destructs, and (re)constructs and has done so for generations. War in South Lebanon is by now a part of the living environment; it is generative of a kind of life that continues to be lived here.

In a place like South Lebanon, it is impossible to parse war and life; they are copresent, they coexist. In South Lebanon, war's subjects, infrastructures, economies, technologies, geographies, and temporalities coalesce into ecologies of living in an agricultural borderland that is also a battlefield. The processes of cultivation and harvests, the profits as well as the risks involved, are always entangled with the ongoing condition of war, despite intermittent periods of calm. This is not a matter of choice but of survival. In this seasoned battlefield, agricultural cycles and seasons of war are interwoven, enmeshed, and together they shape the lived world: agriculturally based livelihoods premised on known and predictable agricultural seasons and harvests, *mawasim zira'iyi*, are sustained across and through seasons and harvests of war, *mawasim harb*. In South Lebanon, life and war are rooted in the land, and hence landscape, as the environment (Sloterdijk 2009)—medium and substance—of both living and warring, is the portal and method of this inquiry into the life of war. Described by Ingold (1993, 156) as "the world as it is known to those who dwell therein, who inhabit its places and journey along the paths connecting them," landscape attunes us to the ways in which war is lived and the

Figure 1. White horse in a tobacco field in late summer. The tobacco has been denuded of its leaves, and the stalk is crowned by the pale-pink tobacco flower.

living worlds that war creates, without coloring war solely with the brush of violence. I chose the medium of landscape—or perhaps it chose me—for its varied tempos and different textures, its gathering qualities, its fragmented, manifold natures. This heterogeneity is key. Landscape as encountered and unfolded from a "dwelling perspective" (ibid.) allows me to weave together an object of analysis across multiple scales, temporalities, affects, and dimensions and to keep in view a lived—and loved—world. In this book, war is the object, landscape the medium and method. It is hard to press a single narrative into landscape[4] (although perspectival painting tried!), which remains to its dwellers the substance and place of life, the various ecologies that make it in every season, tangles of affective and vitalizing relations. Landscape as medium diversely anchors being and becoming within and across the twin forces of destruction and creation, threading a continuous fiber through seasonal storms, rain and shine. Similarly, war is never a singular story of destruction. For those who

Figure 2. The sacred and the profane: olive trees are eternally rooted amidst the fleeting cash crop of tobacco.

live it, as many do in the Global South, war is also the colorful and complex, contradictory and challenging environment of living.

Like dew upon a stalk of tobacco at dawn, this study condenses into what I call resistant ecologies the vitalizing, more-than-human "survival collectives" (Tsing 2015) that sprout around agricultural (and other) practices sustaining life in frontline villages through seasons of conflict. These "ecologies of practice," a hopeful and open-ended attention to subaltern life and its radical possibilities, I borrow from Isabelle Stengers (2005). In South Lebanon they include ordinary arts such as cultivating the "bitter crop" of tobacco (chapter 3), traipsing with goats through deadly (and delicious!) borderland minefields (chapter 4), enshrining the landscape and honoring its lively spirits (chapter 5), and collaborating with human and other beings across a variety of borders to resist and survive (chapter 6). "Resistant ecologies" are those life-sustaining practices that "become with" (Haraway 2016) and thus—unexpectedly, to northern theory—thrive within, the deadly environments of war. Life and war are *not* ontologically opposed. My focus on life neither normalizes nor romanticizes war. It consciously and pointedly recognizes the way in which war is lived by those with no available exits.

I call these diverse relations ecologies to emphasize their vitality and rootedness, and I describe them as resistant because I theorize their ability to thrive in necropolitical worlds as such. Additionally, I call them resistant to recuperate the relevance and utility of resistance for scholarly theory *and* for a politics of life in South Lebanon and other "unlivable" worlds of the Global South far removed from our metropolitan comfort zones.

MUQAWAMA/RESISTANCE

A song entitled "The Lebanese National Resistance," composed in 1985 by Ziad Rahbani,[5] lists the many ways in which the suffering of those who live in war is summoned and instrumentalized—in songs, in poems, in political speeches—by those at a safe distance from those worlds. A child's plaintive voice sings: "Those who speak today / Are not the ones who have died /The wretched of the earth are always the same." The song, named for the leftist coalition of Lebanese and Palestinians that heroically resisted the (1982–85) Israeli invasion and occupation, reclaims resistance for all those who live/d it. The song, simultaneously a lamentation and a celebration, is a Brechtian (and Fanonian) recognition of the unacceptable gap between history as lived and history as narrated and mobilized to various ends. The song having said this, suddenly closes with these words: "This is not a song / This is simply a salute/ That's all." The song (which is not a song but a salute) points to the place where silence is (Trouillot 2001); it enacts a gesture of respect toward those who have lived resistantly and died resisting. In another song, entitled "Speak Up!" (1981), Marcel Khalife sings: "Our story is not written in History / It is lit up in the *sahrat*, nights, of people with no histories."[6] The song continues: "We aren't waiting for someone to write it! Our story, we will speak it!" It is hopeless to try to wash off the stain of "those who speak today." Instead, I will offer this: This is not a book! It is a salute. It begins and closes in the lit *sahrat* of those who have lived and died in South Lebanon.

Resistance in South Lebanon is not one thing. It is much more than a political ideology belonging to this or that group. In South Lebanon, resistance remains a military reality, but more importantly, resistance is a vital existential orientation to the consuming and annihilating realities of capitalism, nationalism, and war.[7] Locally grown armed resistance in South Lebanon (Kassir 1985; Chomsky 1984) successfully expelled the Israeli occupation (Norton 2000), an unprecedented historical event. But—and this must be spelled out—the ability of life to persist in these farming villages amidst ever-returning gusts of war is also (key to that) resistance. Resistance *is* staying rooted through the thickness of adversity, like Bou Sahel's beloved trees. They famously call it *sumud*.

As Ian Shaw (2016) has pointed out for Vietnam, resistant military capabilities and ordinary village life cannot be disentangled; they are an inextricable social-military ensemble that feed each other (in many ways literally). Sahel, Bou and Im Sahel's eldest son, constantly invokes these genealogies and similarities as he strives to show me how war is ordinarily lived here:

> It is the same here as it was in Vietnam: the farmer who is planting his rice is also carrying his gun. When he finds it is time to use his gun he uses it, and when he finds it is time to continue planting he continues planting. The farmer considers that the planting of rice and the gun are twin weapons. And in South Lebanon it is the same.

Not only do frames of trauma, suffering, and degradation (or their opposite: resilience and endurance) fail to contain the pugnacious multi-species vitalities ensnared in necropolitical materialities that "pulsate" (Lyons 2016) through waves of war, but southern villagers still proudly refer to their continuing presence in place and to their sustainable life-making practices in the face of apocalypse as resistance, *muqawama* (which includes steadfastness or *sumud* as a kind of stubborn being). I refuse to take this from them. Resistance can be politically and analytically subsumed (and too often is) under the mantle of Hizbullah, the "Resistance" and current political and military hegemon, but I think that it should not be. Hizbullah actually draws on home-grown and heterodox genealogies and various vernacular practices of resistance as a vital source of its ongoing social and military fluency and continuing power and salience. As I show in chapter 5, through the long years of war in South Lebanon, armed resistance was taken over and is by now almost entirely dominated, monopolized, instrumentalized, and narrated for political and military purposes and ends by Hizbullah (Norton 2014; Blanford 2011; Saad-Ghorayeb 2002; Qassem 2012), who are known as *the* Resistance, *al-muqawama*. But when summoned by frontline villagers in reference to their lives, resistance, *muqawama*, shakes free of the lofty political signifier and is once again humbly and variously rooted in life ongoing—and oriented toward defiant life. It is existentially and affectively important to many villagers (who are largely a vulnerable demographic of elders, women, children—the rural poor) to own the power, dignity, and praxis of *muqawama* and the hope for a better world that comes with it. Neither politics nor scholarship can take that from them—nor should they. My insistence upon resistance as a meaningful frame and banner for the humble (yet heroic) life of war acknowledges and respects its continued local currency, returns it to its manifold histories and multiple presents, wrests it from both singular political/ideological uses and recuperates it from the wastepaper basket of scholarship.

Like my interlocutors in frontline villages, I am convinced that resistance remains empirically, analytically, and morally illuminating about the ways in which life carries on in the battlegrounds of South Lebanon—and I resistantly hold on to this assertion. Lila Abu Lughod (1990), in her seminal piece "The Romance of Resistance," questions an enduring and dated attachment to a term that may analytically misdiagnose the actual workings of power. Similarly, Sophia Stamatopoulou-Robbins, in *Waste Siege* (2020), suggests that "resistance" does not exactly account for the ordinary ways in which life is cobbled together by Palestinians in Gaza within the toxic environment of the Israeli occupation and endless war. I agree that one must not adhere to a simplistic understanding of resistance as that which stands up to crushing power: I am fully cognizant, as this book will show, of the deep roots of resistance, of the complexity of power, and the many gray zones within which inhabitants of war make lives. In this book, resistance (in South Lebanon today) is both of the following: it is the Resistance/*al-muqawama* (the military resistance, its politics and ideology), and it is the multiple, layered, and deep genealogies of resistance against war and occupation but also poverty, neglect, and oppression.

Resistance is not one or the other but rather both. Yet the resistance I am consciously committed to (as are my friends in South Lebanon) is that which exceeds/escapes all-consuming (and annihilating) processes and systems such as the nation-state, capitalism, and war. Resistance is not a political slogan; it is the grounds (and the very possibility) of life. This understanding of life as resistance applies to more than warzones.

The creative, more-than-human ability to stay alive in such conditions—and not merely despite them—is what I am calling resistance (not resilience or endurance!). War as a lethal environment (like other lethal environments of capitalism and the Anthropocene) must be actively resisted by all of those who live it—and it is. This flips the approach from the depressing and defeatist optics of death and degradation to the hopeful commitment to defiant life against all odds. And in this vital struggle on this doomed planet, humans are by no means alone. Resistance is premised on what I call ecologies (perhaps because my battlefield is a bucolic one), which is another way of saying all kinds of relations, connections, friendships, collaborations: the standing fight to stay alive.[8] By carefully attending to the agency and life-making strategies innovated by all of those who have no choice but to continue to live in blasted and deadly worlds, another theory of life and war rises, from the South.

.   .   .   .   .

Life during the occupation was dreadfully hard, but since they were a household of two elders and their unmarried daughters, Bou Sahel and his family were mostly left alone. They adapted their everyday routines and rhythms to the harsh limitations on life under military occupation: curfews, restriction on movement, random searches, abductions, detentions, torture, roadblocks, military operations, bombardments, and the generalized thuggery or "terror as usual" (Taussig 1992) of military occupation and militia rule. Bou Sahel tells me:

> When the boys were in Beirut we would send them from here semolina and oil from the orchard. We would work me, and the girls and the hajji, and so we stayed. Any work requires effort, *Ayya 'amal baddo jahid*. With *flaha*, ploughing, one ploughs in the freezing and in the cold and the rain to plant the ground, and one harvests in the heat! But we chose this difficult path

because we wanted to continue to live here. And it wasn't only us who stayed! Those who could, stayed.

During the occupation, the family, like many others in the border strip continued to farm tobacco for the Régie Libanaise des Tabacs et Tombacs, the Lebanese state-owned tobacco monopoly. One of the hardest rules to live with during the occupation was the Israelis' strict interdiction on movement from sundown to sunup, because it meant that they—and all the inhabitants of the occupied strip who depended on this cash crop—could no longer harvest tobacco in the cool, damp darkness of dawn.[9] "The Israelis would kill anyone violating their rules. We could not leave the house before sunrise, and so we had to pick tobacco in the blazing heat of day. We got roasted alive! It made our hands bleed! But we did it—we had to," recalls Khawla, the eldest of the unmarried sisters with whom I am close. "Harvesting in daytime was also bad for the tobacco leaves, which immediately wilted in the heat," she adds. What is bad for humans is also bad for their plants, that is clear—but together plants and humans persisted, and in staying collaboratively alive, bitterly resisted.

The battlefields of South Lebanon are the landscapes of everyday living and of livelihood. An ethnography of life and war must approach this matter-of-factly, just as southern villagers do, and with a conscious commitment to carrying on, to *living*, as Nazim Hikmet, the poet whose words open this book reminds us. Sahel says:

> War is something that people have gotten used to and have come to live with and perceive as normal. If you say that Israel is there on the border and that there will be wars every now and then, this is something that has come to be normal here, something like the wind. Say the wind will blow from this direction today or there will be bombing, it is the same thing. It is a consideration that the person here will take, to plant this piece of land rather than the other one in response to the direction of the wind or the bombs.

In illuminating war as a place of life and the active agency of its dwellers in resisting this deadly condition through ordinary arts and acts of living, I source a theory of war from the South. I color war with the brush of life, while retaining a stark, lived understanding of its brutal, deadly intention. As 'Am Dawud, who lives in the shadow of an Israeli outpost in a nearby village, sputtered in exasperation as I kept asking him about the buried mines while he described to me in loving detail how he cared for his beloved olive trees along the borderline: "*Ya binti, al mawt bi rizq al insan!* Daughter, death is in human livelihood![10] That is simply the way it is. *Min il bahr lal Mtulleh, min hon la akher m'ammar allah.* From the sea to Metulla![11] From here to the very end of God's earth! *Khalas,* what can you do?" (In the meanwhile, I have come to share 'Am Dawud's impatience with me.) Far from illustrating a fatalism often ascribed to "passive" peasants, the quintessential subalterns (Scott 1990), or more famously the "weak" (Scott 2000), such "acceptance" of the dimensions of surviving in this place, the "making do" (Certeau 2013) of just continuing to live here demonstrates an active form of life making. This is the everyday "art of doing" (ibid.), the cultivated capacity of ordinary people on the margins of the nation-state, of history (Trouillot 2001), and of the social, the economic, and the political, but too often at the center of violence, to navigate, inhabit, and in this way resist, an always precarious, enduringly lethal terrain that remains the primary place and source of life and living. The risks are known; they are managed, domesticated, inhabited, and thus resisted. War becomes a part of the lived world.

In Sahel's words:

> Now look here at the southern farmer who plants tobacco and olives and wheat and lentils and beans and grapes and figs. If you live in a city and you have a young child you tell it "mama, watch out for cars and don't play with glass or you will get hurt!" Here when we were small and began to go outside to play on our own, to pasture with the goats, or to the tobacco fields, our parents wouldn't tell us to watch out for cars because here there aren't many cars—we ride on donkeys and mules! They would tell us instead: "Watch out you don't step on a mine!" or "Don't go near the border fence or the Israelis will shoot you!" They fed us this with our mother's milk—that this is an enemy who will not spare you. So that is why I say that our understanding of war is an education that we absorb from childhood and thus we come to believe that our fight is a duty for honor and humanity.

DECOLONIZING WAR, ECOLOGIZING WAR

For those who must live in war, resistant life carries on in its midst. I do not want to normalize war here—far from it. While I begin in the presence of war, this is not a naturalizing move: it is an ethnographic and a political one. Again, I must stress: I am not naturalizing war. The way in which I describe how those who live in war inhabit it may *appear* to be naturalizing because I ethnographically depict war as a structure that is generative of lifeworlds. If bombs are like the wind, then considerations must be taken in relation to these realities (wind or bombs) to optimize life within them and in this way resist them. "Naturalizing" war draws our attention to war beyond the event and shows us how war nests within violent structures and infrastructures such as capitalism, nationalism, and empire. We naturalize these latter violent structures all the time – they generate the very worlds we inhabit, and we struggle to make meaningful lives within them and simultaneously to resist them. War is no different. Except that war remains far from the experience of most in the Global North, as it has been outsourced to other, "savage" worlds since the end of the Second World War.

In this book, I want to describe life in war without rendering war as other, an exotic elsewhere, a negative space where the social is suspended and violence and chaos rule. Instead, I grasp the stubbornness of life from within the lethal realities in which it grows, and I argue for an ecological and thus decolonized understanding of lifeworlds of war. To ecologize war is to approach it differently (Guarasci and Kim 2022). When it is wrought from the worlds of those who must live it, war becomes more than militarized destruction viewed from afar: it becomes an environment of living.[12] War targets life and life's vital environments (Sloterdijk 2009). Ecology here refers to sustainable and strong and vitalizing relationships that nurture life (in deadly environments). When one must exist in war, one strives with all relationships and resources available to live. To successfully stay alive is to resist the necropolitics of war (and capital and other modern disasters). In *Out of the Dark Night* (2021), Achille Mbembe defines decolonization as "an active will to community" (2), which he says "is another name for what could be called the *will to life*" (3). Thus to think of life in war as rooted in resistant ecologies is not to romanticize but rather to decolonize, by insisting—counter to more common framings—on the (resistant) *will to life* in war and of that life as a source of a theory of war. Here we shake off war's persistent cloak of death, of exotic otherness, of singular violence, savagery, and barbarity and insist that war must be analyzed and resisted (by those who must live it) like other annihilating processes of capital and modernity.

Experiencing war, its rearrangement of the world, its lethal impact on mortal lives, is a shock to the senses. Yet this shock says more about the researcher's expectations and habituated, normalized sensibilities than it does about those who experience and inhabit cycles and seasons of war, especially over lifetimes. For those who inhabit war, it manifests and is experienced differently. Of course, this is not to say that the event of war is not terrible, or to underplay its vexed and lethal qualities; war is terrible and must always be resisted. The political and intellectual task is to recognize (decolonize, unsavage) war as a process integral to the "normal" workings of capitalism and the nation-state. Our awareness of the violence of war (which, unfortunately, is most apparent us to when it happens to those we see ourselves in) should be grasped as an obscured and removed dimension of our more comfortable, normalized realities. Life on this planet continues to be waged amidst the ongoing violence of war, industry, capitalism, nation-state, and empire. War (like violence) must be placed at the heart of our "peaceful" worlds—and in this way more accurately grasped and more effectively resisted.

In *Life and Words: Violence and the Descent into the Ordinary,* Veena Das (2007) writes:

> In contemplating . . . much recent work on violence, I am struck by the sense voiced by many scholars that, faced with violence, we reach some kind of limit in relation to the capacity to represent. Often this argument is staged through the trope of "horror." We are then invited to consider how human beings could have been capable of such horrific acts on such large scales, as in Rwanda or the former Yugoslavia . . . . It appears to me that we render such acts as shocking and unimaginable only when we have a given picture of how the human subject is to be constructed. Thus these descriptions serve to reaffirm the boundaries between civilized and savage, while allowing our picture of the human subject to remain intact. (79)

The hidden domination of a normalized (and legally recognized) human subject centered on the experience of the privileged and the hegemonic—which we shorthand and bundle into the "West" or the "Global North"—obscures the reality of the many who live in war. Too often, war is narrated from its other (imperial) end (Wool 2015; Stone 2018; MacLeish 2013).

War is dominated by the accounts of those who wage it (who are the agents of empire more often than not; just think of US wars in Vietnam and Iraq—faceless, nameless millions of Iraqis and Vietnamese are at best irrelevant to but mostly just absent from the dominant narratives). A theory of war must be sourced from where it is lived and not from worlds far removed from the action. We must decolonize our epistemic terrain, adjust our political stakes, source our theory and ground our ethnography and other representational genres in worlds and words that do not comfortably inhabit hegemonic imperial geographies and tropes (Connell 2019). This is a tricky task for those of us in the heart of empire, who write too comfortably from that location,[13] as was recently pointed out by Bulushi, Ghosh, and Tahir (2020). Plus, as important as it is, this is hardly a new realization—calls to decolonize through new ways of thinking and writing in anthropology have been ongoing (Said 1979; Trouillot 1991; Harrison 1997; Cooper and Stoler 1997; Tuhiwai Smith 2012). Yet even as it appears that decolonization is coming into its own and rearranging the intellectual and political terrain (Appadurai 2021; De Sousa Santos 2018; Mignolo 2018), some things, sadly, remain the same. We are still more or less mired in a conceptual and ethnographic topography that is coherent with empire, as was pointed out by Edward Said back in 1989 in the article "Representing the Colonized: Anthropology's Interlocutors": "There is an almost total absence of any reference to American imperial intervention as a factor affecting the theoretical discussion. It will be said that I have connected anthropology and empire too crudely, in too undifferentiated a way; to which I respond by asking how—and I really mean *how*—and when they were separated. I do not know when the event occurred, or if it occurred at all" (214). Clearly, this event still has not occurred. And despite the calls everywhere to decolonize everything—right now!—scholarship remains insidiously beholden to empire, despite its better intentions.

Since the end of the Second World War (with the exceptions of Northern Ireland and the Balkans and now Ukraine) wars have largely been confined to the Global South. Although they are as globalized (and as unequal) as any process in capitalism—and apart from the unwelcome migrants and refugees they generate—militarized conflicts, "hot" wars, have been successfully outsourced to other worlds and hence are not immediately experientially and imaginatively accessible to those of us complacently inhabiting more "cold" or "peaceful" quarters in the Global North.[14] The ways in which this riven reality has shaped war as a conceptual object is profound and has not been sufficiently acknowledged—or adequately corrected. The naturalized fact that wars take place in far off elsewheres determines how war is thought about, researched and written, felt. Writing from worlds where wars actually take place and having lived through actual wars, I want to think and write about war differently. Living and writing and speaking from the Global South, where wars are real life struggles shaping being and time and driven by ongoing imperial and capitalist projects, contests, and interests, I insist that war—as experience, as analytical object—must take its place alongside other more recognized sites of modern, industrial violence and ruin that many beings have little choice but to inhabit and thus contend with as part of their lot on this damaged, dying earth. War is *not* an elsewhere. War is here and now and fellow beings makes lives in war every day.

So with the aim of pushing anthropology (of war) beyond its persistent Northern bias and enduring epistemological trench, I take up Michel-Rolph Trouillot's call for an anthropology (of war) beyond the savage slot. Trouillot (1991) writes, "We owe it to ourselves to ask what remains of anthropology . . . when we remove this slot—not to revitalize disciplinary tradition through cosmetic surgery, but to build both an epistemology and semiology of what anthropologists have done and can do" (39). He continues, "At the very least, anthropologists can show that the Other, here and elsewhere, is indeed a product—symbolic and material—of the same process that created the West. In short, the time is ripe for substantive propositions that aim explicitly at the destruction of the savage slot" (40). This book on war shapes my refusal of anthropology's "savage slot" for the "irreducible historical subjects" (ibid.) of war. War should not be safely relegated to "other" worlds (and conveniently forgotten about until refugees wash up on Northern shores)—war should be grasped as a globalized process—just as capitalism and industry (and now climate change) are. Bulushi, Ghosh, and Tahir (2020) remind us: "Alongside and in relation to the plantation, there is the colony, the reservation, the borderland, and the garrison, among others, each with its specific mechanics, logics, and forms of overwhelming colonial and imperial violence and linked by

Figure 3. With Im Sahel, her granddaughter, and great-granddaughter in the warm embrace of their village home.

systems of racial capitalism, imperialism, and white supremacy." Through loving, engaged ethnography grounded in an active warzone (a familiar place), I want to show that war is a human experience that is continuous and coherent with the worlds we comfortably inhabit—even if these worlds of war appear temporally, spatially, existentially removed from ours. It is politically relevant—especially to those of us researching, writing, *and living* in such worlds—to show that our ethnographic subjects are much more than mere illustrations of our academic arguments and stepping stones in our illustrious careers. Inhabitants of war are fellow beings with whom we share this wretched earth. They are us. Their lives matter.

The object of war that I hold and behold in this book is an ethnographic composite of intimate experience (mine and others) and engaged scholarly labor. By shining light on life in war, I want to explode the boundary between civilized and savage, to decolonize hegemonic understandings of war (and peace!) To decolonize war we must source our theories from war's lived experience and not our untheorized, normalized distance from the killing fields. As Richards (Richards and Helander 2005) writes "The best analytical approach to war as process is through the ethnography of the actual practices of war and peace" (12). Alongside innovative scholarship on violence (Feldman 1991; Das et al. 2000; Scheper-Hughes and Bourgois 2007), the experience of imperial soldiers (Wool 2015; MacLeish 2013; Stone 2018), and the suffering of victims of war (Nordstrom 1997; Gourevitch 2004), we must also pay attention to how those who continue to live in war actively make their lives within it (Lubkemann 2008; Hoffman 2011). When we understand war as a condition emergent from the same social, political, economic, ecological processes that make "our" peaceful worlds, only then can we recognize our shared humanity, our collective vulnerability, and our complicity and begin to grow a collective (decolonized!) politics that can challenge this insidious, unequal ranking of life (Fassin 2009) and humanity (Asad 2003). This is what it is to decolonize in this moment. Decolonizing war has implications for all of us dwelling on a damaged planet amidst swirling, layered violent systems that we are only beginning to recognize as deeply interconnected and existentially threatened and threatening. For those who inhabit it, war is—whether they want it or not—a living environment on our earth today. In such a lifeworld, one always hopes, but one can never be sure that the sun will rise tomorrow. The creative survival strategies that grow in these deadly worlds of war are the resistant ecologies that underwrite life and that grow in all of modernity's wreckages. For a large number of those we share this planet with, who are less fortunate than us, the end of the world is nothing new.

WAR AS OBJECT

In Lebanon, Palestine, Syria, Iraq, Yemen, Somalia, Angola, Mozambique, South Sudan, Sierra Leone, the Congo, Afghanistan, Kashmir, Sri Lanka, Cambodia, Colombia, El Salvador, Northern Ireland, Yugoslavia, Chechnya, and other locales where it spans generations, war is experienced as an enduring condition that makes worlds even as it destroys them—worlds that continue to be lively, if also deadly. Indeed, war must be counterintuitively understood as generative—and not merely destructive—of life. While the violent spectacle of war monopolizes our attention and fuels our imagination, this book understands war beyond the violent event. Recent important work on worlds of war in the region transform war into a more stable and recognizable object: war is illuminated as structure (Hermez 2017) and infrastructure (Nucho 2016; Stamatopoulou-Robbins 2020; Bou Akar 2018); it is embodied and gendered (Aciksoz 2019; Yildirim 2021); it is grasped through the lens of public health and governmentality (Al-Dewachi 2017), understood through the materiality and logistics of capital and globalized trade (Khalili 2020), and sensed through nonhumans (Navaro et al. 2021). The resistant art of living in the world extends itself across the existing, existential terrain, melding the false-binary categories of war and peace. And war—like peace—is ethnographically and analytically graspable (with a little imagination) as a place for life, and not only its destruction. Herein, though, lies the paradox that feeds the qualifier *resistant*: if modern warfare is understood as targeting the environment of life, and when life insists on thwarting that purpose by finding ways to carry on within lethal environments, then that life—the relationships it is premised upon—is resistant.

Sourced from my experience of life in war, drawing upon years of fieldwork and friendship in the enduring warzone of South Lebanon, and building on recent studies of war from the region, I approach war as a habitable place not because it is a desirable or a "natural" habitat, but because for those who live in it, it has to be (a habitable place). I demonstrate how war, a key dimension and driver of capitalist industrial modernity (Sloterdijk 2009; Bonneuil and Fressoz 2017; Grove 2019; Bond 2022), is lived—and in this way (often bitterly) resisted—by those who do not have available alternatives or easy exits. In the following chapters, this book turns to the lived detail of this observation by considering war as a living environment. By insisting on war as a lived environment I foreground the vital dimensions of worlds of war—humanizing them—while still recognizing war as violent event and force of destruction. The copresence of forces of destruction and creation generates the peculiarities of life in war (but also elsewhere). In a place like South Lebanon, where a condition of war has simmered and exploded across generations now, impacting life and land even in times of calm, it is only fitting that war is analytically and ethnographically treated as continuous with life. It is lived that way in the (Global) South.

Because of its spectacular qualities, violence in its destructive capacities most often takes center stage in accounts of war. In such framings, violence becomes the dominant frame of analysis, coloring all else: agency and action, subjectivity, space and time. Indeed, as Nordstrom, an ethnographer of the war in Mozambique argues, "it is in the act of violence . . . that the definition of war is to be found" (Nordstrom 1997). Violence has—to some—come to saturate war's very definition, to exhaust its essence, to constitute its very nature. To Nordstrom the very presence of violence entails a qualitative transformation, a dismembering or an "unmaking" of the world. She writes: "war is about existing in a world suddenly divested of lights. It is about a type of violence that spills out across the country and into the daily lives of people to undermine the world as they know it. A violence that, in severing people from their traditions and their futures, severs them from their lives. It hits at the heart of perception and existence" (132). War, according to Nordstrom and others, negates the possibility of life, of being. I disagree with this rendering. War, like life, is full of light (and not only darkness).

Foregrounding violence gives us a picture of war that is dominated, driven, saturated by "violent things," argues Lubkemann (2008).[15] "Processes (such as war) that are so implicitly and interreferentially intertwined with violence tend to be discursively constituted as analytical objects of a particular sort. Violence is not only highlighted as their central feature, but the analytical framing itself is more often than not imperceptibly altered so that the object considered seems to coincide only with that part of itself that is violent" (10). Furthermore, the violence-riveted gaze on war not only highlights "the most acute, outrageous manifestations of violence" but also illuminates "only certain capacities of violence, most notably its capacity to unmake and undo—to hyperactively disorder, disorganize and destabilize—with little if any reference to other possible effects" (11). I do not want to lose sight of violence of course, but like Lubkemann I do not want to see everything through its fractured prism. What about the many other processes that necessarily, ordinarily continue throughout wartime, such as cultivating, nurturing, learning, loving, living? In such framings, they are subsumed, effaced, overwritten by the fixation upon violence that organizes all else around it, an attention that reduces vibrant lifeworlds in all their complexity, color, and confusion to violence-driven monocultures that Nordstrom ropes, undifferentiated, into "warzone cultures" (1997). Not only is the emergence and unfolding of war as a historical process and occurrence denied when it is perceived as a primarily violent event, but also, in collapsing war into a violent essence, many other processes and happenings that constitute life in war are not given sufficient analytical attention or ethnographic place to breathe. This diminishes our ability to relate to lives lived in such unlivable quarters. When violence is perceived as the prime characteristic of war, it saturates everything. For example, it comes to define the warscape, and so all we see in terms of actors on the war-stage are either perpetrators of violence or victims of violence, and the observer inevitably takes on the role of assigning clear moral roles for these human players. Yet when other than violent things are considered, and other than human beings (Kohn 2013) are allowed into the limelight of theory, new, unexpected, and eclectic formations and more historicized, nuanced, grounded, and complex (and relatable!) living landscapes (of war) materialize. In chapter 5 I tell the story of Jihad, who did not let war or occupation (or liberation!) stand in the way of his pursuit of a living in his borderland village. Presently running a busy building-supplies and contracting business, Jihad's jolly adaptability and brazen opportunism amidst changing political circumstances is frowned upon by many as indicating a lack of moral integrity, but that doesn't bother him much, and neither does it adversely impact his life. Quite the contrary! He embraces his contradictions with gusto and a belly laugh and carries on. Jihad loves to regale me (and others) with his provocative ideas and opinions to get a rise out of his listeners. It is from him (and the mutterings of those around him) that I also learned to embrace the contradictions, inconsistencies, ambiguities, and many shades of gray that color the everyday choices and worlds of those who strive to survive in morally charged and existentially challenging environments such as war. Attending to life in its fullness within war opens up a more vibrant, recognizable scene than one in which all we see is bruised and cracked by the destructive handiwork of violence.

Equating war with violence as event precludes an analytical grasp of its more prosaic and structural dimensions. When we think of war in terms of continuity rather than rupture, tracing ongoing, substantive relations rather than their definitive rending or dissolution, we can then reconcile an understanding of life in war with life in places *not* "at war," where the social is seen to tumble along uninterrupted. We must recognize war as one site among others of modernity's ruinous processes. We see war as violent because of the way in which we are normatively conditioned to see certain kinds of violence (Scheper-Hughes and Bourgois 2007). We mostly do not see the violence in normalized violent processes (theorized as structural violence; Farmer 2004). But war, as an exotic (nonnormative for the Global North after the Second World War), dramatic form of violence is easy for us to see, less so what goes into its waging. The inhabitants of war struggle to make lives in conditions made unlivable by nationalist, capitalist, imperialist, classist, racist, sexist projects. Theirs are not so very unlike the everyday struggles of those who strive to live with hope and dignity amidst the ongoing (largely normalized) violence of industrial modernity and its resulting, ongoing wreckages.

War is never an easy condition to inhabit, yet it cannot be theorized as merely destructive; it contains many gray zones (Levi 1989). War may disorder and disrupt, but it unfolds within lived and livable worlds. To those who live in the midst of war, its dimensions become the dimensions of their everyday worlds and are navigated, resisted, lived as such. This is ethnographically significant. As Lubkemann (2008) writes, "Anthropologists who work in the growing number of societies in which armed conflicts span entire lifetimes, need to trace the unfolding of social relations and cultural expression through the social condition of war, rather than treating it as a period in which social process is suspended" (24). To think of war in this way places it upon a continuum with "peace" (the "peace" that at the end of the Second World War became the default position of the Global North and of theory), to which it is most commonly opposed, which pushes war's ethnographic and analytical framing into the realm of the exotic, the exceptional, and the "savage." War and peace should not be conceived of in this way. Rather than apprehending war in negative terms as the chaotic unmaker of worlds, it is more generative to recognize war as a part of this world and in this way apprehensible. This necessarily confuses the clear distinction (and ranking) between war and peace (which is the normative position of theory and privilege) bringing them closer together. With

Richards (Richards and Helander 2005), I urge an ethnographic approach that "stress[es] that war is a social project among other social projects," and I also believe that "we do the ethnography of war best . . . not by imposing a sharp categorical distinction between 'war' and 'peace' but by thinking in terms of a continuum" (5). As Korf, Engeler, and Hagmann (2010) write, "It is . . . difficult to draw a clear line between the social conditions of war versus those of non-war as social actors continue to struggle throughout both conditions in a peace-to-war continuum" (386). Writing about the Troubles in Northern Ireland, Begoña Aretxaga (1997) observes, "Peace and war are not so much two opposed states of being as they are multi-faceted, ambiguous, mutually imbricated areas of struggle (4). And as Achille Mbembe (2002) argues, "Getting beyond a consideration of its empirical aspects . . . the state of war . . . should in fact be conceived of as a general cultural experience that shapes identities, just as the family, the school and other social institutions do" (267).

In South Lebanon, an impoverished margin of a small and disastrously dysfunctional state (Salibi 1988; Fisk 2002; Hirst 2011; Traboulsi 2012; Arsan 2018; Wimmen 2021), war is better grasped as a "deepening of structural violence" (Lubkemann 2008, 37). Structural violence is especially hard to perceive in warzones, where acute violence offers itself up time and again in spectacular formats to the observer. Structural violence experienced as normalized forms of the everyday (Farmer 1996, 2004; Kleinman 2000; Scheper-Hughes 2009) is often overlooked. "However, it is precisely such forms of mundane, unremarkable and routinized structural violence that are the most significant factors in constituting the social condition of war, particularly in prolonged conflicts that span and socialize entire generations," writes Lubkemann (2008, 37). And, like elsewhere, it is the structural forms of violence that inhabitants of wars must contend with on a daily basis to survive. "The most pervasive and perverse effects of acute violence were not necessarily realized in the moment of their performance but through their indirect effects on sociality and subsistence" (38). Indeed, diverse relations of sociality and subsistence are key to survival in war (as in other places), and these are the various ecologies that I ethnographically describe in the perennial warzone of South Lebanon both to compose a picture of war that is about life and to show how war as a lethal condition is vitally inhabited and, in this way, bitterly resisted.

My research was conducted following the 2006 "July War" on Lebanon, in which Israel unleashed the might of its arsenal to destroy and devastate Hizbullah, an enemy that was not differentiated in the eyes of the Israeli war machine from the very landscape of life in South Lebanon (Deeb 2006, HRW 2007). In the wake of this war, I went into the field, following the path of destruction, and surveyed a smashed moonscape where villages once were, crossing makeshift bridges and gingerly navigating crackled and cratered roads to get there. In villages with fresh graves and hidden explosives, recently visited by violent events, I could have easily collected stories of death and devastation and made ready use of frames like trauma or violence. But having grown up in war, I knew that what I was beholding should not be grasped as event but instead approached as structure, environment, landscape, lifeworld (I am not trying to justify war by normalizing it; rather I want to point to the way that war does not merely disrupt but continuously folds into ways of being that have taken shape over long time in these war-seasoned parts). Life was already rebounding in the rubble. In the different chapters of this book, by tracing the various strands of what I call resistant ecologies that grow in worlds of war (and other wreckages), I consider the vitalizing relations or ecologies of practice composing a landscape of war. It is in their configuration, temporalities, forms, and substances that "war" is shown or brought to life in theory and writing—outside of violence and tropes of otherness and across (unexpected) times of calm.

In this book I want to recognize and render war as a place of life: a landscape alive with ecologies that unsettle commonplace oppositions such as war and peace, catastrophe and normalcy, event and structure, destruction and creation. Life is always excessive, and it holds many contradictions. How do we honestly describe this? Ethnography, with its immersive methods and attention to detail, helps us traverse the discrepancy between a dominant understanding of war as unlivable and the experience of war as lived. War is a startlingly unexpected landscape to navigate and one that requires creative energy and gumption to survive. Literature, poetry, memoir, and ethnography are intimate, descriptive, and expressive genres of writing that can breathe life into war's depths and contradictions. My theory of war is contained in the writing. I do not romanticize; I humanize, I vitalize, I recognize. I share relatable scenes, describe familiar characters, draw out details that draw us in without exoticizing to bring war home to those who have not experienced its intensity, brutality, and passions, its sharp, shifting times and breathless fragility.

This is where landscape comes in.

LANDSCAPE AS METHOD

To show the ways in which life and war are entwined in South Lebanon, this book utilizes landscape as method, medium, and material for gathering the diverse and often contradictory aspects and matters of living within a context of ongoing, recurrent war. Landscape has recently come into anthropological purview as enabling multidimensional, more-than-human perspectives. As Tsing, Mathews, and Bubandt (2019) write, "The multidimensional crises of our times call for an anthropology . . . that takes landscape as its starting point and that attunes itself to the structural synchronicities between ecology, capital and the human and more-than-human histories through which uneven landscapes are made and remade" (186). Inspired by the inclusive, more-than-human approaches of landscape theorists (Makhzoumi 1997; Olwig 2008; Wylie 2007; Nash 1996) and cultural geographers (Casey 2001; Jones and Cloke 2002; Tuan 2011; Woodward 2005; Gregory 1998), I came to appreciate the methodological utility of landscape as I wandered in the bucolic battlefield of South Lebanon and sought a way to pull its many strands into a picture that was neither romantic, reductive, nor constricting. "Landscape" honored the complexity, breadth, and depth of this place and of life in general. Not only does landscape generatively hold the tension between contrapuntal forces; it moves us to think structurally—in terms of space and time—about the "event" of war. An admirable picture and an uncomfortable bed, something distant and intimate all at once, powerful image and patchy matter—the analytical and ethnographic potential of landscape lies in the creative tensions it threads between such differences, the colorful, dynamic milieus, practices, and presences that compose it. Landscape as method defines the field of analysis without trapping it in cookie-cutter categories coherent with dominant power. Landscape opens up life as lived to complex description and critical analysis and to a new

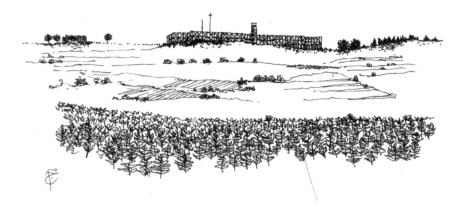

Figure 4. Tobacco exuberantly flourishing in fields over which an Israeli outpost keeps belligerent watch.

understanding of (a planetary) politics beyond what appears as natural, primordial, given. Relational, indeterminate, unfolding, landscape is a methodological hesitation in face of concluding too much. As a method that works with jumbled becomings (Biehl and Locke 2017), content rather than set form, landscape allowed me to ease sideways into the thorny maquis and the lovingly tended, explosive-riddled terrain of my field, war. By placing myself in a landscape alongside (or stumbling behind) its habitual dwellers, I began to make out features defined by what appear as patterns, practices, tendencies, textures, rhythms, proclivities, loves, edibles, interdictions, imaginaries, desires, fears. These made themselves apparent to me in time. They gave life to the peculiarities of this place, composing it.

Agriculturally based living is rooted in the land; dependent on the seasons and local networks and long traditions of practice, knowledge, care, conventions, and trust; defined by cyclical rhythms; in tune with the seasons and geography. Guerrilla war (Ho and Bello 2007; Nkrumah 2015, Mao 2000, Guevara 2013) is also dependent on the physical terrain and upon local networks and traditions of practice and intimate knowledge, while at the same time driven by the element of surprise, shock, sudden shifts, ruptures, and obstructions. To weave diverse relationships and variable tempos into a partially legible scene, landscape allows me to access, observe, collect and examine the peculiar synergy of life and war here.

Embodied and unfolded—grounded—in dwelling practices, landscape allows me to ethnographically grasp war's continuing presence in the warp and weft of living after conflict has (for now) abated. When one approaches the South Lebanon landscape from the perspective of dwelling, one enters an existential realm akin to an impressionist painting where edges and colors and textures blend and blur, or better, a place (and moral space) akin to what Primo Levi (1989) has called the "gray zone," where actors and morals, oppressor and oppressed, friends and enemies, humans and nonhumans take on ambiguous roles and new colors in a space of intensified power conduits—a charged nervous system (Taussig 1992). As I show in chapter 6, it is hard to say exactly where one order begins and the other ends, here in a bucolic battlefield at a nation-state's political and physical edge.

And yet despite the entanglement, there is a polarizing undercurrent. Whereas the Israeli military and the fighters on the Lebanese side who these days are Hizbullah (who mostly are but some are not villagers) enroll the landscape in war, effectively transforming it into a battleground, those whose livelihoods are tied up with farming the land (who are and are not separate from those doing the warring) seek in ways available to them to reclaim the landscape as the site and source of continuous living. Battlefield or bucolic countryside? Both, and neither is reducible to the other. Landscape enables, undergirds, structures, and engages the practice and performance of life and war. The combinations, collisions, and collusions of these networks and projects generate interesting configurations: ambiguous yet resistant formations that cannot be easily parsed, judged, attacked, or annihilated. Like the fire-resistant, nay fire-dependent (Kadmon 1999; Malkinson 2011), scrub maquis that coats the terrain (Tomaselli 1977; Carmel and Zev 2003), this Mediterranean landscape[16] and ecosystem is an earthly expression of these flows, rhythms, practices (Makhzoumi 1997). Shaped by and adapted to pastoral and farming practices and to recurrent conflagrations (like summer and autumn wildfires)—even dependent on them—the evergreen sclerophyllous and phrygana ecosystems also known as maquis shrubland that cover the southern hills can thus be seen as responsive to brushfires, like as to phosphorous and napalm: resistant ecologies premised upon—and arguably revitalized by—powerful forces of destruction.

In "The Temporality of the Landscape" (1993), Tim Ingold elaborates a "dwelling perspective," a method that attends to the practical activity of the dweller, and through this attention gathers knowledge about the world. Landscape to Ingold is the tangles of practice, the tactile, affective, resonant materials that the researcher must be fully alive to in the pursuit of knowledge about the world within which she thinks and dwells (and writes). In this book I utilize a dwelling perspective to describe a living landscape of war. Far from a fixed frame (Olwig 2008; Mitchell 2002), I dynamically approach landscape as in-habitation, experience, and embodied practice, and I encounter it in and as the resonant, layered, always becoming, unfolding, unruly sediments of being in this world. Landscape portals usher us into exuberantly more-than-human lifeworlds that are constituted and composed of heterogeneous rhythms, processes, agents, affects, species—human, animal, plant, spirit, stone. Landscape as dwelling embroiders strands of life as lived and felt and narrated; it gathers across fractured spaces and multiple times and offers up new ways of apprehending life and war. Both a picture and all that is in the picture, landscape lends itself to analytical framing but also pulls us into scrubby and uneven and awkward ethnographic experiences and pathways. Landscape as medium and method allowed me to gingerly and honestly enter the thorny terrain of war. The actual and metaphorical paths of most conversations I had with people in frontline villages inevitably led into the landscape, where people, events, and places were located (from biblical times to the present, this world and the spectral—all equally vivid). Certain places in the landscape gather stories (Basso 1996), hold them, and generate them, and it was to those places that I was taken and to which I return time and again, physically and discursively. Ethnographically, I carefully attend to the way the landscape is inhabited, inherited, enacted, related, recounted, cultivated, claimed, consumed, destroyed.

Land, *ard*, is potent material, metaphor, and medium in South Lebanon, both as a source of life, identity, and power and as property, possession. A major player in the history of oppression and dispossession as narrated by subalterns vis-à-vis the big landowners and the state, land and claims to land occupy a prominent place in local discourses and long histories of power struggles and transformations both between imperial projects (Ottoman, British, French) and national ones (Lebanese, Israeli, Palestinian) and between social classes and, of course, neighbors and (perhaps most contentiously!) kin. Land, as it transforms into property, becomes a basis for new social, political, and economic orders; its possession another way of remaking worlds (Mundy and Smith 2007). During my time in the field in the post-2006 era, the borderland (the former occupied strip) was undergoing a cadastral survey for the first time (Khayat 2004).[17] I observed the strategies employed by villagers in (re)claiming land. War-fueled class struggle over the generations, transformed the capacities and capabilities of the peasant-farmers of South Lebanon, and (in many cases) improved their social and political standing; it also aided their struggles to (re)claim land from their long-absent former overlords. But land is not landscape. Landscape is something more.

Many have described landscape's inescapable relationship to power, but landscapes can also be grasped as an eclectic assemblage (a nervous system or labyrinth) (Taussig 1992; Rose 2002) excessive of (singular) power. This ethnography plays out along the limens of two enemy states, in a friction zone (Tsing 2005) of nationalist and capitalist exploitation and extraction and of the present with the past. What follows is an imperfect account of the unexpected life that thrives in a limen or *barzakh* (Pandolfo 1997), "betwixt and between" (Turner 1995), a gray zone. And it is through an appreciation of landscape's multiplicity that I have assembled an account of the South Lebanon borderland (a physical limen and a gray zone) through seasons of war and of relative calm, where the arts of living entwine with those of warring, tightly braided. In this book, practices, affects, narratives, and all kinds of beings and nonbeings (Povinelli 2016) are among the threads I grasp to weave a landscape of everyday living in war, in counterpoint to the heroic and hegemonic edifices offered up to speak in their place.

Far from the perspectival framing device developed in the emergent capitalist/imperialist order of sixteenth-century Europe (Olwig 2008; Cosgrove 1998; Hirsch and O'Hanlon 1995; Buttimer and Seamon 2016; Casey 2002, 2005; Matless 1998) landscape in this book is scattered into dynamic, affective assemblages (Navaro-Yashin 2009). Here, landscape is a verb (Mitchell 2002) contained in the practical arts of living and the more-than-human collaborations that enable life and its perpetuation and that shape ongoing presence and horizons of continuous, resistant hope in a place of always-replenished natural bounty and perennial human-made ruin (Sebald and Bell 2004; Santner 2006). Connecting places ravaged by war with places buckling under industrial, capitalist, extractive, nationalist, imperial, and settler-colonial hubris, landscape is a methodological portal (Mathews 2018) into defiant and ever-radiant life in the disastrous Anthropocene. Landscape as method enables us to think about scales of destruction that are indeterminate and open-ended. It shows us how these cyclically destroyed worlds continue to be inhabited. And in this way resisted. How can one describe the bloody-minded insistence on building and rebuilding, living, and living the best way one can, through wave upon incessant wave of destruction, and those to come? To grasp the sharp ends of fate and bend them into opportunities? To continue to stubbornly care for and cultivate life amidst the ever-present reality of a shattering return to war and certain death? This book offers ethnographic evidence depicting the resistant arts of living in an at once brutal and beautiful, bitter, and beloved landscape of war.

Not usually verbose, Bou Sahel warms to the bubbling energy of this peaceful midsummer eve's gathering. He says to me:

> I have watched on TV how Japan and America or Britain were at war, and when they fought in boats the sea turned red with blood. They had their wars, and then they reached a point when they were done. Now in their countries there is calm. Here, you don't know how things will end, because war is ongoing. There is a sectarian struggle. There is the struggle of capitalism. There is the struggle to power. There isn't a leader who comes to power in Lebanon who cares about the country as a whole. And that is how the story goes. We have gone through a war, through two, three, four. Israel invaded a first time, a second time, a third time, a fourth. Maybe another war will happen, but what will be the result of that war? What more could happen? We continue to live. We have no fear.

Here in South Lebanon, in this bucolic battlefield where we will dwell awhile, war is as generative as it is destructive—a "naturalized" force whose powers and materials and beings have constituted ways of living and of making a living on this sliver of earth. Likewise, dwellers of this embattled borderland have found ways of domesticating war and continue to inhabit and to (re)create their lifeworlds across and through seasons of military destruction. War is creative of subjects, space, and time, embroidered into the tangible and intangible textures of oft-resurrected villages, embodied in the flora and fauna of cultivated fields and wild pastures, embedded in the shapes and stories and spirits of the land. Tracking the unfolding of the ordinary in a landscape of war, moving through home, village, and countryside alongside human and nonhuman dwellers, this book illustrates how life is waged in war and how war is lived as life.

The *sahra*, the ebullient evening gathering, winds down. Goodnights are exchanged and we stand and press our right hands to our hearts in the Islamic gesture of greeting and farewell. The warm, humid night is inky and spattered with stars. Jasmine, in riotous flower, releases its heavenly scent. Many left the South through endless cycles of wars across the decades, but Bou Sahel stayed. Why? I ask him. He doesn't immediately answer. He closes his eyes, breathes in the damp night air and holds the question inside for a heartbeat. Then, opening his eyes, he says brightly: *Walla hayk!* "Just so!" He continues, after a pause: '*Andna karm, 'anda ard wa mnizra' wa mniflah.* "We have an orchard and we have land and we plant and we plough." He opens his gnarled and calloused palm and gestures upwards to the bounty, *rizq,* of God. Then he gathers his shaking hand into a firm fist and with a warm and misty smile says, "The one who has some land, has a path, has a home."

1 A Brief History of War in South Lebanon

The earth has the face of massacre
And the sky rains gray
There remains no branch but pillaged
No face undefiled

—Marcel Khalife, *Ard al Janub* (Land of the South)

What was once Galilee is now divided. The landscape remains a crumpled, thorny stretch of crimson earth hugging a borderline where the highland plateau defining the southern ridge of Lebanese territory tumbles into the lower rolling hills of northern Israel. A hardy Mediterranean maquis, whose scrubby appearance conceals a resistance, this landscape has thrived through rhythms of destruction and regeneration for the better part of a century now. Poetry and songs such as the one above have described these years of suffering and devastation (see Y. Khayyat 2023). This is *janub lubnan* (South Lebanon), *jabal 'amil* and *al-jalil* (Galilee).

Unfurling along a militarized border and mined frontline into rocky elevations crackled with deep and crooked gorges, the borderland is dotted with villages whose dwellings condense along the glittering slip of main road, perch on hilltops, and crouch in valleys. In winter the hamlets are quiet, all but empty; the earth is deep red and the vegetation tender. Pools of rainwater collect in crevasses and hollows and quietly mirror the sky. The cold air is clean and sharp and smells of pine, sage and thyme, red earth, and wood smoke. Spring approaches as the sky takes the water back from the earth, relenting often in passionate, restorative showers. As the world warms, the soil is ploughed in preparation for the planting, exhaling

Figure 5. The southern Lebanese borderline extends from the Mediterranean Sea to the foot of Mount Hermon in Syria, which rises above the occupied Golan Heights.

ancient sighs of loamy breath. Flowering wild meadows offer themselves to foragers and other beings. Summer is tobacco. The "bitter crop" saturates every flat surface from front-yards to cliff-side terraces: its electric color pops out of the ochre and brick palette and draws the topography together in a unity of profit, practice, and purpose. Villagers are yoked to the time-space of tobacco. Outside every household, women and children cluster in pools of shade and rhythmically, endlessly, through the three months of high summer, thread the rubbery, black-blooded leaves for drying. Earlier harvests are strung in geometric rows near homes and on rooftops in a spectrum of green to gold and dangle from ceilings in loops like tinsel. The sweet poison of tobacco dust suffuses all interiors. Olive trees sparkle like blessed silver halos around villages, filling the middle ground between built-up habitation and the bristling border fence. In the *tashareen* (October and November) the laden branches are beaten with sticks to collect the fruit that rains onto burlap sheets spread on the ground, to be pressed for oil or preserved. Tangles of thorns, wild pistachio, thyme, and sage coat the rocky slopes along the borderline, and solitary, often spirited figures of oak, carob, juniper, hawthorn, fig, and laurel trees stalk across the pastureland where flocks of hardy goats are herded from sunrise to sunset. Dovetailing with these pastures and all along the border fence are minefields where the purple grasses grow. Beyond them begin the phalanxes of cypresses along the final border, Israel.[1]

It is hard to get past the romantic, pastoral, rustic, biblical, almost eternal imagery offered up by this bucolic countryside at the very edge of the earth. Yet such idylls have been and are shattered often enough. This place is at once a margin of a troubled and neglectful state where tobacco farmers toil for their miserable upkeep and, since the establishment of the state of Israel in 1948, an enduring geostrategic and very bloody battleground. Since the 1960s the southern borderland has been used by successive groups of fighters as a stronghold. In intimate alliance with the knolls and valleys, natural caves and ancient fortresses,[2] spirits and beasts, and the thick and prickly, ever-regenerating maquis shrubland coating the terrain, guerrillas and resistance fighters have enrolled the earth of South Lebanon in their project and practice. It is their refuge and their weapon.

For a while now, the presence and practice of war has entwined with the thrum of life and the lay of the land, its patterns of vegetation and habitation, its seasonal rhythms. For today, underneath and above and across and through this pastoral pastiche and seemingly idyllic countryside, several military formations continue to flirt, fight, and cohabit: Hizbullah, the Lebanese Army, the United Nations Interim Force in Lebanon (UNIFIL), the United Nations Truce Supervision Organization (UNTSO), and the Israeli Army[3] (there are other, unseen networks, of spies and smugglers and other murky things). The military elements blend into villagers and livestock, fields and orchards, and the rocky maquis. In the earth, especially along the borderline, are planted mines from previous rounds of war and in woodlands and commons nestle unexploded cluster bombs that rained from the sky by the millions, most recently in 2006 but on many other occasions, too. Subterranean battlefields are an open secret in the current phase of battle or preparation for the ever-expected "next round" (Blanford 2007; AP 2011): nature reserves (*hima*) and maquis scrubland (*wa'r*) outside villages are naturalized military spaces; villages are organic barracks and vernacular defensive fortresses and their human population an always ready supply system to "the boys" in the field. War is woven into this fertile countryside, sutured into its natural/ized life-forms: a landscape of war (and of living). This is a bucolic battlefield, a lifeworld strung between the arts of cultivation and the sciences of devastation (not to mention histories of oppression and politics of apocalypse).

A LANDSCAPE OF WAR

The southern borderland was drawn and defined on the ground beginning in 1923 by the imperial powers France and Britain, who created and administered Lebanon and Palestine, respectively, in the wake of the First World War. The area that came to be Lebanon's southern frontier was historically the hinterland of Palestine's coastal cities, and its market towns burgeoned as vital nodes linking Damascus and the Syrian interior to the Mediterranean coast. Networks of trade, governance, and kinship extended throughout the region. When France and Britain defined the border creating the nation-states of Syria, Palestine, and Lebanon, Jabal 'Amil, the South Lebanon borderland was cut off on all sides. From that moment began the modern chapter of South Lebanon as trapped, impoverished periphery (and soon battleground), a period from whence the South's present day geopolitical, social, historical, moral formation and identity is genealogically traced, sourced, narrated (Weiss 2010).

The drawn-out considerations and deliberations concerning where the border would fall, like most border-drawing events, had everything to do with the geopolitical interests of the empires doing the drawing and nothing to do with the concerns and livelihoods, families or fields of the people and lands being drawn upon. As Frederic Hof (1985) puts it in *Galilee Divided: The Israel-Lebanon Frontier, 1916–1984:*

> It is not likely that the British and the French diplomats who partitioned Upper Galilee and the adjoining regions imagined the impact their action would have on the inhabitants of the area. Had they known, it is even less likely that they would have cared. The area was an economic and social backwater, a depressed region populated almost entirely by Arabs (except of

course for those few Jewish settlements around the Hula valley) engaged in subsistence agriculture. It hardly seemed possible that the drawing of an international boundary through such an area would have much of an impact, positive or negative, on anything. (17)

Little did they know! After a tussle between the British and the French to control the territory in a way that would best suit their geopolitical interests, they finally decided upon a border whose passage through the landscape was premised on the presence of the Iraqi oil pipelines (the Tapline) that were evenly distributed along the Lebanese and Palestinian coasts and secondarily on rail networks and water resources (a key concern of the Zionists who were pressuring the British). In 1923, Britain and France signed the Anglo-French agreement defining the borders of their respective mandates, and the French Mandate of Le Grand Liban and the British Mandate of Palestine were simultaneously born.

At first the impact of the new geopolitical reality was not dramatically felt on the ground. The borderline was largely ignored by the locals, who continued dwelling in the new borderland as if there were no such thing as a border. In 1926 the Mandate powers grudgingly accommodated this situation by signing the "Agreement of Good Neighborly Relations," which gave privileges of (controlled) movement to the inhabitants of the Palestine-Lebanon frontier, even as the Mandate powers proceeded to mark on the ground the line separating their territories and, when the occasion arose, to educate the local population about the border's conceptual, political, and physical existence and reality.

This era of border-demarcation is a foundational moment in the current geopolitical-demographic formation of South Lebanon. Hence it often manifests as a beginning point in narratives. Slapstick stories of the era were often recounted to me in the field, especially by the older generation whose lifetimes span this period, and those stories usually involved villagers following the accustomed routes of their lives and livelihoods, only to be pounced upon by British troops on a civilizing mission. Many stories involved border markers being casually moved by locals unsatisfied with their position: "It looked better in my neighbor's field." One story was related to me by a man in Aitarun, a member of a band of brilliant, old communists who only half-jokingly call themselves "the marginalized," *al muhammasheen*. They gather every day in Abu Gebrans's tiny bookshop facing the municipality; they were always more than happy to share their wisdom and many stories with me. Laughing, this man, let's call him Rida, declared that his father, Abu Rida, was South Lebanon's first *shaheed* (martyr), for perishing with the first shot fired across the border in 1948. Before his untimely death and around the time that the British and the French were mapping the shared border of their dominions on the ground, Abu Rida was arrested and taken to a police station in Akka/Acre for a sound, civilizing lecture by disgruntled British officers about the consequences of casually transgressing the newly realized frontier. Abu Rida, a cameleer, was suitably perplexed about what he had done wrong, for he had been apprehended by the unamused *ingleez* (English) at a place he had traversed with no issue his whole life. He could not for the life of him fathom why this "border" had suddenly materialized, let alone why the British would not let him cross it. Abu Rida allegedly told the magistrate, or whoever it was who was impressing upon him the existential and practical dimensions of this new political reality, "Who are you to decide what a border is?" Grabbing a pencil from the desk of the official he continued demonstrating with the pencil on the desk, "You can't simply move a border from here to there the way one can move this pencil from here to there!"

Well, they could and they did. So it was that perhaps because of this encounter and his resistance to the idea of *ajanib*, foreigners, dictating and enforcing unwelcome, unwieldy new earthly and existential realities that when the first shots were fired in May 1948, as Israel declared itself a state on the former land of Palestine and moved on the Lebanese borderland, Abu Rida ran home and collected his ancient blunderbuss (most likely issued by the Ottomans during the First World War) to defend his (national, village) turf. He ran up to the highest hill of the town, beyond which lay what was Palestine only yesterday but no more . . . and was summarily shot dead. This event—and not the comic retelling of this man's encounter with the stuffy British officers that elicited guffaws from listeners— illustrates the powerful repercussions of this border situation upon the newly minted "southerners" and the generations to come. The border was not at all a funny affair. It was a violent and imposed line of power that caused major disruptions across the entire region and would for years to come.

But for a line of power that has caused so much disruption, the curious thing is that this border has never been completely marked on the ground, nor has it been ratified as border by international agreement. This is because the two states that need to agree about this border have been officially at war ever since one of those state's inception. During the 1948 war, Israeli forces entered Lebanon and took control of eighteen border villages, and when they withdrew an "Armistice Demarcation Line" was drawn over the 1923 boundary. In the period between 1949 and 1967, the Israel-Lebanon Mixed Armistice commission (ILMAC) was set up to continue marking the border under the observation of UNTSO. But by the time the 1967 war began and ended, six days and a whole new world later, only twenty-five noncontiguous kilometers of the border had been marked and signed by both sides. Like other things (like the cadaster), this border-marking process was suspended, and it remains so today, despite the fact that the various confrontations and wars that those states have been involved in have left a rainbow of colored lines interpreting the border: the Green Line is the 1948 line; the Purple Line, the ceasefire line at the end of the 1967 war; then there was the Red Line that defined the northern edge of the twenty-two-year Israeli occupation that collapsed in 2000; after which the UN added a Blue Line (that is heavily disputed but will have to do for now) (O'Shea 2004). All these lines have left various traces on the ground and in the lives of communities upon which they were imposed. Until the 1967 war the border had remained more or less porous to civilians and smugglers and other kinds of border beings (like sheep and goats) and largely quiet. Only the wind, butterflies, seeds, bees, and birds continued to cross it unhindered. The UN "actually has a report form referred to as a 'Sheep-rep' or 'Goat rep' because of [their] frequent coordinating role to help shepherds recollect their flocks that transgressed the lines" (Norton 2006). But by the late 1960s the blood-red star of guerrilla warfare was on the rise, and the border was well on its way to becoming a frontline and the borderland a battlefield.

GUERRILLA GENEALOGIES

The inhabitants of this rural front have since 1948 weathered recurring cycles of militarized conflict, including decades of intensive guerrilla warfare and Israeli attacks in the 1960s and 1970s, two major Israeli invasions (Operation Litani in 1978 and Operation Peace for Galilee in 1982), and numerous Israeli aerial bombing campaigns (such as Operation Accountability in 1993 and Operation Grapes of Wrath in 1996). Persistent military violence punctuated a simmering war of attrition between the Israeli Army, their Lebanese proxy militia, the South Lebanon Army (SLA), and the various local guerrilla resistance groups both Palestinian and Lebanese that grew out of and lasted throughout (and beyond) the twenty-two-year (1978–2000) Israeli occupation of the Lebanese borderland and the Lebanese civil war (1975–90). The war with Israel outlived the Palestinian armed struggle in Lebanon (1967–82) and became a local one (Lebanese and southern) with various home-grown resistance groups doggedly fighting the occupation. Along the southern marches of the country, the conflict encompassed repeated Israeli scorched-earth tactics (environmental warfare) targeting the agricultural communities living in the arid but fertile highlands of the border region, as well as other forms of attack, counterattack, aggression, occupation, exploitation, and paranoid military rule that shaped the lifeworlds of the farming communities inhabiting this warzone (Beydoun 1992; Hirst 1999; Mowles 1986; Kassir 1985). This warzone has been at the heart of the geopolitical struggles of the modern Middle East since the inception of the Zionist state of Israel in 1948, and conflict there has repeatedly recalibrated the acrimonious relationship between Israel and the rest of the region. As normalization with Israel, inaugurated in 1978 by Egyptian president Anwar Sadat and Israeli prime minister Menachem Begin with the Camp David Peace Accords between Egypt and Israel, continues to be unevenly imposed upon the Middle East's political terrain, some wars simmer on (and sometimes explode) within, across, and beyond the borders of Israel/Palestine. South Lebanon remains the last live *international* front of this ongoing bloody regional war. South Lebanon is perhaps the only place in the long Arab-Israeli conflict where the mighty Israeli war machine was militarily repudiated and repeatedly humiliated (Khoury 1985). *It is the only place where Israel has unilaterally ended an occupation.* South Lebanon's continuing significance as a live battlefield and geopolitical pressure point remains, and this reality is actively cultivated by the anti-American axis of powers spearheaded by Iran (including Syria and Hizbullah), often referred to as the "Axis of Resistance" (or "Axis of

Evil" depending on the side one is on). South Lebanon is a fertile land-scape of biblical beauty, heavy with history, alive with spirits, and crosscut with layers upon layers of militarized infrastructure and materiel. It is where war resides, it is where war remains.

Fida'iyeen in South Lebanon

With so much attention focused on Hizbullah, who are the present-day hegemon of South Lebanon, other narratives and histories get silenced and subsumed. The period of Palestinian resistance in South Lebanon that gained momentum by the mid-1960s and was finally usurped with the second Israeli invasion of 1982 consecrated the South as battleground. The *fida'iyeen* must be given their due,[4] for their successes and their fail-ures are a critical part of the South's (and Hizbullah's) genealogy, land-scape, story, and sociopolitical formation and present-day reality.

Of course, outside of the historical, demographic and geographic conti-nuity of what is now South Lebanon and what was once Palestine, it was during the Palestinian Nakba, when Palestinians from the Galilee and beyond came streaming over the border to take refuge in Lebanon's closest villages from the armed Zionists "sweeping" them out of the Promised Land (Khleifi and Sivan 2003). Many of southern village elders recall the time when the Palestinians lived among them. As the Nakba took place in late spring (early May), the Palestinians sheltered under the trees in south-ern orchards, or those with relatives, among relatives. Naturally, everyone thought the situation was temporary. Some Palestinians would sneak over the border at night to visit their emptied villages and some remained there (the family of the Palestinian poet Mahmoud Darwish is among those who did so). Days stretched into months, and months became years, and it did not look like they were going back home anytime soon. So in the early 1950s the Lebanese state rounded up the Palestinians living in southern villages and put them into refugee camps, empty lots appended to the large coastal cities, where they (or rather many of their descendants) remain, in sprawling, walled, concrete jungles, in a permanent temporary state, until today (Sayigh 1979, 1993; Khalili 2009; Peteet 2005; D. Allen 2013)

The Catastrophe/Nakba that brought Palestinian refugees to South Lebanon brought the first taste of historical injustice to an as of yet politically unmobilized and residually subaltern Lebanese peasantry. A common cause was transmitted from the displaced *fallaheen* of Palestine to the *fallaheen* of the South Lebanon borderland.[5]

Before they were given carte blanche by the 1969 Cairo Agreement to operate militarily in South Lebanon, the armed Palestinian guerrilla groups needed to tread a delicate warpath. So through the 1960s, Palestinian fighters depended heavily on the sympathy, hospitality, and most crucially the practiced knowledge of the terrain possessed and offered by the local inhabitants of the borderland. The guerrillas recruited local guides who intimately knew the many hidden footpaths into Palestine (that were formerly used for trade and pilgrimage and other networks). With the help of the locals, the fighters sought (following Mao's dictum) to blend like fish into the village waters to escape the Lebanese authorities, who at this stage did not approve (to put it lightly) of armed Palestinians operating along their frontiers. The guerrillas used the villages of the South as organic bases and as inconspicuous places to conceal their weapons. Yet the harsh crackdown of the Lebanese authorities, especially the feared and hated Deuxieme Bureau, the intelligence wing of the Lebanese Army, on the Palestinian militants and their supporters could not be sustained after the Arab defeat of 1967, which gave birth to an Arab Nationalist firestorm that the Palestinian Revolution managed to harness. At this time

> hundreds of Lebanese militants, especially from the South, poured into Fateh training camps to prepare for the next armed struggle against Israeli occupation. From August 1967 until mid-1969 Palestinian armed presence and activities in southern Lebanon grew slowly on stable ground. This was counteracted by many Israeli mass retaliations on towns and villages accused of cooperating with the "terrorists." (Sharif 1978, 15)

By now the Palestinian liberation struggle, or Revolution, *thawra*, had coalesced under the Palestine Liberation Organization (PLO or Fatah) into a powerful and generously funded political movement with massive popular support.[6] And when the PLO was expelled from Jordan after the infamy of 1970's "Black September," there was nowhere to go but Lebanon (Hirst 2011). And thus the Palestinian Revolution entered the disheveled and disempowered landscape of the Lebanese South. Suddenly the poor villagers had a cause. More importantly they had cash flow; suddenly villagers could replace their yokes and ploughshares, their twine and *maybars* with AK 47s and RPGs;[7] suddenly South Lebanon was a strategic geography and was taking on a vital military role with existential significance to the region and reverberations around the world. War had come to stay; it was digging in, making itself at home, growing new worlds. It reconfigured the landscape of the South, transforming it from a disinherited and dispossessed and marginalized place of poverty, oppression, and neglect into one of regional and global power games and international media attention.

Killing Fields

The Cairo Agreement of 1969 sanctioned South Lebanon as battlefield. This agreement, among other things, freed the Palestinian liberation struggle from the persecution of the Lebanese authorities and, most significantly, gave the Palestinian *fida'iyin*/militants use of South Lebanon borderland as base for military missions against Israel. Although this was at best a mere formalization of what already existed on the ground, it gave the Palestinian guerrilla presence in the South unchallenged authority and free rein, a combination that—with the moral sanction that goes hand in hand with revolution, weaponry, machismo (Genet 2003)—encouraged an attitude among the militants such that they came to barely recognize the existence of the lowly peasant-villagers plying their earthly toil upon *their*—the guerrillas'—battleground. Soon the guerrillas established effective control of the border area. The *fida'iyeen* militarily reconfigured the borderland, dividing it into three sectors.[8]

Of course on the ground the Palestinian guerrillas and their local allies did not adhere to these rules; at best they paid them lip service as they spread out across the borderland in varying degrees of visibility and invisibility.[9] The weaving of Palestinian resistance into the daily life and landscape of the South altered it in many ways, giving an economic boost to many languishing towns and impoverished villages and a new military meaning and utility to the landscape. Ideas of social and political empowerment were planted and disseminated among the heretofore disempowered peasantry. During this time many village youths joined the resistance. Many of the highest cadres of Hizbullah today had their first taste of warfare and their first military training among the Palestinians.

As mentioned, southerners at first welcomed Palestinian guerrillas into their midst, providing them with invaluable support, especially in terms of facilitating their blending into the terrain. But the relationship eventually soured, and a crucial local alliance and symbiosis broke down. As Palestinian funds and hubris grew, and as the fighters dug into the South, transforming it into a battlefield (some parts of the borderland started being called "Fatahland"), their consideration for the impoverished and endangered lives of the villagers among whom they were conducting a guerrilla war (and who were also critically enabling this guerrilla war) diminished. Palestinian guerrilla presence came to chafe at the limits of village tolerance as it degraded already difficult lives and exacerbated suffering. If the guerrilla, according to Mao, must move through the people like a fish moves through water, the South Lebanon waters were turning hostile. After September 1970, as guerrilla presence and activity intensified in South Lebanon so too did Israeli attacks (Farhat and Saleh 1978).

The Israeli military began the practice of relentless strikes against the guerrillas operating from southern villages, exacting high death tolls (de Goede 2009). It was an Israeli tactic from early on (and still) to undermine guerrilla activity through attacks on noncombatants. The logic was that this would weaken the incentive of villagers to aid and abet the guerrillas. As the Palestinian guerrillas were also actively contributing to their own diminishing popularity among the Lebanese villagers, this "circular pressure" tactic began to work. The ties—of class, of cause, of Pan-Arabism, of anti-Zionism, of kinship, of political being and agency, social mobility, manliness, money—binding the Palestinians guerrillas to their Lebanese counterparts began to unravel as the violence increased in frequency and intensity. It began to be said that the Palestinians would continue to fight Israel until the last Shi'a (Abukhalil 2001, 90).

Les Miserables: Al-mahrumeen

Augustus Norton (1987) writes:

> The people of the south, including the Shi'a, have given the Palestinian cause more than all the Arabs combined have given it. They have given the cause their land, their children, their security, their orchards—everything but their honor and dignity.

Endless suffering, burning resentment, and the resulting increasing alienation of Shi'a villagers from the Palestinian cause were gathered into "the movement of the disinherited and dispossessed," *harakat al-mahrumeen*,[10] that initially coalesced around the charismatic figure of Musa al-Sadr, an Iranian-born Shi'a imam of Lebanese descent who appeared on the scene in the 1960s. Sadr's initial success and popularity had to do with staking claims for Shi'a presence in Lebanese government and politics, stepping into the role neglected by the hated feudal families,[11] and also, probably most significantly, luring the mobilizing Shi'a, who were drawn into the Palestinian and leftist thrall, militias, and payroll, into a new sect-based political tradition and formation. As Norton argues in *Amal and the Shi'a: Struggle for the Soul of Lebanon* (1987), "Musa al Sadr set out to establish himself as the paramount leader of the Shi'i community, and his arrival could not have been more timely. He did not single-handedly stimulate the community's political consciousness, but he capitalized on the budding politicization of the Shi'a invigorating and rationalizing it" (39).

Sadr drew his rhetoric from the leading thematic tropes of Shi'ism (the followers of Ali, or *ahl al bayt*), its historical and ongoing dispossession at the hands of the power-hungry (Sunni) establishment and the subsequent massacre, suffering, and impoverishment, exile, and dispossession of its followers. Sadr was the first modern-day political figure to give Lebanese Shi'a peasantry and urban poor a personalized political voice that drew upon the potent mixture of their sectarian identity, perceived and real historical oppression, sociopolitical dispossession, and recent militarization. Sadr launched *harakat al mahrumeen*, the movement of the dispossessed, in a massive rally in Baalbek in 1974. With the run-up to the civil war gaining intensity and the increasing militarization of Lebanese politics, Sadr's movement begat a military arm, *afwaj al muqawama al lubnaniyya*, detachments of the Lebanese resistance, better known by its acronym Amal (which in Arabic means "hope"). Amal was the first Shi'a-based resistance movement in South Lebanon, and although its first adherents were trained by Fatah, it soon eclipsed and then overtook the secular-leftist alliance of Palestinians and Lebanese in the borderland and elsewhere (by the time of the second Israeli invasion of 1982, some Amal villages were in a nasty and often petty open war with the leftist-Palestinian guerrillas). The movement gained force and momentum with the beginning of the Lebanese civil war in 1975, when many poor Shi'a were expelled from the Christian areas of Beirut and flocked to the protection of their "own" militia. Norton (1987) sums up this process:

> As the conflict in Lebanon progressed, the Shi'a were increasingly isolated as a community. In the early stages of the civil war, the Shi'a provided the cannon fodder for most of the groups aligned with the PLO. Indeed, as a dispossessed people they were often and aptly described as the natural allies of the Palestinians. However, they increasingly became the communal victims of the Palestinian-Israel war for Palestine-Israel. In a mean dialectical process, the Shi'a found themselves targeted by the Israelis for their geographic propinquity to the *fida'iyin* and viewed with increasing contempt and suspicion by the *fida'iyin*, from whom they attempted to distance themselves. It needs to be stressed that Israel's campaign would not have been nearly as successful had it not been enhanced by the unpopularity of the *fida'iyin*. The [Israeli Army's] intensive campaign, beginning in 1978, served to bring the latent contradictions and tensions to the surface, and the resultant alienation of the Shi'a from the Palestinian resistance served as a fertile context for the growth of an organization, Amal, that promised to fill a most basic need, security. (51)

Be that as it may, in the first phase of the Lebanese civil war Amal remained a relatively weak military presence and political player, as a newcomer to the field of battle and still in the process of wresting its constituency from the feudal lords and the leftist pro-Palestinian parties. As a rubric for the disenfranchised Shi'a in the process of forming a political identity and place for themselves in the Lebanese theater it was robust and well-funded by merchants, the small agrarian middle class, and overseas Shi'a (ibid., 61), but its infrastructure was weak, it was disorganized militarily, and its supporters and adherents were scattered. Yet three occurrences within less than a year invigorated and consolidated the sweep and goals of this movement. These were the first Israeli invasion of March 1978, followed in August of that year by the mysterious disappearance of Musa al Sadr in an official state visit to Libya, and finally the Iranian revolution in January 1979. Within the context of the ongoing civil conflict in Lebanon that was being increasingly waged by sectarian-based militias, Amal's popular support, political strength, and military expertise began to grow. Amal thus formed the first wave of Shi'a resistance in Lebanon, from which the kernel of Hizbullah formed in the bloody crucible of the second

Israeli invasion (1982) and subsequent occupation. Sweeping away the enduring clout of feudal structures across the South and undermining the burgeoning leftist alliance across the borderland, the movement of the dispossessed consolidated a Shi'i social revolution and set the stage for communal politics and military resistance in South Lebanon ever since.

Christian Cadres

The Shi'a were not the only group in the borderland who had developed disaffection for the Palestinian guerrillas and the war games and power politics being played out at their expense and in their villages. In addition to fraying through acts of violence the already tenuous alliance between Shi'a villagers and Palestinian guerrillas, Israel had been making inroads in the deteriorating sectarian situation across the border villages by pandering to the Christians. Playing on the boiling opposition of right-wing Christian forces to Palestinian presence and activity in Lebanon (where a nasty war had been raging around this explosive theme in the capital since 1975), Israel had been courting the South's Christian villagers with a "good fence" policy while simultaneously building up a military force of local allies around a core of Christian Lebanese Army officers (the First Infantry Battalion, stationed in Marjayoun) who had splintered with their men from the army when it disintegrated with the outbreak of the civil war. In addition, many demobilized military men had flocked back to their villages (the Christian border villages had provided many sons to the Lebanese Armed Forces) when the war erupted in Beirut, and they too became the objects of Israel's recruiting drive for a local proxy force to wage their ongoing war against Palestinians and their Lebanese allies. By 1978, Israel's practice of divide and conquer had worked its way into the multisectarian villages of the South, and by then the borderland was divided into a pattern of enemy village enclaves wrought along sectarian lines.

1978

A little after midnight on March 15, 1978, Israel launched "Operation Litani," its first large-scale land invasion of Lebanon. Heralded by barrages of artillery that began just after midnight, armored columns of tanks and around 30,000 Israeli ground troops barreled over the border and into South Lebanon, flattening fields and villages, sweeping terrified human and other beings ahead of them, setting orchards and fields alight as they went. The guerrillas swiftly withdrew to the other side of the Litani River, and it was the sleeping villagers who bore the brunt of this massive military assault.

Sweeping across the landscape without facing insurmountable resistance, the Israelis achieved their stated objective—to flush the Palestinian guerrillas from the borderland and (their hidden objective) establish what they called a "security belt" along the entire border, ten kilometers deep. It was the beginning of spring, and the earth was in the process of being sapped of its winter moisture, and the tender tobacco seedlings were quivering on their stalks; in many fields the planting was still in progress: the red earth was freshly churned and awaiting tobacco, its "bitter crop." Those who worked this land were asleep, to get up before dawn when the dew was heaviest, softening earth and vegetation, and so begin another labor-intensive day of transferring the tobacco shoots to fields. During the seven-day operation around 2,000 people were killed, a quarter of a million were displaced, and around 2,500 homes were completely destroyed across 100 Lebanese villages. Particularly devastated were a small cluster of *bedu* villages. They were wiped from the map and their inhabitants (supposed "militants") were massacred or displaced (Hirst 2011). On March 19, 1978, the UN Security Council passed Resolution 425, which called on "Israel to cease its military action against Lebanese territorial integrity and withdraw *forthwith* its forces from all Lebanese territory" (Nasrallah 1992, emphasis added). It also established "immediately under its authority a United Nations interim force for southern Lebanon for the purpose of confirming the withdrawal of Israeli forces, restoring international peace and security and assisting the government in Lebanon in ensuring the return of its effective authority in the area, the force to be composed of personnel drawn from member states of the United nations" (ibid.).

The "forthwith" would take twenty-two years to be honored, and UNIFIL has been renewing its "interim" status in the border zone every year ever since then. That same day, with the operation supposedly over, the Israelis suddenly broke out of their newly created buffer zone to reach the Litani River, demonstrating their utter disregard for such international resolutions. Finally on June 13, 1978, Israel began its withdrawal. It left behind a ravaged field of battle and, significantly, for the first time a landscape strewn with unexploded cluster bombs, weapons that they would use time and again, reseeding the Southern landscape to target the cultivator, the dweller, the unarmed, and thus enhance the lethality and price of pursuing an ordinary agrarian living on this (coveted) land. As the Israelis withdrew they suddenly stopped ten kilometers from the borderline and turned over the entire swath of borderland to Lebanese Army major Saad Haddad, who led the pro-Israeli militia that would rule what would come to be called "the strip," *al shareet*. Then named the Free Lebanon Army (FLA), this Israeli-allied militia was the precursor of the SLA. Israel then supposedly withdrew, leaving a proxy force in its place to ensure a Palestinian- (and UNFIL-) free "security zone" on seven hundred square kilometers of Lebanese land. In any case the Israelis would soon be back.

Thus began Israel's long and harsh occupation of South Lebanon.

1982: Making Enemies in South Lebanon

Between 1982 and 1985, during its second invasion of Lebanon and subsequent three-year occupation, Israel expanded the border strip to include offensive geography and consolidated it with the establishment of the SLA under the command of General Antoine Lahd. The 1982 invasion, the infamous and terrible "Operation Peace for Galilee" was a long-planned assault (Israel's "chosen war") that set out to exterminate the PLO in Lebanon once and for all (it had other "hidden" goals, such as setting up an allied order in Beirut, which failed) (Schiff and Ya'ari 1985; Laffin 1985; Yermiya 1982; Khalidi 1983; Fisk 2001). This time an invading force of 90,000 Israeli troops, with 1,300 tanks and 1,500 armored carriers, covered by the Israeli air force and navy carpet-bombing humanity into surrender and cities into rubble, ploughed through the country in a three-pronged attack all the way to the gates of Beirut. There the invaders were halted at the Khaldeh junction, on the coast ten kilometers south of Beirut, by a valiant and temporarily effective resistance comprised of Palestinian and leftist militias who had formed themselves into the Joint Forces, a ragtag but determined defensive fighting force. At this point the invading Israelis stalled and regrouped, with some officers taking up residence in the plush homes on the low hills overlooking Khaldeh and Beirut (among them my uncle's villa, where they shot and killed his dogs, our pets, before entering—just as described by the narrator of the animated film of this invasion, *Waltz with Bashir*). From there the Israelis launched the infamous siege of Beirut that many Israelis see as a turning point in Israeli military history (van Creveld 2002). The invaders demanded the "disappearance" of the PLO (Hirst 2011), and after seven weeks of strangulating blockade and a relentless bombing campaign that made the city a living hell, Beirut, exhausted and depleted and in the throes of a full-blown humanitarian disaster, finally gave in. The PLO got out; Ariel Sharon implemented his (hidden agenda) puppet-government plan, which ended with the September 14 assassination of the young Lebanese president-elect Bashir Gemayel, scion of the Phalangist party. The massacre of Sabra and Shatila (September 16–19) soon followed, facilitated and overseen by the Israelis and implemented by the Phalangists and the Lebanese Forces. Around 2,000 Palestinians and other poor souls were brutally killed over three days of carnage (Nassib and Tisdall 1983). The death toll of Operation Peace for Galilee topped 20,000. The absolute number is quite large, but for a country of a mere 2.5 million at the time, it is monstrous.

The 1982 invasion has been called by Israeli military historian Martin van Creveld (2002) Israel's "greatest folly," for in entering the "quagmire" of Lebanon, Israel, through unspeakable acts of violence and destruction, tarnished the "pure" military reputation it had forged in the numerous Arab-Israeli wars. Most crucially though, through this violent invasion and occupation, it created its most formidable foe to date. Israel invaded Lebanon to destroy the PLO and upon defeating it rode a wave of hubris to create another much more dangerous and effective one: Hizbullah.

It was Israel itself that changed the Shiites, which turned rice and flowers into grenades and homemade bombs. Indeed, observers never ceased to marvel at just how thoroughly unnecessarily and counter-productively it managed to achieve this. At bottom their metamorphosis was a completely natural—if initially delayed—response to what Israel had done to them, beginning with the invasion itself. They had not been the specific target of that, but they had nonetheless suffered more than any other community if only because, as inhabitants of the South, they stood directly in its path. Mainly theirs were the villages—nearly 80 percent of them—that were damaged and destroyed, theirs the majority of the 20,000 killed. They formed the overwhelming bulk of yet another great exodus from the South, further swelling the capital's 'belt of misery', and contributing to the fact that in the massacres of Sabra and Shatila, perhaps a quarter of the slain were actually Shiites, not Palestinians. (Hirst 2011)

After the Sabra and Shatila massacre, Multi-National Forces (MNF) took over Beirut, and Israel withdrew in stages, leaving carnage in its wake as the various Lebanese factions went at each other's necks in the ensuing vacuum. The Israelis eventually entrenched themselves in the southern half of Lebanon beginning from Awwali River on the northern entrance of Saida/Sidon (this is when my personal experience of war first came into focus—we would often cross the Israeli checkpoint to visit our grandmother in Saida; we were, like everyone, roughly handled by red-eyed, olive-clad occupiers, stranded for hours, pushed around, taunted, humiliated, made to feel expendable, like animals, threatened). In the vacuum of the PLO's withdrawal and the continuing messy and violent Israeli occupation of the southern half of the country, a context was created for a homegrown Lebanese resistance to come into its own; Norton calls it "making enemies in South Lebanon" because that is in fact what the Israelis did. Overstaying their "welcome" by a stretch, and through their heavy-handed dealings with the southerners, they personally crafted an enemy they are still unable to get the better of.

Thus, among the seasoned militants and resistors already on the scene, a new group made an appearance: Hizbullah, then still known as Islamic Jihad. A core of Iranian-inspired clerics and Amal cadres—among them present-day secretary general of Hizbullah Hassan Nasrallah—who broke with Amal and recombined, taking their followers with them, it was catalyzed in the vortex of rampant violence ("the economy of terror"; Taussig 2004) visited upon Lebanon, and particularly the South, during this invasion. Hizbullah literally burst onto the stage in November 1982, first with an attack on the Israeli occupation headquarters in Sur and then with the October 1983 suicide attacks on the US embassy and the US marines and French soldiers who were part of the MNF "keeping the peace" in Beirut in the wake of the Israeli withdrawal from the capital. The double attack on the barracks near Beirut Airport took the lives of 241 American marines and 58 French troops and ended the presence of the

MNF. As Hirst puts it, "It was an impressive debut for this latecomer among Lebanese militias which would in due course surpass and then long outlive them all" (Hirst 2011). In 1985, for the first time in its military history, Israel unilaterally withdrew from an invaded Arab country under pressure of armed resistance. Norton (1987) writes:

> No other facet of Israel's misadventure in Lebanon is a clearer case of bad judgment and self-defeating policy than Israel's mishandling of the Shi'i population of south Lebanon. . . . Of all the blunders committed by Israel in Lebanon, those committed in south Lebanon were the most unnecessary, the least easily excused by the dumb luck of history, and, perhaps, the most far-ranging in effect. For the first time in the history of the Arab-Israeli conflict, the IDF was defeated, and not by a standing army, but by a loosely organized, poorly equipped resistance force.

I remember watching people celebrating in the streets behind the retreating Israelis. A young girl my age—nine—was dancing and singing behind a line of armored tanks carrying its sullen, expressionless soldiers away.

An Occupied Place: Normalizing the Exception

In 1978 Israel did not withdraw completely but rather ensconced itself in an expanded and improved "buffer zone" (including offensive geography now), the occupied borderland that came to be known as "the strip," *al shareet al hududi al muhtall.* By now the Israeli occupation of the South Lebanon borderland ensnared 1,200 square kilometers, around 10 percent of Lebanese national territory.

> The "zone" . . . stretches from the mist-shrouded foothills of Mount Hermon, with its apples, walnuts, and cherries, through lower-lying olive and tobacco-growing regions, down to the Mediterranean and a lush coastal fringe of oranges and bananas. More than just a ten-kilometer-wide "defensive" buffer zone, it includes a salient, offensive in nature, running north to the mountain resort of Jazzin. It comprises a good 10 percent of the country, with about 150 small towns and villages. Its mix of religious communities— overwhelmingly Shi'ite, but including Sunni Muslims, Druze, Maronite, and other Christian sects—is perhaps even more intricate than in the rest of the country. (Hirst 1999, 6–7)

And no description of the occupied borderland can fail to include its landscape, a key ally to resistance warfare:

> The . . . zone runs for 70 km from Al Bayyadah on the Mediterranean coast, south of the ancient Phoenician port of Tyre, eastwards to the slopes of Israeli-held Mount Hermon, where the borders of Lebanon, Israel and Syria converge. The 2,224 m peak is of exceptional geostrategic value because it provides a commanding position overlooking south Lebanon, the Golan plateau and much of northern Israel and Southern Syria. The eastern border of the security zone abuts the northern end of the occupied Golan Heights. At its deepest point, the zone is 15 km wide. At its western end, a thumb-shaped salient juts northwards to the mountaintop Christian town of Jezzine close to the Awwali River, the northern boundary of south Lebanon. The country is rugged, cleft by ravines and studded with craggy mountains and hills: classic guerrilla terrain. *(Jane's Intelligence Review)*

The Israel-funded and controlled militia formerly known as the FLA had been until 1984 composed of around 3,500 men in six battalion-sized infantry formations, a tank battalion and an artillery battalion. In 1984 Saad Haddad, the FLA commander, died of cancer, and many members of the surrogate military force defected in the wake of the 1985 Israeli Army pullback. This is when Israel restructured, reorganized, and revamped the force under former Lebanese Army major general Antoine Lahd, renaming it the South Lebanon Army (SLA). The SLA ruled the small towns and villages of the borderland, fielding around 2,500 soldiers who were mostly drawn from the villages of the zone —ideally one from every village *beit,* house or family. Some formerly disenfranchised or merely opportunistic souls jumped on the bandwagon to participate in militarized empowerment, and others were forcibly conscripted.

In 1989 two new brigades were formed, with three territorial battalions each (three infantry battalions, two batteries of artillery, and two tank companies). The brigades corresponded to the two regions of the zone, the Western Brigade under the command of Colonel Aql Hashem (a Maronite) and the Eastern Brigade under Druze command. The Western sector (encompassing the Central sector of the Cairo Accords) extends from the coast to Bint Jbeil and is the area that I conducted my fieldwork in. It was the more turbulent sector of the zone, with the largest concentration of Shi'a villages. The military headquarters of the zone was Markaz 17

(Position 17), housed in the former (and today once again) Bint Jbeil hospital. During the occupation it was a terrible place, where many were taken for interrogations, beatings, and detention and imprisonment. This part of the zone is also the heartland of tobacco farming. Its high elevations and lack of irrigation make only rain-fed and dryland crops viable. Geographically it is crinkled with deep valleys and gorges—some of which extend into the Israeli north, facilitating guerrilla warfare (the kidnapping that launched the 2006 July War happened in one of those sharp and deep border valleys). The administrative headquarters of the zone were housed in the former Lebanese Army barracks in Marjayoun, a graceful Christian town on the side of a hill overlooking a wide fertile plain that extends north into the Bekaa and then Syria and south into Israel and beyond. Antoine Lahd, the commander of the SLA, inhabited a stone villa not far from the barracks (which I visited, among other freshly deoccupied places, on the first day of the withdrawal). This sector is mainly Christian and Druze, with a pocket of Sunnis around the Wazzani springs area and the currently disputed Sheba'a farms. Across the fertile and irrigated plain on a low hill right on the border perches the town of Khiam. There the SLA established their infamous Khiam detention center in the building of a French Mandate–era barracks, where the inhabitants of the zone were dragged and imprisoned: men, women, and children. This prison was a place of illegal detention, torture, fear, and terror (Bechara and Levine 2003) and a site of control and power (Khalili 2012) that also generated stories of terror, enhancing the occupation's "economy of terror" (Taussig 2004).

The occupation zone was separate from the rest of Lebanon, with several tightly controlled crossings where people could enter and exit. Only those registered as residents of the villages there were allowed regularly in and out, and even they needed permits that were issued by the SLA administration; the permits, issued and permanently revoked at will, were an insidious mechanism of governance and control. All kind of movement in and out as well as within the zone was severely restricted and monitored.

The Israelis consistently maintained that they were merely overseeing their "security zone" and not directly involved in an occupation, but this conceit did not hold out. It may be true that at first they did not involve themselves in the day-to-day control and governance of the occupation zone—that was the job of the SLA—but they provided the means, more than $32 million a year to cover the $500–$600 average monthly salaries of the SLA soldiers and other sundries of military occupation, and they maintained 1,000–2,000 troops there ensconced in fortified highest-hilltop locations, in particular those where hundreds of years ago the Crusaders had built hardy fortresses that soared above the landscape like Beaufort and Blat. More involved in daily developments in the zone were the various Israeli intelligence agencies that cooperated closely with the intelligence arm of the SLA to keep a heavy lid on the local inhabitants.

The occupation was a paranoid and violent order that harassed its subjects constantly. Monopolizing the skies, the Israelis utilized their technologically advanced arsenal to compose a detailed intelligence picture of the South, and they depended on the SLA to rule the villages as they saw fit. The following passage from *Jane's Intelligence Review* describes the nervous landscape of occupation:

> Despite their overwhelming firepower, SLA and IDF troops fear the South Lebanese bandit country. Villages in the security zone are subject to curfew and most nights are disturbed by artillery and small arms fire as jumpy sentries sound the alarm. In retaliation for attacks, SLA compounds rake nearby villages with small arms fire. IDF artillery fires warning salvoes at or around suspect villages and Cobra helicopter gunships use TOW missiles to destroy buildings used by Hezbollah or other militias.

One could argue that the occupation inherited and slipped into a structure of power in this borderland that did not deviate radically from the patterns of years past, with only a changing of actors: farmers in villages living off the land with some more entwined with the ruling order and some less so and at the mercy of armed men doing the bidding of those in power. People often repeat that there was an atmosphere of pervasive fear, suspicion, and insecurity throughout the hamlets and villages; a situation that was exacerbated the more Hizbullah infiltrated the area with increasingly painful blows against the occupation. During the occupation the tables began to turn in favor of the guerrillas, and the transformations described above became palpable as Hizbullah honed its warcraft and consolidated its social base; it soon gained the upper hand.

Yes, the occupation was a paranoid and violent order, a time of depopulation, expulsions, house demolitions, interrogation, imprisonment, and militia/military rule, but on the other hand, for some it was a time of relative peace and prosperity. For those remaining on a slip of land that had been ceaselessly wracked by multiple forms of violence and warfare for decades, the post-1985 occupation inaugurated a more or less stable framework, a period of relative calm. For those who for whatever reason threw their lot in with the occupiers and those who simply remained in their homes and on their land because they fell outside the snare of the militia and the military in terms of service and suspicion (generally, old men, women, and children), the Israeli occupation was simply another chapter in an ongoing cycle, and they accommodated themselves to it accordingly. Bou Sahel, who remained in his village and in his home throughout the years of occupation, farming tobacco, olives, and grain and consistently practicing a form of resistance by staying, described this play of life and war to me as "rain or shine."

Hizbullah, Hybrid War, and the "Hybrid Collectif"

Hizbullah, the Shi'i militant organization that took shape in the crucible of the deadly 1982 Israeli invasion (Norton 2014; Saad-Ghorayeb 2003; Daher and Randolph 2019),[12] came to perfect and monopolize resistance and guerrilla warfare in the South during the Israeli occupation and beyond. The Israeli occupation of Lebanon was a laboratory where Hizbullah honed its warcraft, transforming into the formidable military adversary it is today. As Norton writes, "the occupation had been a fantastic training ground, during which Hizballah became an incredibly effective fighting force. By the end of the occupation it had managed what is virtually unheard of in guerrilla warfare: it was basically at parity with Israel in terms of casualties: for every Israeli (or allied SLA militiaman) killed, a little more than one Hizballah fighter died. Typically the ratio of guerrilla to conventional army losses is ten to one" (Norton 2006). Because of their technological inferiority to the Israelis, who with their air force command the skies, Hizbullah had to resort to earth-boundedness to succeed in their domestic battleground (see chapter 5). The landscape was their ally, their weapon, their source of strength. Absorbing the lessons of their fighting forebears such as the Palestinian and leftist fighters and groups (who learned from the Viet Cong the ways of successful rural guerrilla warfare with Soviet weapons such as the Kalashnikov and the

Katyusha), the Hizbullah guerrillas, known now as *al-muqawama*, the Resistance, harnessed the landscape, becoming a part of its nature (see Pearson 2008; Gregory 2016; Gordillo 2018). Funded and armed by anti-American powers (such as the USSR and Iran) but shielded, enabled, fed, and sustained by local kinship networks, homegrown ecologies, intimate terrains, natural formations, and supernatural presences, the resistance "melted like salt," as some of my friends in the South describe it, into the landscape and successfully undermined the occupation. Sahel, who fought with the resistance, first as a Communist and now with Hizbullah, put it thus:

> In these rock formations and crevices, if a group of resistance fighters are hiding there, Israeli elite troops, Apache helicopters, and Israeli infantry all wouldn't be able to touch them. Imagine: if in a place with a surface of 100 dunums [10 square kilometers] three soldiers are hiding, one with a rocket launcher, one with a medium machine gun, and one with personal weapons, what are the Israelis going to do? It is like finding a pin in a haystack! This whole area needs just thirty soldiers to militarily tie together the valleys and the plains.

The form of warring that Hizballah developed in the laboratory of South Lebanon over several decades has been dubbed "hybrid" by military scholars (Brun 2010; Bearman 2010; Friedman and Biddle 2011; F. Hoffman 2009, 2007) for the way it combines guerrilla-type tactics with classical battlefield practices. I extend the descriptor *hybrid* to acknowledge the ways in which this style of warring enrolls nonmilitary and nonhuman actors into a resistant, more-than-human assemblage, or what Callon and Law (1997) call a "hybrid collectif." Converging upon this hilly geography are resistant forms of life where the human and nonhuman, the military and the mundane, are deeply entangled, often indistinguishable. It is no secret that agents of war are domestic to the village nexus, as organic to the place (and as implicated in this war game) as the scrubby *maquis* that coats the terrain.[13] As dwellers of frontline villages who make ordinary livings in times of calm, resistance fighters are more than military actors, for many of them live their lives and pursue their livelihoods in the selfsame spaces that they fight for in times of conflict. As Norton (2006) observes, "One of the salient features of the system . . . is that the permanent full-time cadre [is] quite small. During the occupation period it was 450 or 500 men. Today it is probably between 1,000 and 1,200. Basically, it is a reserve system. People undergo periodic training and when they go out on an operation they just close their shops and businesses. It's an accordion and drawing on reserves it can stretch rather large." Exum (2006) also observes that "in contrast to its political wing, Hizballah's military wing is horizontally organized and can be divided into two types of fighters: the so-called "elite" or regular fighters—numbering around 1,000 men and often given advanced weapons training—and the village fighters, whose numbers cannot be estimated." Fighting then, to these fighters, is more than a military career or a dreaded draft. In these wars, it is their very lifeworld that is at stake, their livelihoods, loved ones, livestock, and all. This kind of intimate entanglement makes a formidable enemy, as the US Army realized in Vietnam (Shaw 2016).[14] A fatal misrecognition akin to that of the US in Vietnam took place in Israel's South Lebanon "quagmire": "Hizballah's tenacity in the villages was . . . the biggest surprise of the war . . . . The vast majority of the fighters who defended the villages . . . were not, in fact, regular Hizballah fighters and in some cases were not even members of Hizballah. But they were men . . . who in the words of one Lebanese observer 'were defending their country in the most tangible sense—their shops, their homes, even their trees'" (Exum 2006, 10).

Resistance is staying rooted in a deeply familiar landscape, as Sahel says:

> Now there is something I want to tell you: the resistance won, but one of the main reasons for their victory is *geography!* This terrain is for wars of small groups and guerrilla resistance. This is what breaks the backs of the Israelis and of classical warfare.
>
> The Vietnamese have taught a beautiful lesson to any people who want to be liberated: you dig a hole in the ground and you sit in it and wait. No need to go to the enemy, the enemy will come to you. You stay where you are comfortable. He will oppress and colonize you anyway, but when he comes to you *that* is when you shoot him. The enemy seeks his own annihilation and the Israelis are just like that.

But of course, the Israeli war machine, following the environmental logics of modern warfare, took on the landscape as adversary: attacking the physical terrain, squatting upon hilltops (atop ruins and shrines), uprooting entire forests of pine, pistachio, and ancient olive, burning broad swaths of woodland, mining the red earth south of the borderline, and maintaining vast areas as no-entry zones. The landscape tells the story. The mundane lives and too-often difficult loves of people here are waged and fought within this landscape. The diverse and entangled relations that nurture, root, and vitalize the ongoing fight for life in a repeatedly scorched landscape of war are the resistant ecologies that I examine in this book.

Liberation and "Interregnum"

Despite Israel's scorched-earth tactics and increasingly desperate measures, in time the resistance got too good at playing within the rules, and so Israel played without them by launching two major assaults on the unoccupied rest of the South and Lebanon in "Operation Accountability," July 1993 (140 dead, 350,000 displaced), and "Operation Grapes of Wrath," April 1996 (165 dead, 500,000 displaced). These two operations inaugurated a shift in Israeli war-practice from ground war to air war. It was a vicious cycle: control of the skies, flaunting the rules of war, and clamping down ever more violently on the inhabitants of the zone while the resistance was only getting better at its game. Israel's rule wavered; paranoia and insecurity increased.

After twenty-two long years, the Israeli occupation of South Lebanon collapsed over the course of two days (Norton 2000). The end was a long time in the making, but it came suddenly and swiftly, beginning on May 21, 2000, and ending at dawn on May 24 (and I was there from beginning to end). The Israeli Army withdrew unilaterally from the borderland they had ruled—violently and expensively—for more than two decades. In the end, no political deals were won by anyone, and in the final run to the border, the great Israeli war machine could barely cover its rear as the jubilant crowds rushed in. Many proclaimed it as an ignominious rout. Yet most Israelis were relieved to be out. And surely Hizbullah, who (rightfully) claimed the withdrawal as their greatest victory to date and proclaimed themselves as the sole authors of the liberation (*tahrir*) of the long-suffering South, rejoiced (along with the rest of the country)—and moved in, consolidating their hold on the borderland and the majority of its population.

The end of the Israeli occupation had been heralded and foretold for some time, ever since Ehud Barak was voted into office as Israeli prime minister and found himself having to honor his campaign promise to leave Lebanon by July 2000. The promise created a nervous arc of anticipation that resulted in a spiral of insecurity and fear, especially among the SLA foot soldiers (who by the time the occupation ended were 70 percent Shi'a villagers), who were not sure that their Israeli masters had any secure future in mind for them (more precisely: if they had them in mind at all). The existential core of the occupation had been doubly shaken in the past year or so, first with Hizbullah's targeted (and filmed) assassination of Brigadier General Erez Gerstein, commander of the Israeli Army in South Lebanon, whose armor-plated Mercedes was blown up by a roadside bomb near Hasbaya in the eastern sector on February 28, 1999, and the assassination (also filmed) less than a year later (January 30, 2000) of the commander of the SLA Western Brigade, Aql Hashem, outside his home in Dibl in the central sector of the zone. Defections and surrenders began to eat at the rank and file of the forcibly recruited and mercenary militia, and morale continued to plummet as tensions rose.

Seeing that their network of control was fraying, by the spring of 2000 the Israelis began evacuating forward positions and heavy weaponry along the northern border of the strip (having already left the Jezzine salient in the hills overlooking Sidon the year before); these moves only added fuel to the fire of collapse that had already taken over the occupation. On May 21, 2000, an entire brigade of SLA soldiers in the central sector surrendered, and by the next day villagers from Qantara along the northern edge of the central sector simply walked past the UNIFIL roadblock, across the border separating Lebanon proper from the occupied strip, and back to their long-lost homes, paving the way for Hizbullah and the rest of the country to swarm in. An inexorable collapse was at hand. Israel scrambled to get its troops over the border as they destroyed their fortified positions and arms depots behind them. Full-blown panic took hold of the SLA, with entire families fleeing helter-skelter across the border into Israel. The wildly discarded paraphernalia of this hasty retreat was visible everywhere by the time I entered the liberated strip early the next day, the first dawn of a free South Lebanon. I witnessed this and recount some of it below.

The border fence at the Fatima Gate near the village of Kfar Kila was strewn with abandoned cars, luggage, and especially clothes, a rainbow of colors festooned the barbed wire fence separating and containing the enemy territories like disembodied bunting. It was an unnerving sight, the suspended clothes hung like colorful effigies, deflated scarecrows, mutely expressing the terror spurring the chaotic, headlong rush across the border by the no-longer-needed and now unwelcome SLA rank and file and their terrified families. Full-blown celebration gripped the rest of Lebanon, with people rushing South in a spontaneous "return" (for many, like me, it was their first time). Civilians streamed across the zone, with crowds rushing to the abandoned prison in Khiam accompanied by television crews who documented live the freeing of the prisoners by their families, bare hands tearing at stone walls and metal grilles. Frenzied reunions. It was an absolutely astonishing historical moment that I consider myself lucky to have been witness to.

The moment of collapse was also a moment of intense uncertainty, for no one knew how it would unfold, whether there would be spontaneous acts of retribution, looting and pillaging, and other things expected in the wake of such precipitous crumbling of entrenched power. But none of that happened (much to the chagrin of the media who had gathered like sharks at the smell of blood). The return of the borderland to Lebanon after twenty-two years of occupation, of the southerners to their villages, although spontaneous, chaotic and somewhat uncontrollable, was something that Hizbullah appeared already ready for. Among the effervescing celebrations, rice and rose-petals and ululations, the strewn-about, abject matter of hastily retreating troops, some wary villagers lurked along the walls of their village squares and took in the advancing crowds with wide, scared eyes. They were starkly counterposed to the hysterically joyous borderline encounters of long-separated families (both *bedu* and Palestinians long imprisoned in nation-states not their own and at war), jubilantly pledging sons and daughters in betrothal as if that act would bring them back together across the cruel political divisions of time and space. Hizbullah quietly inserted itself in the wreckage of the occupation (as a matter of fact, they were already there by the time of the collapse), spreading out across the landscape, securing infrastructure and materiel, rounding up and handing over surrendered, disoriented, disheveled SLA soldiers to the Lebanese authorities, marshalling the crowds, policing the border, and consolidating their grip on the(ir) borderland.

Hizbullah[15] remain ascendant in South Lebanon politically and militarily, everywhere and nowhere, everyone and no one: through the July 2000 deployment of UNIFIL to the borderline (in fulfillment of the twenty-two-year-old Resolution 425) and the post-2006 beefed up UNIFIL presence, as well as the belated Lebanese Army deployment to the border after the 2006 war (today the border zone is patrolled by 11,000 UNIFIL troops and 15,000 Lebanese Armed Forces soldiers who monitor compliance with the post-2006 UN Resolution 1701 forbidding "any armed personnel, assets and weapons" in the frontier area south of the Litani). South Lebanon is among the most densely-militarized strips of earth on this planet.

Six years of dead calm ensued in the former occupied strip in the wake of its sudden liberation.[16] At first people triumphantly swarmed back to their long-lost villages with dreams of reclaiming a lost and long yearned-for way of life, but they quickly realized that those dreams had nothing to do with reality. The borderland had altered dramatically in the intervening years of constant war and heavy-handed occupation and could not be miraculously reconnected, revived, or restored: for twenty-two years, the vital dimensions of the borderland were finely attuned to the reality of the unresolved and ongoing war situation that had been suddenly removed ten kilometers to the south. The persistent war condition, now into its sixth decade, had kept this raucously reclaimed sliver of Lebanese sovereign territory nervously apart from the rest of the nation, even after liberation. South Lebanon continues to occupy a liminal space and "gray zone" in time, space, politics, and practice (as I describe in chapter 6). Aside from the droves of 'umala, collaborators, who had escaped over the border when the occupation collapsed and uncomfortably burdened their former masters with their unwelcome presence, there remained everybody who had lived under Israeli and SLA rule, making-do, "surviving." How did they fit into the new environment? (Jihad, my friend from chapter 6, embodies this awkward reality; he inhabits its contradictions audaciously.) A new order—that of Hizbullah—took over the border-strip, and there were (re)arrangements to be made. Hizbullah wasted no time; they consolidated their hold on the borderland militarily, politically, socially, economically, and geographically. Thus, much of what I describe in the following chapters implicitly and sometimes explicitly intersects or coincides with Hizbullah and the Hizbullah-dominated scene. I acknowledge the hegemonic presence of Hizbullah in the border zone, but like all formations of power, it is not the whole story, as I show in chapter 5. My aim in this book is to show how life in war overflows the strictures of accepted and acceptable categories and narratives and thrives, as Navaro (2017) evocatively puts it, "in interstices—in the gaps, creaks and crevices not entirely smothered by the bombastic politics at play nor flattened by the conflicting governmentalities in the region" (211).

In the meantime, in August and September of 2000, municipal elections were held in the former occupied villages in South Lebanon and the Western Bekaa[17]—158 villages in total—for the first time since 1963. Such (mostly symbolic) moves of "reuniting" the neglected southern margins with the sovereign body of the nation proceeded apace. But at the same time that South Lebanon was clasped close to the beating heart of the Lebanese nation's glory in victory over its longtime foe, it trenchantly remained a marginalized and neglected agricultural backwater whose main function was as battleground and whose inhabitants regarded the central state with more than a little suspicion and quite a lot of hate. In short, in the wake of its sudden liberation, not much took place in terms of political, economic, or infrastructural development in South Lebanon, and it was left, as always, to drown in its many and assorted miseries and, as always, in the meantime to somehow get by. Loudly trumpeted pledges of international aid during a massive donors' conference[18] held right after the end of the occupation never materialized, and thus after the collapse of the occupation economy even more people, especially the youth, migrated out, never to return. Some lamented with a strange nostalgia the end of the occupation era, which for many was more stable and lucrative than the present "return." So despite reverting to the national fold, the southern borderland remained a politically exceptional, economically marginal, and infrastructurally underdeveloped place with war constantly clouding the horizon, despite an unprecedented period of calm—what one could think of as "peace."

I invoke here a question posed by Das (2007) that echoes throughout this book: "What is it to pick up the pieces and to live in this very place of devastation?" (6). Many in fact did just that, moving back to their villages to rebuild their homes, to plant tobacco. And in the meantime Hizbullah was at work preparing the ground for the wars to come. The selfsame ground that southerners lived from and that too many were abandoning. The guerrillas expanded and extended their networks, infrastructures, fortifications, technologies. Tangled up with the lives of the villages and among (and of) the topography and lifeforms of this earth, they dug in,[19] built up, hunkered down, and got ready. "Melted like salt."[20]

2006

The morning was warming already when Mariam heard the first shots. She was sitting on the flat roof of her home, like all mornings at this time of year, threading tobacco, the morning's pickings. The July sun, intense even in the ante meridiem, was beginning to warm her bowed head as she threaded the fresh leaves. Suddenly a plume of smoke rose from Rose Valley just below where she sat. She heard the crackle of gunfire and heavier artillery. She didn't know it yet, but the kidnapping operation that sparked the 2006 war was underway.

It was an operation designed to fall within the grammar defining the "war dance" along the borderline and to realize a pledge made by Hassan Nasrallah, the secretary general of Hizbullah, to bring home Lebanese prisoners in Israeli jails. But it came at a volatile moment. It provided the spark needed by a highly combustible configuration: an inexperienced Israeli leadership and a military establishment confident of its powers of annihilation and itching to get even with Hizbullah (Matthews 2006; Brun 2010). Almost immediately, Israel launched a massive campaign against the very weave of life south of the Litani river: smashing villages, targeting homes and fields, tobacco and livestock. In thirty-four days of incessant bombardment from air, sea, and land as well as ground battles, many southern towns and villages along the borderline (and the southern suburbs of Beirut) were flattened, and large expanses of the landscape scorched, ravaged, and rained upon with unexploded bomblets. The 2006 war was remarkable in its magnitude of destruction (some argue it was

Figure 6. Bint Jbeil, the largest town in the central sector of the border strip, was almost completely destroyed during the July 2006 war.

the most destructive war ever waged in Lebanon): an Israeli maritime and air blockade, incessant bombardment from the sky and sea—with a particularly annihilating focus on the South and the southern suburbs of Beirut—and in the last week, ground incursions along the borderline and toward the Litani River. The war continued (with a brief pause on July 24 when Condoleezza Rice made an entirely unhelpful surprise visit to Beirut to meet with the prime minister) until a United Nations–brokered cease-fire went into effect on the morning of August 14 and then formally came to an end when Israel lifted its naval blockade on September 8.

In those thirty-four days of warfare 1,123 Lebanese civilians were killed, 30 percent of whom were children under the age of thirteen; 4,409 were injured, 15 percent of whom were permanently disabled, according to the Lebanon Higher Relief Council. Material damage was assessed at $3.6 billion and comprised 640 kilometers of roads, 73 bridges, and 31 other targets, such as Beirut's international airport, water and sewage treatment plants, electrical facilities, 25 fuel stations, 900 commercial structures, 350 schools, two hospitals, and 15,000 homes. Another 130,000 homes were significantly damaged. The Lebanese coast was left in dire environmental straits with an oil slick that resulted from the bombing of the power station in Jiyyeh just south of Beirut; its storage tanks seeped 15,000 tons of oil into the sea, the largest-ever oil spill in the already threatened, polluted, and dying Mediterranean Sea. Another 25,000 tons of oil burned at the station, creating a toxic cloud that rained oil downwind and upon the beleaguered landscape (standing in my parents' garden and clutching my eight-month-old baby, I watched that menacing cloud with horror; there was truly nowhere to run).

Mariam, like many bound to the brief but intense tobacco harvest that was peaking in July, was at first hesitant to leave home and field, despite the quick and violent escalation of the conflict. Right away, as movement became the recipe for instant death, she and those like her no longer had the choice to leave and stayed put. Mariam is unmarried and hence did not have to think of the safety of dependents, and so she remained in her village for as long as she could, keeping an eye on the homestead and baking bread for "the boys," with whom she also shared her larder. She also occasionally acted as lookout, warning the fighters concealed in the built environment of the village when she saw enemy movement. Mariam—and many women like her—played a part in the war events unfolding in the landscape of her everyday life. Her and other civilian presence in the field of battle is a key component of Hizbullah's tenacity in (this) war.

Much of the ground battles of this war were fought in and around Mariam's village, among the houses and between the streets. The village was subsequently almost entirely flattened, in particular its old core (Al-Harithy 2010). The Israeli war machine recognized the difficulty of fighting in the dense weave and tangle of ancient village streets and thus flattened all old village centers in the last days of the conflict as they withdrew their ground forces. When the Israelis took the town in the last week of fighting, Mariam finally left to the nearby Christian village, where many Shi'i villagers from the surrounding area had taken refuge from the incessant shelling. Christian towns were pockets of safety in this warzone, because they were not directly targeted. Of course, the influx of refugees drastically stretched the resources of even the biggest Christian villages, which despite not being targeted, were also caught in the middle of this monstrous and terrifying war.

Destruction and (Re)Construction

As always in the wake of violent eruptions like 2006, a period of return and recovery ensued while the international community scrambled to do good by the latest headlining humanitarian disaster. This time though, the amount of international attention in the form of hard cash was unprecedented. The South exploded into a (re)construction frenzy as the international community fell over itself to pledge millions of dollars of direct aid to the blighted villages to assist beleaguered villagers in rebuilding their homes. Every eligible southerner jumped at the chance of money, and thus many villagers actually put the finishing touches on the destructive handiwork of Israel as they went about destroying the remains of their old family homes to get the maximum compensation prize of $40,000 per residence unit. This is how many ancient and deeply layered village quarters were wiped from the map of history by the bulldozers of the postwar (re)building boom. Various villages were "adopted" by donor nations whose flags advertised this fact across the South (Qatar was an especially desired donor). This humanitarian-fueled frenzy—which also included short-lived campaigns to rid the South of unexploded ordnance—lasted as long as such attention lasts: about three years. Frenetic activity then ground to a halt again, although the long-term effects of war remain: ongoing military activity and a looming threat of war; lack of infrastructural development (apart from the travesty of the uncoordinated and wild and now stalled (re)construction drive) and jobs; "symbolic" governance in the shape of impoverished, understaffed, and incapable or corrupt municipalities; unexploded cluster bombs and mines still seeding the southern earth; and a complete lack of any sustainable projects outside of short-lived, showcase development initiatives donated by Western countries, such as a smattering of Italian-donated olive presses and a scattering of cracked and torn and unused USAID PVC-covered water reservoirs. This landscape of enduring war was the (dusty) context of my fieldwork.

.   .   .   .   .

Since 2006 and for now, Israel is contained behind the Blue Line, the disputed withdrawal line demarcated by the UN in June 2000 (Makdisi 2011). And a state of war continues to glower and grumble. Yet on this wretched earth, life goes on through seasons of war, and through seasons of life war goes on; people live on in this place and cultivate the earth themselves. It is to some an unremarkable, peripheral village life premised on the land, in particular the household-based labor of tobacco farming combined with olive cropping, goat herding, and subsistence agriculture.[21] To stay rooted in place and to stay alive, the inhabitants of this borderland battlefield cultivate relations—with other humans and across species and with the earth and its flora and fauna—that "become-with" (Haraway 2016) and resist (in part, by embracing, as I will show in the following chapters) the lethal dimensions of war and poverty, the structural violence of capitalism. These are the vitalizing relations that I call resistant ecologies. Strung along a barbed constellation of difficulties (stemming not only from the acute violence of war but also the slow, grueling structural violence of war, such as poverty and violent histories of empire, nation-states, and sectarian and clientelist politics) and upon a thin and rocky topsoil and uneven terrain, resistant ecologies thrive and in many ways sustain those who live here.[22] Such as tobacco, a global market commodity and Lebanese state monopoly has sustained the inhabitants of the southern borderland throughout many seasons of war and devastation. Tobacco is above all reliable. As I describe in chapter 3, to the people still inhabiting the frontline villages of South Lebanon, the accumulated tasks of the tobacco year always pick up and carry the pace (and the economy) of daily living again, as yet another round of awaiting *al harb al atiya*, the coming war (Hermez 2017; Bou Akar 2018), ticks by and regional storm clouds grow gloomier and more imminently threatening. Similarly, as I show in chapter 4, goats and their human companions reclaim explosive geographies infested with mines and cluster bombs over many years of war. Having no choice but to live alongside these deadly objects of war, those clever, nimble beasts and their humans daringly make their lifeways together with the "rogue infrastructure" (Kim 2016) peppering the treacherous terrains of war. It is a bitter life. And so it is more as a result of the constant wars that they have had no choice but to live with and through, rather than political ideology, that the inhabitants of the borderland have become the "war society," *mujtama' harb,* called for in the early days of Shi'i mobilization (Ajami 1987; Daher and Randolph 2019). Although *mujtama'* most often refers to *human* society, it is an Arabic word meaning "collective" that is derived from the root *j-m-'*, "to collect." To recognize and make a place in history, theory, and politics for the more-than-human collectives constitutive of this resistant "war society" I call it: a landscape of war.

2 Battle/field

War studied at home as inhabited, as tangled with the textures and temporalities of life as lived, is a different object and endeavor than war studied
as an imperial or national military campaign or project. While anthropological accounts (Lutz 2001; Wool 2015; MacLeish 2013; Stone 2018)
that make the US military their focus bring war palpably "home" to
(American) audiences accustomed to watching (mediatized) war unfold
elsewhere, such accounts (perhaps unwittingly) reinforce a bias that centers the experience of imperial agents and erases the experiences of those
millions whose lives imperial armies have violently impacted, rearranged,
and tragically ended. The "collateral damage" that is packaged as a necessary and "unfortunate" aspect of the global US-sponsored spread of
"democracy" remains vague and unexamined when "war" is experienced
primarily as a media event that always aligns with the experience of US
soldiers (this is perhaps where the sense of "surprise" at the atrocities that
US soldiers commit comes from—no one is thinking of those wretched
others!). Framing war as the experience of imperial agents is complicit with
a widespread acceptance of war as something that happens (perhaps

deservedly) to people in far off elsewheres. Unacceptably smothered in such accounts are the lives of those who are on the receiving end of imperial (and other) wars. In her recent book *Combat Trauma* (2022), Nadia Abu el Haj exposes the dangers of these entrenched perspectives and insidious elisions: "There is far more at stake here than overlooking or misrepresenting the other. This genre of recounting war endangers the very possibility of political critique" (4). As a child in wartime Beirut of the 1980s, a place that was constantly in the eye of the international media, I was always puzzled by the discrepancy between war as represented by the Western media and war as lived. They rarely aligned. Which was more real?

In post-2006 Lebanon I became a student of war, and I had to find my own truths, my own path, my own way of finding and telling in a field without many helpful signposts. I was a young anthropologist (with a brief but formative background in journalism) who knew war intimately, intuitively, yet I sought to grasp it anew—analytically and ethnographically—in a field site that was also a fresh and active field of battle. In this field, where I was simultaneously guest and daughter (Abu-Lughod 2016), welcome and not, I had to make my way with care. To compose an ethnographic account of war that faithfully followed the contours and conduits of war as lived in the immediate aftermath of a major conflagration in an always unstable social and political environment, I required a method and approach that respected the field's sensitivities and potentials, its hard limits. Also, there was the question of what indeed was knowable and what disclosable, questions and choices that clung to my research and writing and ultimately pushed me to shape an inquiry and narrative that tells the most suitable story.

I began fieldwork in the summer of 2007, a little under a year after the July War of 2006, as (re)construction, fueled and funded by a flood of international aid, boomed. The first period of research was a time of dusty and frantic (re)building in the South, where many villages were literally bursting forth from the rubble. This was also a time of political upheaval in Lebanon, where the fallout of the February 2005 assassination of Prime Minister Rafiq Hariri and the subsequent withdrawal of Syria from Lebanon after decades of military occupation merged with the repercussions of the 2006 war and resulted in an acutely charged environment that erupted into the "mini civil war" of May 2008, as well as other kinds of explosions (actual ones). The headlining issues, alive since the brittle closure of the Lebanese civil war, continued to gurgle menacingly and are presently manifesting in another level of catastrophe, as Lebanon slides into a calamitous vortex of financial and economic meltdown and political and civil unrest. On August 4, 2020, 2,750 tons of ammonium nitrate unsafely stored in Beirut's port blew up in a massive explosion, dealing a shockwave of devastation to a city and population already reeling. Disasters in Lebanon are ongoing (Khayyat 2020).

But in the 2006 war's immediate aftermath, I went deep into the country, away from the city to the edges of the nation-state, to look for answers to my (scholarly and personal, these always deeply entwined) questions about life and war. Though the effects of the 2006 war were felt in the metropole as well as in the margins, and its reverberations continued in Beirut (and elsewhere) in eruptions of violence throughout the entire initial period of study, I turned away from ongoing orchestrations of political contests and rivalries and organized, "model" utopian (violent, centrally designed, and implemented) reconstructions in the Beirut central district, Solidere, and the southern suburbs, *al-dahiyeh* (Sawalha 2010; S. Makdisi 1997; Fawaz 2009), and I headed instead to the physical and existential edges of the nation-space, taking cues from, among others, George Bataille (1985), who wrote, "Life must be examined in its empty and peripheral forms rather than in the monuments and the monumental vistas that are at its center." So back-tracing the path of a Benjaminian war-storm, I traveled deep into the "epistemic murk" (Taussig 2004) of a "gray zone" (Levi 1989): the well-seasoned battleground of South Lebanon. I traveled into the heartland of war, where a repeating historical cycle of cultivation, devastation, ruination, and regeneration had composed a curious countryside collage where unevenly inhabited, almost rudimentary villages or remains of villages subsist side by side with intact sections of the same villages, or entirely new villages actively sprouting from the rubble or upon abandoned agricultural land, mushrooming along the very edge of the earth. It was my hope that at the edge I could grasp what was obscured at the center: that in the creative destruction of the violence just revisited some things could be discerned that would lend themselves to a less scripted account of such happenings. That was my hope. But also my problem.

This book is rooted in lifelong solidarity and friendship and long-term fieldwork conducted in villages along the Lebanese side of the Lebanese-Israeli border since 2000, but especially for two years (2007–9) in the wake of the July War of 2006, with regular short annual visits in the interim and more extended stays in 2018 and 2019. The area in which I worked, a handful of small, neighboring villages in the district (*qada'*) of Bint Jbeil, had comprised the "central sector" of the occupation zone. It saw the biggest ground battles, and many of its villages were reduced to rubble by the Israeli war machine during the July War.[1] As that war occurred at the height of tobacco season, everyone's livelihood in the borderland tobacco-farming country was affected. The 2006 war resulted in massive losses in the agricultural sector (FAO 2006; Save the Children 2005) that is the grounds of life for the inhabitants of the southern Lebanese borderland. Yet barely was the final ceasefire declared when the devastated villages were doggedly back to life, with villagers once again picking up the pieces and carrying on, shrugging off the latest violent irruption as "normal" and "habitual," *'adi, ta'awwadna*.[2] This book describes the dimensions and difficulties of this everyday living in a place of seasonal war. It illuminates the ways in which life has embraced war and war has embraced life in South Lebanon. The enmeshed nature of life and war has been long in the making, for this area has been a battlefield for more than seventy years.

NAVIGATING MINEFIELDS

It is never easy doing research at "home"(Altorki and El-Solh 1988), especially when one is simultaneously an insider and outsider to the field, flitting between the tensed social roles of guest and daughter (Abu-Lughod 2016). To counter the ease of access afforded by a lack of language barriers and a more intuitive understanding of the realm of the unspoken, many thorns emerge that make the going rough. Familiarity, inclusion in a sociopolitical system, breeds its own set of problems. I will relate an illuminating encounter below, but there were many like it, differently configured, that presented themselves throughout my research: shifting sands of traps and taunts that I had to deftly negotiate.

The South Lebanon border strip, the landscape that concerns this book, is an active warzone watched over, fought over, and jealously cared for by several armed networks. This reality, placed within the constantly bubbling Lebanese political cauldron, spiced with ongoing brinkmanship, and peppered with shows of force and episodes of violence, made the already confounding undertaking of fieldwork in the immediate after-math of the 2006 war just that much more delicate, dangerous, and difficult to navigate. Yet being Lebanese, I do not find such contexts insur-mountable, just existential, and so to me, the delicate (and possibly dangerous) task of researching along an active front had much to do with sensing sensitivities and allaying suspicions, treading a path of least resist-ance and aggression and always nurturing a sense of ethical integrity in the face of constant challenges and questions.

Sectarian identity (Makdisi 2000) is key to social navigation in Lebanon, as in the wake of the civil war and the demise of ideological parties it has more and more become shorthand for social and political identity. The social (its possibilities and limits) in Lebanon is shaped by institutionalized political sectarianism, familism, patriarchy, and patriliny, as has been exten-sively documented by Suad Joseph (2000, 2008, 2011). Lebanese citizen-ship is premised upon inclusion in sectarian and gender categories, and this deep bind colors all social being and political expression across the viscerally linked intimate and public dimensions and domains. The state is set up as the portal and access point for a limited set of resources and services that are distributed across the various Lebanese sectarian communities in return for political allegiance by the *zu'ama*, the traditional sectarian leaders (Nucho 2016). Treading the fine line between consociational democracy and obstructionist politics, and descending into communitarian violence for the duration of the Lebanese war (1975–90) and beyond (Hanf 1993; Wimmen 2012), the Lebanese setup has never been a happy one, consistently serving the interests of the elites at the expense of their vulnerable constituents. One of the results of this configuration is that Lebanese citizens manage their personal encounters in keeping with these charged sectarian logics.

To maximize my welcome, in the field I was a pragmatist: when prod-ded, I would enhance my identity markers differently yet always truth-fully, depending on who my interlocutor was. But in terms of difficulties, sectarianism was not all. To add to the sectarian/political minefields, I also had to manage the distances of social class. My obvious place of privilege was not lost on anyone, least of all myself. I straddled this uncomfortable gap with much heartfelt empathy and respectfulness and always insisted on deferring to others in terms of age, knowledge, and experience (this didn't always work). As a final hurdle, my place of study, the United States, was not very high on most peoples' popularity lists. My way out of *that* one was to crack the joke among those who would find it funny (it was originally said to me in jest in a Shi'a village when I identified my university as Columbia) that I studied at the University of Ahmedinejad.[3]

Awareness of the terrain I had to traverse in study and observation were vital in shaping the object of inquiry, its medium, and its methods. Fieldwork focused on a strip of the border encompassing several neighboring "frontline villages" dovetailing with minefields and the bristling border fence. An arid highland of rolling scrub-covered hills overlooking the lower elevations of Israeli Galilee, these villages constitute the heartland of tobacco farming and asymmetrical warfare. The southern borderland remains a semiclosed military zone under the control and surveillance of several militaries including the Lebanese Armed Forces (LAF), the Israeli Army (also known as the IDF), Hizbullah, the United Nations Interim Force in Lebanon (UNIFIL), and the United Nations Truce Supervision Organization (UNTSO), to name the known ones. Only Lebanese nationals are allowed in and out of this area without a military permit, and everyone is considered suspicious.

One day I was driving with my sister and we were heading to the village that came to be a home base in the South. Today we took the coastal road south of Sur and drove until we hit the end of the land in Naqura, where the UNIFIL headquarters have taken over, then turned inland away from the infinite sea and eastward to trace the borderline (a coastline, but of a different sort; Wylie 2007). Ever since my first moments of encounter with this route some twenty years ago, I have never ceased to be amazed and inspired and weirded-out all at once as I dip and rise through the hallowed hills of northern Galilee and trace the southern extremity of Lebanon. which feels like the very edge of the earth, so pretty and precipitous, so idyllic and wholesome, so desolate and cracked all at once.

We reach Naqura, a seaside town overtaken by UNIFIL on the last rocky outcrop of the Lebanese coast; once a tiny fishing village, it is now a booming center dominated by shops and restaurants catering (in idiosyn-cratic English) to an international mix of UNIFIL personnel, who work in complexes hermetically sealed behind tall fortified walls. We climb a hill sprinkled with little homes entangled in nests of grapevines, basil, roses, and jasmine. As we crest the hill, a sea of scrubland heaves to our right and then is suddenly and inevitably interrupted by the border: aerials stabbing at the sky. There is Israel: the end of the land (Grossman 2010). We turn northeast and pass a UNIFIL position hunkering in the desert-colored bedrock and leave it behind with the borderline cutting through the geography to our right and follow the asphalt, its rubbery smell mixing in with warm whiffs of thyme, to a tiny Christian village. Although it is partly abandoned—falling-down stone houses and overgrown gardens tell that story—it retains some present life, because many of its current inhab-itants work for UNIFIL. Thus the roads are paved and the inhabited houses are pretty, painted, and well-tended. After a brief visit to the municipality, where I chatted with the mayor, we stopped to take a break at a roadside minimarket with a few plastic chairs scattered in a front garden under some trees. We bought some water and sat in the warm embrace of the morning sun. Soon the market's owner joined us by sitting at a nearby table; eyeing us, he asked us who we were, where we were from, and what we were doing here. We told him our names, said we lived in Beirut, and I told him I was doing research. He had an aggressive demeanor and a cynical look on his bearded, blunt-featured face. He was smiling but it was an unfriendly smile, and his eyes were calculating and hard.

He said: "*Well* if you want to know anything about this place let me tell you something about it: half of this village is over *there* in the *dear sister*," pointing with his nose behind our shoulders in the direction of Israel. He was referring to members of the South Lebanon Army (SLA), Israel's aux-iliary militia during the occupation, who were abandoned by Israel upon their withdrawal from South Lebanon in May 2000. Some managed in their desperation to escape over the border in a headlong rush in the wake of the sudden collapse of the occupation. When the Liberation-frenzy sub-sided, and realizing that they would not be vengefully slaughtered, many eventually returned, but a handful—those with good reason to—remain there to this day, bundled into camps in northern Israel, finding no way

back home outside of an official pardon or political settlement after collaboration with the enemy.

The man continued: "Every time there are elections some politician
comes and says that he will bring them back, but no one does, and in the
meantime they are stuck there. A girl who was ten when she went there
with her family is now twenty years old. Who is she going to marry? It will
have to be either a Palestinian or an Israeli!" [subtext: both options are
horrible]. He asked us again what we were doing here and I repeated that
I was doing research and elaborated a little on my theme of life in war and
indicating my interest in agricultural practices to lend my research a hint
of tangibility. I added that we found the village charming and that we were
going to take a walk around. "You can't," he said abruptly. "You know, our
villages are *closed* to outsiders and people aren't accustomed to seeing
people, *strangers,* walking around. People will stop you and ask you what
you are doing. This area is no place for tourism."

His message was clear—he was pushing us into the category of outsiders, "*strangers*" and closing the door of friendliness before our very noses. I
of course chose to ignore this, text and subtext, and said "But you must be
accustomed to 'strangers' here." I was referring to the UNIFIL, the "interim"
multinational peacekeeping force that has been patrolling the borderland
since 1978. I don't know if he deliberately misunderstood me, but he got
decidedly agitated and cutting me off said: "Do you think that we haven't
seen anything? Do you think we are living in jungles here and haven't seen
anything of the world? What do you take us for, savages?! We have been to
Israel and have *seen* civilization!" That was an open taunt. Speaking of any
contact with Israel is still very much taboo (and illegal), but he apparently
felt secure enough in his own garden sitting with two "strangers" to test the
limits of discourse and explore our reactions. He was unable to figure out
our sectarian identity from our already disclosed names and place of origin,
the usual "casual" way of knowing, but he simply *had* to know, since that is
usually all that is needed to uncover much about a fellow Lebanese citizen,
in particular affiliation, in the fractured political landscape. He was trying
to provoke a reaction to figure out who he was talking to.

I did not bat an eyelash and repeated levelly and with a pacific smile
that *that* was obviously *not* what I meant and that what I had intended to
say was what with all those UNIFIL soldiers about, inhabitants of the

former occupation zone must be used to *ajanib, ghuraba,* "strangers" (foreigners, outsiders), in their villages. He didn't back down but instead pursued his track: "Well the UNIFIL are strangers but they are like us, *Christians* as you know, and if you don't mind me saying, this is a Christian village. You are obviously Lebanese and we aren't accustomed to *Lebanese* strangers wandering about. You know you might see a woman dressed as you are walking down the street, and further down the road she will go into a shop and come out veiled. [Subtext: you may be Muslim, for all I know]. You never know who people really are." He added: "I'm not from here. I moved here fifteen years ago from the north during the days of Aoun and Geagea [the last major conflict of the civil war in 1989–90]. There was a nun here who is related to me and so I came. I was an outsider, but now I am considered a fellow villager, especially since I stayed here during the [2006] war making bread for people. Now I have a badge of honor, and I am considered one of them. I also plant tomatoes and cucumbers in my garden; want to watch me?" he sneered.

My sister and I took our leave without satisfying his curiosity as to our sectarian identity. We did not heed his advice or succumb to his unwelcoming commentary and still went for a wander through the village, peering into ruined stone houses and reading the writing on the wall: "Bye-bye *hara* [old neighborhood]." As we wandered down a narrow road crowded on either side by thick, towering cacti bearing orange prickly pears and crowned with pink flowers, a woman came out of her home and offered us freshly picked baby strawberries from her garden, cradled in her palms. She smiled at us and did not appear in any way ruffled by our "strange" appearance on her doorstep. Behind her sweet little home with a vegetable patch beside it from where the strawberries came, began the land of Palestine/Israel.[4] The road ended in a clump of shady pines sheltering a Lebanese Army roadblock. Impasse.

These two encounters in one tiny village indicate the unevenness of the social and physical terrain I would constantly navigate in the field. Both encounters reflect the conditions and realities defining the borderland: suspicion and bitterness and anger, spontaneous generosity and unquestioning welcome. Later that day as we drove back toward the coast, we heard on the radio that someone in that very village had been arrested on suspicion of spying for Israel.[5] The ongoing war is never far in space or time. It is up to those inhabiting the here and now to find a way and a place to be within the prickly and treacherous givens.

LANDSCAPE PORTALS

The South, being a warzone for most of its existence as a part of the Republic of Lebanon, has not been extensively explored by anthropologists. Other than Emrys Peters's (1977) ethnography of an unnamed southern village in the 1950s and '60s, not very much else in terms of anthropological fieldwork has been conducted there. Michael Gilsenan (1996) relates in the introduction to *Lords of the Lebanese Marches* that he had wanted to do fieldwork there in the early 1970s but was discouraged because of the guerrilla war ongoing in the southern borderland, and thus he ended up in the northern borderland instead. I did not have much to build upon in terms of anthropological literature or established networks, so I have had to make my own. It was hard going at first both to find my theoretical bearings and practical footing and to break into the field.

My actual way in was, like many things in this research, serendipitous. One day in the summer of 2007, I went to meet Rabih Shibli, an architect and urban planner, who had set up an NGO to assist southerners in navigating the cutthroat reconstruction market that had boomed in South Lebanon the wake of the 2006 war and the millions in international aid that were flooding into the area for this purpose. After chatting for a while, Rabih asked me to come with him to meet Jala Makhzoumi, a professor of landscape architecture at the American University in Beirut with whom he was setting up a collaborative project in which he thought I could take part. At that very moment I simultaneously met two of my closest collaborators, friends, mentors, fellow *maquisards* in the field (and beyond).

Through following the work of Beit bil Jnoub (House in the South, Rabih's NGO) for the UN Habitat–funded project "Good governance in Post-war Reconstruction in South Lebanon" and through my participation in Jala's AUB observatory team that assessed the impact of this project, I gained exposure to people and places across the war-ravaged South beyond my immediate circle of friends. My role was to interview villagers about their participation in this project and assess its impact. Through the project's uneven and sometimes rocky unfolding and its ultimately (in my opinion) unsatisfactory outcome, my eyes were opened to the deep problems both faced and created by the international development and humanitarian aid sectors in South Lebanon. But this experience and interface eased me into the field. It was through the many experiences afforded me through my participation that the borderland first came into analytical focus. Through extended trips in the South and conversations with Rabih, himself a southerner, the borderland unfolded in its textured detail, its many contradictory facets. In particular, it was under the guidance of Jala (Makhzoumi 1997, 2008, 2009, 2016), architect and landscape architect (and the brilliant artist who has illuminated this manuscript with her drawings), that I developed my first ideas: it was she who first led me to the magical portal of landscape and it was from her that I first heard that wonderful word *maquis*. Frustrated at times by what I could not ask and what was (loudly) not being said, I began to look at and question and probe the landscape—its beings, forms and features.[6]

As time went on and I did not find myself obstructed, I decided that this meant that my presence was not considered threatening. I took this as a good sign and followed the oblique, ordinary, organic trajectory that I found myself upon, and it led me down interesting, colorful, and varied paths. I spent a lot of time in the field talking and walking: observing village life, dwellings, and farming practices. I would meet someone in their village, in their home, in their workplace, and we would begin by talking. Inevitably this talk would lead us *into* the landscape, and we would start walking, and in walking we would arrive at new paths, places, revelations, meetings, encounters, clearings. It is fascinating how often this occurred. It emerged then, in an unremarkable and also unremarked sense, that the landscape was a crucial medium, a necessary object, practice, performance, and experience, as well as a metaphor for staying, surviving, speaking, and just being in South Lebanon: landscape generated and gathered life, made its unique local cadences vibrant, tactile, and material.

In the villages I conducted interviews; collected oral histories; got caught in webs of kinship; absorbed stories of the land, agricultural wisdom and local lore; discovered a fast-ebbing world of customary law; and encountered cultural and actual ruins, reverberating remains, rubble. I saw patterns of daily and seasonal rhythms emerge across the seasons, both sacred and profane. I was shown memory places, holy places, haunted places; I visited homes, shared meals, gingerly skirted minefields and slinked along the borderline, discovered known and hidden military sites and spaces. I visited mosques, churches and monasteries, Muslim, Christian and Jewish shrines. I encountered the Régie, the tobacco monopoly, from the experts in the field buying tobacco from villagers to the warehouses and regional and national headquarters. I sat in gardens, traversed fields and orchards, walked hills and valleys, petted donkeys, was herded alongside goats, ate wild fruit, collected wild herbs, prayed at graves and shrines, communed with trees. I kept a field diary throughout this time, recorded many interviews, took many pictures, and made some drawings. I had to rely on written notes and memory when things just happened (as things tend to do; Stewart 2007) or when I sensed a recording device appeared unwelcome or counterproductive. Often, I would head off on my own to revisit places I had been to before to see if there was something more I could discover unaccompanied, or simply to uncover new places and unearth new paths, new experiences and encounters. I also benefited from the expertise of professors, researchers, practitioners in the development and humanitarian sectors and at NGOs, heads of municipalities and those involved in reconstruction, and some politicians. Their narratives, concerns, and insights added new layers, angles, and contexts to my fieldwork.

And thus my research rolled on. I am not exactly sure when I was doing crazy things, traveling alone across miles of emptiness, wandering through fields alone with men I was not related to in a setting where women did not move alone very often if at all, wandering too close to the technical fence defining the borderline, with Israeli Humvees dustily zooming past on their rounds. My little blue Fiat must have been a common sight to Israeli soldiers on border duty as I drove up and down the borderline (not to mention the Hizbullah and UNIFIL guys on our side of the border); I often wondered what kind of intelligence they had on me. In general though, I used my common sense and applied a few basic precautions, like never walking across an unknown field (to pick red and purple poppies in spring, say, no matter how magical or enticing they were). And so, through many serendipitous encounters and winding paths and lots of black coffee, sweet tea, and various homegrown and homemade edibles, and many, many stories and encounters, I came to inhabit and know my field. As I came to inquire about the practices, processes, relations, places, objects, assemblages that gather and make life in the borderland, I was led into a landscape of war and dwelling slowly unfolding in its myriad details. And this is how the landscape became the material, medium, and metaphor of my research.

DEFINING THE FIELD: KNOWNS AND UNKNOWNS

From the outset it was clear that my field was composed of areas I am calling knowns and unknowns. These swaths of epistemological and methodological access and obstruction defined the field for me in large strokes and put me on the path of observation, inquiry, and experience that composed my research and produced much of the material and memories I now have at hand to work into this book.

The knowns emerged from the guiding questions around the ongoing entanglement of war with life. Presumably, in a place just (re)visited by war those would not be too hard to find. But the difficulty of my endeavor was underlined to me early on by two illustrious scholars of (and from) the South: Munzir Jabir, the author of an encyclopedic tome on the occupation of the border zone (Jabir 1999), and Ahmad Beydoun, a Lebanese sociologist who has written beautiful semiautobiographical pieces (Beydoun 1992, 1993) on the South, along with other highly regarded work on Lebanese society and politics. When I told Jabir about my project and my research he looked at me with a mixture of sympathy and pity and said that one of the most difficult things about doing social research in the South is that people there "know how to talk." So long have they inhabited the harsh realities of war and so often have they rehearsed political ideologies of oppression that they are by now old hands at representing themselves in ways that people have become accustomed to receiving and perceiving them. The sentiment was echoed by Beydoun, who in addressing my questions about the history of tobacco farming and the historical wretchedness of the southerner, said that the story of the "disinherited and dispossessed" was such a common and established trope of southern social and political identity that it had become something of a "song"[7] the south-erner sings. And I knew what they were talking about. So, not wanting to be recurrently caught up in refrains everyone already knew the words to, I decided that the key to my approach would be to orient myself away from such topics, tropes, and themes, but how? Das (2007) provides a clue. She writes on her work on the Partition of India, "I never in fact asked anyone for their stories of Partition. It is not that if asked people could not tell you a story, but simply that the words had the frozen slide quality to them" (11). Das chose instead to inquire into ordinary matters. And for my part, I too resolved to edge sideways ("obliquely" as Rolph Trouillot had advised me years before) into my field through unexpected portals.[8] The most unexpected, when it comes to war, is in fact the most ordinary. Thus I found myself on a practical path of discovery that began with the daily concerns and activities of the inhabitants of the southern borderland as they went about their lives. And that led me unexpected places.

The unknowns that came to define my method and the reach of my investigation, had to do with the warzone realities that define the strip, the borderland, the former occupation zone, my field site today. Because of the reigning state or condition of war, because of the twenty-two-year occupa-tion that ended not so long ago and the difficult predicament of those who "collaborated" with the enemy, because of the (openly?) secretive nature of ongoing guerrilla warfare, there were so many things I *could* not know, and should *never* ask—even if I were dying to! The hard truth of the matter is that it is a highly problematic and also sometimes dangerous pastime to poke around and pose pointed questions in a live battlefield where knowl-edge is a matter of life and death, steadfastness/resistance or annihilation. Constantly then, I was afraid of taking that one step too far, of being con-sidered too ignorant of what I could know or too clumsy and curious, a liability or an object of suspicion that would lock me out of my field. This is another reason why, as will become clearer, the landscape (O silent speaker!) became the medium of my research.

With respect to the borderland and former occupation zone: in the first instance no one is allowed freely in to this semiclosed area except Lebanese nationals. Anyone without a Lebanese passport has to apply for a permit from the Lebanese Army in Saida and gets stopped at each and every checkpoint throughout the zone to verify their papers and answer tedious questions. Secondly Hizbullah, the organization in de facto control of the borderland usually requires researchers or anyone conducting any business from outside the zone, to make themselves known and get either written or verbal permission from them. Apart from a visit to their research headquarters, the Consultative Center for Studies and Documentation, during the preliminary phase of my research I did not ask for any formal permission as I edged into the field. The reason for this had something to do with my desire to avoid as much as possible politically endorsed and scripted narratives. Hizbullah's research arm and cultural production sectors are highly developed and competent, and I did not want to be coerced, even if gently, into reproducing what I recognized as their hegemonic tropes and narratives. Although I am sympathetic in some respects to Hizballah's cause and project and presence in South Lebanon, I knew that there was something important to be found outside of their political will and imagination in their largely disciplined and well-monitored battlefield.

ETHICAL/POLITICAL QUESTIONS

So my status as "outsider" was attenuated by threads of connection that tied me to my field site. Yet a tension remained. I was a kind-of insider (respectful of boundaries and of the reach or limits of knowledge) but also an outsider (constantly desiring the transgression of those boundaries and reaching for forbidden knowledge), a friend and yet a tireless, perpetual inquisitor, a professed equal but one with an objectifying purpose. Audra Simpson (2017) has articulated the complicated politics of anthropological knowing in her brilliant essays on ethnographic refusal. When the researcher occupies an awkward position vis-à-vis their friends/family/interlocutors and the politics of a discipline (still!) on the wrong side of history, they must make political and ethical choices in their writing clear, because as we all know, knowledge is power! As Simpson points out, at stake is much more than the question of representation. She writes: "I want to reflect upon the dissonance between the representations that were produced by writing away from and to dominant forms of knowing and commitment to what people say. . . . I do so in order to ask what the form of knowledge might look like when such histories . . . are accounted for in disciplinary form and analysis. And further to that, I consider what analysis will look like, or sound like, when the goals and aspirations of those we talk to inform the methods and the shape of our theorising and analysis" (2007, 68). I write through a similar dissonance with dominant theory and with a similar political commitment to the worlds I write from and about and for. I strive to write from the world that I research and for the world that I and my interlocutors inhabit, without losing disciplinary legibility and social credibility. It is a tricky task!

Enhancing the persistent feelings of betrayal that dog big-hearted, well-meaning, world-loving anthropologists (and other seekers) like myself was the fact that I was able to roam around in a place not many others could and that I had access to knowledge that many would love to put to purposes I would never condone. For example I have since read many studies conducted by the US and Israeli militaries on South Lebanon and its feted guerrillas (in particular, their perfection in performance of "hybrid warfare" is the object of much soul- and strategy-searching among the most advanced militaries in the world) and saw that many of those sharp and well-placed researchers were consistently barred access to the borderland as well as to the organization in control of it. I recognize how much remains outside of the grasp of the most eager students, and I realize that much of what I saw and did in the field could be put to good use by such knowledge seekers and the insidious powers behind them, much to my displeasure and discomfort. In a way similar to how knowns and unknowns shaped my field and my grasp, I have fashioned this book to be as careful a presentation of what I explored and witnessed and discovered in the warzone of the Lebanese South with regard to how the information it contains can be further used or mobilized. To put it another way: let us just say that the purview of my research as well as the written form it has taken in this book is the best compromise I could find between the presentation of a certain witnessed knowledge and its full disclosure.

FULL CIRCLE

Toward the end of my initial fieldwork in 2009, when I felt I had exhausted the field on my own (or rather just exhausted myself, since the field is never exhausted), I decided to approach the Hizb.[10] I went back to their center (which in the meantime had been pulverized in the 2006 war and relocated from the cramped streets of *al-dahiyeh* to shiny new premises right off the Beirut airport road) to speak to the new director, a brainy, bookish man who had recently taken the reins of the institute after his formidable predecessor had been elected to parliament. The director commiserated with me on the lack of attention on South Lebanon (on all fronts) in comparison to that lavished on Beirut and its southern suburbs and directed me to his head of surveys and research. A kind and soft-spoken man, he listened to my long-winded description of my research so far and said he would connect me with a local who could show me around. He said that this would take a few days and that once he had found someone and okayed my research with the powers that be, he would give me a call. A few days later he called and said he was connecting me with someone—someone who had herded around researchers before and was from the very village where I had spent most of my time in the field! I took this coincidence to mean that my intuition and careful reading of the field had indeed landed me in the right place. Of course it also probably meant that the Hizb was (as I had sensed) aware of my research all along. Which leads me finally to what connects me to South Lebanon and this particular village in South Lebanon.

MY STAKES, MY PASSION, MY SOUTH

As I have already stated, this academic project draws its specificity and its strength from my life as a witness to and (former) inhabitant of war. So as much as it is a work of scholarship, it is also a life project and a labor of love. Its questions are simultaneously sourced from and directed toward my experience of the Lebanese civil war (including the Israeli invasion of 1982, when I was six) and what came after, including several Israeli aerial bombing campaigns (especially Operation Grapes of Wrath in the spring of 1996, when I was a junior at the American University of Beirut), ongoing struggles within the Lebanese theater, and most pivotally (for this book), the 2006 war. As described in the prelude, this project was conceived after—and unfortunately probably also made possible by—the war of 2006, during which I found myself for the first time in a temporal, spatial and emotional place that enabled me to grasp war as an object of study.

My contact with the occupied border strip began a long time ago (circa 1985), when Abu Jalil, a poor man whose wife had just died, followed soon after by their ailing son, came to our door with his youngest daughter Ghida, who was my age, to ask for work. He had left his village on the very last inch of Lebanon as a young man, years ago, turning his back for good on a place no longer (and never really) home to him or holding him, to seek (eke) out a living in Beirut. He was one in a wave of ongoing out-migration that began, continued, and swelled in the wake of a borderline that put the South on the edge of the nation and in the middle of war. Abu Jalil brought with him to the misery of city life his young children and his wife, who was from Tarbikha, one of the lost "Seven Villages" of South Lebanon,[11] once just over the ridge from his village but now sunken out of existence and out of reach in the high blue grasses behind the border (there is a poignant sign there pointing to nothing on the other side of the border, indicating where this village no longer stands).

During the "golden years" of Beirut in the 1960s and early 1970s, when the well-heeled couldn't decide whether Beirut was Paris or Switzerland (Said 1979), Abu Jalil worked as a ticket collector and janitor at the Rivoli, one of downtown Beirut's ritzy, ultramodern cinemas. When the civil war broke out and downtown Beirut became a battleground and the Rivoli a snipers' nest, Abu Jalil and his family began the hard downward journey into desperate poverty: hunger and homelessness. They would return to their village when there was truly no income or place to stay elsewhere, falling back on family, living off the land, planting tobacco throughout the opening chapters of the civil war until the 1978 Israeli invasion. With that invasion they were, like so many others, flushed out of their village, and after spending some time in a Red Cross camp for the displaced in Sur, they (by now six children in total) eventually made their way away from the occupation that had swallowed their village and back to the "misery belt" south of the capital, where the civil war continued to rage. During some more years of difficulty and into the early 1980s they, along with several other families from their village, eventually squatted an empty place on a low hill hovering above the Mediterranean where a few affluent families had built villas in the early 1970s and then abandoned them as they fled the war to comfort-in-exile abroad.

In June 1982 came the second Israeli invasion that swept up viciously, swiftly toward Beirut. Through the rotten, sweltering months of June, July, and August the Israelis camped on the outskirts of the wretched city and laid upon it a deadly siege. And one of the Israeli's top-brass headquarters, with a birds-eye view of southern Beirut, was Doha, where my uncle had bought a home when he got married in 1979.[12] The siege was a burning hell, and the occupation of Doha is counted among the worst days of this family's life, as they survived on barely more than a piece of bread a day. Soon this ordeal was somehow also survived, and this family continued to occupy this house (and did until around ten years ago) with Abu Jalil for a while making a living as caretaker of some of the empty villas and then living off the goodwill of the handful of better-off families that took up residence in Doha. This is where our families' paths converged, as we moved back to Lebanon from Abu Dhabi, the United Arab Emirates in 1983 and my parents rented one of the empty houses on this hill near my uncle's villa. My mother employed Abu Jalil as gardener and caretaker, and his older daughters also came to help with the housework (we were also a family of five children in a war, albeit with many more means). One of his daughters, Munya, although only twenty-one years old, was already married and divorced and estranged from her infant daughter, who remained back in the village in the occupied strip with her father, who had taken a second wife. It was through Munya's painful attachment to a village that lived in her broken heart and clung to her shattered dreams that brought the occupation into first focus to me as I became aware of the world and of war.

It was not until May 24, 2000, on the day of liberation, that I first clapped eyes on the borderland, this village, and what lay beyond. During that time I was working as a journalist. The day before I had been in Majdal Silim, a pretty village built on a sloping hillside and the verdant agricultural plain that lay adjacent to (just south of) the border of the occupation zone. On the frontline of the occupation, the village had absorbed much bombardment, including phosphorous and cluster bombs—munitions banned by international conventions—throughout the years as the war of resistance against the occupation gathered force and momentum. The day the occupation ended, I was fixing for Tony Birtley, a freelance war journalist who was completing a piece on the occupation and had just spent a week inside the zone. I saw some of his footage of his evening drinking and dancing at a café, as the sun set on the occupation, with some Christian youngsters in Marjayoun who spoke of their attachment to the occupation order[13]—the only lifeworld they knew. To give his story balance and context, he wanted to interview the family of a martyred Hizbullah fighter from outside this "comfort zone," and that is where we were that day the occupation ended. As we were speaking to the father of the martyr, who Tony had placed in the camera frame sitting alone on a chair under the picture of his dead son ("Our eldest son was martyred to liberate our soil, our younger son is now in the Resistance thank God *al-hamdulillah*"), the steady sound of shelling began. Usual fare in these parts, so we didn't pay it too much attention.

Wrapping up the interview, I asked to use the restroom before the long drive back to Beirut. The old man discreetly directed me to his daughter-in-law, married to his younger son, the one now in the Resistance. She took me upstairs to her home, built atop of her parents-in-law's ground floor level; a neat, freshly furnished flat, adequate for a young family with a young child. As she opened the door to the bathroom she paused, and turning to me, looked me in the eyes said: *Ma tkhafi,* "Don't be scared!" I looked back at her questioningly, wondering what she meant. But as soon as I stepped into the pink-tiled bathroom, I understood her warning: the bathtub was piled high with ammunition, battle gear, machine guns, grenades and small rocket launchers. It was her husband the Resistance fighter's weapons cache. I didn't tell the journalist.

We went to visit the graveyard where the martyrs and the victims of this long war are buried. A young man with blonde hair and blue eyes showed us around. While we are there among the graves, an Israeli jet flies low over the village. "It's low," says the young man squinting into the sun as the jet flashes across the blue, "they are going to hit." Almost instantly, a huge crash tears open the sky and beige smoke billows out of the hillside. The jet loops over the hill above us and comes back, dropping another bomb. Another shattering crash. We rush towards the car, which is parked outside the house of the Resistance fighters, not to safety, but to get a better perspective for Tony's hand-held footage! He stands on the roof of the car. I goggle at the sky, my heart beating fast. The young woman whose husband is in the Resistance rushes out of the house excitedly brandishing a transistor radio, her black *shador* billowing around her like batwings. "Did you hear the news?" she shouts gleefully, gesturing expansively with her arms. "We have liberated Qantara! The Israelis are retreating!"

As the occupation swiftly crumbled, Tony's story for BBC Channel 4 fell apart around his ears, much to his chagrin, and a larger news team was sent to cover the major story, headed by Gaby Rado, a renowned war correspondent (who later died in mysterious circumstances in Iraq during the 2003 US invasion). I joined the team the next day, and we returned. But we were not the only ones heading South: almost everyone in Lebanon was. It was a magical, once in a lifetime experience, a truly festive occasion, spontaneous celebration bubbling all around as a hated occupying power crumbled and slunk away like foxes in the night, locking the border gates behind them, a move that struck me as queerly domestic, like someone bolting a garden gate.[14]

The traffic was appropriately monstrous. The feeling was appropriately giddy: the feeling of power crumbling is positively, physically electric. People were silly with emotion. Of course, those jaded journalists I was with were impatient to get their take and get out. But then we reached Kfar Kila and the Fatma Gate and there it was: the border! And more than that, what lay beyond the border: *PALESTINE!* A landscape that I had held in my heart for so long and lived under the political imperative of my whole life was unrolling *before my very eyes*. I could barely breathe. It felt unreal. As if I were looking at a painting or a picture, that thing that had solidified in my imagination over many years—that had suddenly turned *real*. I blinked: there it *was*. People around me were equally overwhelmed and in a similar state of shock and disbelief. There were shouts of "Palestine! Look at Palestine! That is *Palestine!*" as people shared the moment. A guy next to me smacked himself on the forehead and staggered backwards then turned to his companion, who was also reeling, and pulled urgently at his sleeve, pointing at Palestine. It really was quite an overwhelming state of affairs, and the feeling has not left me. I still feel the same ripple of excitement and disbelief when I look across that border, even after all those years. I never imagined that I would be so close—to touch with my own eyes!—Palestine, a place that had all the concentrated emotion and tactile reality of a dream in my life thus far.

The next day I shook those hard-nosed journalists, who had spent the evening after filing their stories sitting around a restaurant table in Sur, drinking and griping about how the event's relevance was sinking like a stone because none of the expected (desired by the media!) violence had erupted. Instead I connected with people who felt the occasion like I did. With my mother and sisters and with Abu Jalil's daughters (Munya and her younger sister Ghida, who was eight months pregnant) we headed to their beloved village. As we entered the village, Munya felt her heart was going to explode with happiness. She walked through the streets with her arms held up in the air, embracing the world all around her as the villagers—neighbors, kith, and kin tumbled out to greet her. Finally the village she had yearned for for years was underfoot, at hand. In nearby Dhaira (a Bedouin village), in a laurel grove we saw Palestinian families who had been separated for more than fifty years tearfully (re)connecting across the barbed-wire border fence with relatives lost to them for so many years. They were patrolled by young Israeli soldiers, who were put to immediate work by the excited families ferrying bonds of shared blood and affection in cups of thick black coffee across the border fence, at once an intimate new interface and deadly uncrossable divide, brimming with love, laughter and tears.

One scene will never leave me: a frail old woman, pale, ethereal, and waiflike and dressed entirely in white was being carried up the hill by her two strong sons, seated in a chair. Like my grandmother returning home all those years ago, she was also "returning" to as close to home as she could, to see her beloved Palestine at least once more before she left this bitter earth. It broke my heart to see it. She was urging her sons, who were overcome with emotion, to be strong: "Palestine has returned to me," *Falasteen rij'itli*, she said with soft determination, hand on her heart. Elsewhere across the newly free zone the tangible paraphernalia of a collapsed oppressive order was everywhere, and we collected what we could.[15] We flocked to the infamous Khiam prison that had only yesterday been emptied of its prisoners. What a stinking hellish pit, so raw—the rags of incarceration, the stuffed rooms with stacked narrow cots, the writing on the wall of those forcibly detained. The previous midnight I had stood under the stars with crowds in Haret Hreik in *dahiyeh* and watched as Hassan Nasrallah, who would still appear among the crowds in those days (he has been underground and out of sight since 2006), welcomed the prisoners, kissing each one on both cheeks and looking them in the eyes with a smile. There are so many stories and feelings from these days, but I cannot recount them all here. I just want to describe the feeling of what the South is to me. As Fairouz sings in one of her beautiful songs: "Wars erupt and wars subside, but you remain my love, O land of the South."

I grew up with the idea of the South as a beloved homeland, an unconditional love for the South (*ya habibi ya jnoub*), the cause of the South. The suffering of the South. "The sun rises from the South," the poetic life-affirming mantra and slogan of resistance throughout the (endless) cycles and seasons of war. The inescapable identity of the South as a place of suffering and of steadfastness. Hence the moment of its liberation was huge. To me, it somewhat redeemed the suffering of the war years and the death of my grandparents: my grandfather, my beloved *jiddo* Abu Bashar, died during the Israeli invasion of 1982 believing that Lebanon was Palestine lost all over again, and my beloved grandmother, my namesake, the true southerner among us, born into a peasant family in Kfar Melki, a village in the hills above Saida, died in 1994, before the South was fully free. This enigma of the South, this love of the South as an imaginary object, is part of what has driven me to examine it as a lived place and in particular to explore its ambiguity; for maturity also brings with it a sneaking awareness of the strange flatness of such beguiling "songs."

And finally the village again: as strange as it sounds, I reconnected with this village serendipitously as I was exploring the field. Driving along the borderline one day with Rabih, we saw a woman sitting by the side of the road under a large picture of a martyr. We were beguiled by the closeness of the border that for a change rode on an elevated ridge that walled in this village on one side,[16] so we stopped the car and asked her where we were. She answered. I couldn't believe it! I had never seen her before but after exchanging a few words she looked searchingly at me and declared that I looked familiar. It was Zahra. Hers was among the families that had lived for a spell in Doha with the family of Abu Jalil during the years of exile, and she had recognized me somehow. Soon her older sister Khawla arrived and took up the thread of the conversation; they became among my main interlocutors and companions as I explored the landscape of South Lebanon.

3 The Bitter Crop

Al-nabti lamma ti'tini feeha tid'eelak la tul al-hayat.
[When you care for a plant it blesses you for as long as
you live.]

—Southern saying

Along the South Lebanon borderland where it thrives, they call it—not
unlovingly—*al-nabti al-murrah*, the bitter crop. It is also known as the
"crop of resistance," and it is widely embraced as a steadfast source of life
in a perennially harsh and deadly world. An annual dryland crop with a
brief efflorescence, the tobacco plant is well-adapted to the hilly topography and arid climate of the borderland. Tobacco thrives because it coheres
generatively with the limitations on life along the southern border of
Lebanon. Tobacco is a globalized market commodity carefully planted,
plucked, and processed across the homesteads of Lebanese villages in a
regional warzone. It flourishes within conditions of poverty and through
seasons of war. The poor who farm it and the powerful who profit from it
are variously invested in its vitalizing qualities: the wretched labor hard
for its reliable if meager income; the powerful monopolize its political and
economic profits. Through decades of war and occupation in South
Lebanon, the tobacco plant, a creature of niche ecology, industrial agriculture, and globalized capitalism, has proven its mettle: it is well known for
its capacity to grow in adversity, not unlike its human cultivators. Hence,
to those who also cultivate the ability to thrive in suboptimal conditions,
tobacco, a crop long entangled in these highlands with subaltern histories

Figure 7. The hands of Fatima are stained black by tar bleeding from the green tobacco leaves she is threading.

of poverty, oppression, and neglect, is celebrated as the crop of *muqa-wama* and *sumud*, resistance and steadfastness. At the same time, it remains a bitter, wretched lot.

This chapter is threaded around the resistant ecology of tobacco farming in South Lebanon, whose dwellers continue to live amidst the infrastructures, fault lines, and frictions of military violence, state-monopolized and globalized extractive agriculture, and the ongoing wreckage of numerous violent histories and wars, with the promise of more to come. In South Lebanon, life flourishes alongside the tobacco that is grown for the Régie Libanaise des Tabacs et Tombacs, the Lebanese state-owned tobacco monopoly. To those who grow it, tobacco is life. They acknowledge that. This laborious cash crop makes them live when not much else does. It has, they say, allowed them to survive military occupation, endless wars, grinding poverty, and enduring neglect. And so tobacco is passionately clung to by the farmers of South Lebanon's war-ridden borderland. But it is not as if they have alternatives at hand. "Tobacco is what taught us," says Dr. Mahmoud. He grew up in a southern village under the Israeli occupation and then left to study agricultural engineering in the USSR. Like everyone, he admits that tobacco is a necessary evil. "We are near Israel. There is no alternative to tobacco. Tobacco is the only thing that stays. We all live through this plant. It is the backbone of the area." Hajj Abbas, a Hizbullah-affiliated mayor of a Shi'a frontline village that is now amongst the biggest producers of tobacco put it best. Referring to a period in the 1960s and 70s when this village had turned to communism (it was locally known as "Moscow") he admits: "Southerners can live without God, but they can't live without tobacco." Today, tobacco continues to thrive and its cultivators to survive in a landscape continuously buffeted by the fast and slow violences of war. In this chapter, I explore this hardy human-plant partnership as an ecology of resistance and survival that flourishes in the harsh and hardly livable terrain of capitalist agriculture, clientelist politics, and endless war.

Plants "are, like their roots, entangling," writes Myers (2017, 297), and tobacco cultivation has a deep history that has shaped South Lebanon for hundreds of years. Similar to what Gan (2017) describes for rice in Vietnam, tobacco in South Lebanon is an "aleatory formation," an embodied temporal configuration shaped by the (violent) histories of this place. The political economy of tobacco (like most things in Lebanon) is caught in the kleptocratic and clientelist logics and structures of the Lebanese state (Arsan 2018) as well as the imperial and feudal history of tobacco farming in South Lebanon. Tobacco—the plant, its cultivation, and its industry—continues to play a major role, through its multiple affordances, for the different collectivities variously benefiting from it. Tobacco was somewhat wrested from the clutches of the feudal landlords by a burgeoning labor movement in the 1970s, and in the 1990s its means of production were modestly redistributed to the "wretched of the earth" as a way of countering the structural and actual violence of the continued Israeli occupation of the borderland, where they lived. Through years of war and occupation, tobacco cultivation in South Lebanon, always and still a wretched lot, has tipped into the symbolism, rhetoric, and enactment of national resistance and steadfastness (that is increasingly monopolized by the Resistance/Hizbullah). But tobacco's difficult history, heavy labor, and meager profits leave a bitter residue—like sticky black tar coating raw, red fingers—in the lives of those who cultivate it and depend upon it. To its human cultivators, tobacco embodies and holds the tension between oppression and exploitation, on the one hand, and the only means of viable life, on the other. This chapter explores this unresolved tension as "bitter life."

THE TOBACCO WORKERS

In a Lebanese frontline village, life teeters on the cusp of summer. The tender growth of spring is already burnished by the summer sun, with a few tenacious wild blooms hanging on as tangled yellow bushes bunch across the rocky hills and steadfastly channel the zest of springtime. The air is warm and nature is raspy. Tobacco seedlings are already growing up in the fields. They are still short and shy, not yet the confident electric-green army that marches across every horizontal surface big or small and will frenetically work every southern household in another month or so. I am in the courtyard of Im and Bou Sahel with three of their daughters threading freshly picked tobacco leaves. We rose with the call to prayer in the darkest hour of the dawn while the dew was still heavy on the rubbery stalks, making them more tender for picking. Working our way through the family plots in the pink blush of morning, we collect today's harvest by twisting off small handfuls of leaves, stalk by stalk, field by field. As the village begins to stir, we return to the house on foot, carrying the leaves in big cloth bundles slung over our shoulders, which we dump in the courtyard before washing our sticky hands and breaking our fast: *labneh* (sour strained yoghurt) drizzled with deep green olive oil, steaming bread (baked as we eat by Im Sahel, who sits beside the dome of her *saj*, magically transforming soft balls of yeasty dough into wafer-thin disks and piling up the freshly-made, translucent loaves like gold leaf beside her), olives, cucumbers, tomatoes, and mint—everything homemade or from the kitchen garden—*zaatar* made from wild thyme from nearby meadows, all washed down with scorching black tea served in tiny glass cups half filled with sugar. Sated and somewhat restored, as the sun travels across the ante meridiem sky, and still in our work pajamas, we begin the work of *shakk* (piercing/threading), the tiresome, endless labor in these parts of women and children and occasionally the old.

On this morning, like every morning at this time of year, the women are sitting on the stone floor among drifts of fresh tobacco, their legs splayed open before them. They work at a fast clip, bending forward rhythmically with the movement: deftly selecting handfuls of leaves from the pile in their midst and impaling them on the sharp *maybar*, the long, flat needle they hold wedged between their body and outstretched limbs, shoving the green ruffles of leaves down the rusty shaft onto an attached length of twine that trails off behind them. Sap bleeds out of the tears in the rubbery fibers, coating their cracked, red fingers in sticky black tar. All this is done with barely a look toward the work of the hands, as it has been practiced since they were tender yet able. (I am nowhere near as adept; each of my movements is hesitant, clumsy, fumbling). This is the dance of every summer morning in South Lebanon when tobacco is ripe for the picking. Bou Sahel, after greeting his fruit trees and feeding the goats and chickens, takes his seat nearby and looks out dreamily onto the world, leaning his head on his hand. His two sons, who live and work in the city and visit on the weekends, pull up cracked plastic chairs alongside their father and sip the tea served by their attentive, always smiling mother. Tobacco is not men's labor, although it is a source of their life. They too, like everyone, acknowledge the life-giving force of tobacco. They, like everyone, say with ardent fervor and a slightly acid smile: *Al-dukhan m'ayyashna*, Tobacco makes us live.

Bou and Im Sahel, the old hajj and hajji, and the three unmarried of their seven daughters, Khawla, Nawal, and Zahra, are the ones still living in the family's village home, a stone's throw from the borderline separating Lebanon from Israel. Khawla and her sisters Nawal and Zahra are the tobacco workers of this family. The sisters (and their mother who does less these days due to the onset of age-related aches and pains) plant six *dunums* (6,000 square meters) of tobacco, as permitted by the Régie-issued licenses owned by Im and Bou Sahel, who inherited them and will pass them on in time. These six *dunums* generate an income of 9–10 million lira (at the time, around $7,000) a year. The modest income tobacco farming generates sustains the members of the family residing in the village—the elderly and the women and children—who would not be able to earn an independent living otherwise. Tobacco is the lot of those who stay. It is the crop of continuity, of survival in a place of many ruptures and difficulties. And in a world teeming with exploited urban migrant wage laborers, the ability of those on the rural margins to remain in place and depend on the fruits of their own toil on their own land is perhaps a good thing.[1] Tobacco cultivation is known to be the work of the poor, yet it is recognized and celebrated— and not only in ideological ways—as the crop of life and of resistance.

THE (PARA)STATE OF TOBACCO: AN ENTANGLED HISTORY

Tobacco farming predates the Lebanese state by several centuries.[2] It was introduced to the eastern Mediterranean by the Ottoman Empire in the seventeenth century. In the mid-nineteenth century, the empire established a monopoly on the trade of tobacco and then in 1883 turned it over as a concession to the French-owned Régie Co-Interesse des Tabacs de l'Empire. The French monopoly continued until 1929, after the dissolution of the Ottoman Empire in the wake of the First World War and the creation of the Lebanese state under the French Mandate (1923–46). In 1935 the French established a new monopoly granting exclusive rights on tobacco cultivated on Lebanese and Syrian soil to a private company, Société Anonyme de Régie Co-Intéressée Libano-Syrienne de Tabacs et Tombacs (mostly owned by a French colonial bank, Crédit Foncier de l'Algérie et de Tunisie). This monopoly was used by the French Mandate to galvanize the loyalties of the Lebanese landowning elites (the *zu'ama*, grandfathers of today's political class), who in turn consecrated their economic and political gain at the expense of their hungry constituents, the peasants, *fallaheen*. It is during this period that tobacco farming became entrenched, both as a political tool and as the main agricultural activity of southern peasant households who produced the cash crop for their overlords. Ahmad Beydoun, to illustrate the violent enforcement of the tobacco monopoly on the dispossessed southerners and the alienation of their land and labor, told me that during this time "it would be considered a crime for a peasant to even own a *hawin* [tobacco-chopping knife]!" The crop and the land it was planted on belonged entirely to the monopoly and to the big guys, not to those who farmed it. These were harsh times.

After gaining independence in 1943, the Lebanese state focused its attention and resources on Beirut and Mount Lebanon, neglecting peripheral rural areas. The creation of national borders in 1920 had disastrously severed the vital trading networks between Damascus and the coastal cities in what became the British and French mandates of Palestine, Lebanon, and Syria, drastically impacting the villages and towns of Jabal 'Amil and Galilee. This difficult new reality became much worse in 1948, when Israel burst into being upon the land of Palestine and the southern border of Lebanon became a frontier of war. Poverty exploded in the borderland, resulting in urban and overseas migration (largely to Africa, but also to South America and Australia). The time of wars had begun in South Lebanon, adding to the already fraught layers of marginality, poverty, exploitation, and neglect shaping southern life into a growing tragedy of dispossession, hunger, and grief. In the 1950s, '60s and early '70s, as the clouds of war gathered with increasing episodes of military violence across the land, southerners became more politicized, and tobacco laborers formed into cross-sectarian, class-based collectives uniting Maronite and Shi'a tobacco farmers (often under leftist and communist banners)[3] and organizing demonstrations, strikes, and protests.[4] The French monopoly remained in place, but in response to these agitations, minor reforms introduced price subsidies and addressed the question of licenses that had been exclusively in the hands of the *zu'ama*, the sectarian/political bosses/elites that rule Lebanon. As Fawwaz Traboulsi writes, "In the south, the Régie had become a private reserve of the traditional *za'ims,* who packed it with their clients and controlled cultivation licenses, which they distributed to their friends or rented to farmers" (Traboulsi 2012). In 1964 the French-owned monopoly was renewed for another ten years, but in a move to somewhat address the insistent demands of tobacco-farmers, licenses were granted to small-scale cultivators for the first time. Aided by the leftist forces fired by the Palestinian struggle in Lebanon, the southern villages staged a tobacco revolution, demanding the redistribution of tobacco licenses by the Régie. On January 22, 1973, thousands of tobacco laborers occupied the regional offices of the Régie in Nabatiyeh, demanding an increase in the purchase price of tobacco, an end to the speculation in licenses, a limit on the area of cultivation, and nationalization of the Régie, which was still French-owned. The tobacco movement snowballed, and eventually those demands were met, setting in place the order that defines the tobacco cultivation sector and its relationship to the Lebanese state to this day. The arrangement continued de facto throughout the Lebanese civil war that officially began in April 1975 and officially ended with the Ta'if Accords in 1990. The Israeli occupation of the southern Lebanon borderland that began in 1978 continued until 2000.

In 1993, as the dust of the Lebanese civil war (and all those other wars) settled, the Régie was finally nationalized and placed under the Lebanese ministry of finance (not agriculture!).[5] Licenses belonging to the old elites were cancelled, and new licenses were issued for those still residing in their villages and farming their own or leased land.[6] Of course this was framed as a grand nationalist move when in fact it also served the purposes of the state in the ways I have already noted—by keeping poor villagers in their villages through war and occupation and somewhat stanching rural-urban migration. In Hamade's view "the 'democratization' of tobacco licenses was motivated by political aims related to the Israeli occupation of southern Lebanon and postwar reconstruction" (Hamade 2014, 33) and sought to reduce the dependence of southern farmers on landlords or local elites for tobacco-growing licenses. By issuing new licenses to those still on the land and actually farming it, the Lebanese state/monopoly acknowledged the changed demographic reality of southern Lebanon, whose elites had been driven out, never to return, and whose villagers (largely tobacco-farmers) were living under Israeli occupation. One aim of the 1993 license redistribution was to provide Lebanese citizens with a means of income independent of the Israeli occupation to undermine collaboration with the occupiers/enemy. It was absolutely the right thing to do—politically and economically—and tobacco cultivation for the now state-owned monopoly continued throughout the years of the Israeli occupation (as it had throughout the Lebanese civil war that overlapped with it). Tobacco farming kept the frontline villages semipopulated (and the cities somewhat less clogged with desperate and bedraggled refugees). And at the same time that the Lebanese state won hearts for underwriting "national resistance" against a much-hated enemy, the state (its political elite, that is) continued to reap considerable profits off the international trade in tobacco, a cash crop and commodity planted and harvested in a warzone by its poorest and most embattled citizens. In short, this move of symbolic and charitable "strength"

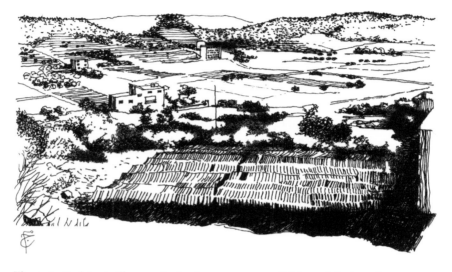

Figure 8. Resistant village ecologies: homes, terraces, fields, and drying tobacco.

by the state incentivized inhabitants of the borderland to stay put and to continue to grow the crop the state (its elites) made a profit from; the living presence of tobacco farmers in the occupation zone continued to shape a resistance to the necropolitics of war and occupation that the Lebanese state by itself was unable to realize.

The long and harsh Israeli occupation of the borderland changed the power configuration in South Lebanon and definitively put an end to the political dominance of absent landlords (the *zu'ama*) that had prevailed for generations.[7] New political parties and militant groups grew out of the histories of dispossession and years of war and occupation and came into their own: Hizbullah (and to a lesser extent Amal) emerged from the crucible of the many wars and the occupation as the hegemonic power in South Lebanon. Through those years Hizbullah came to interpellate the role of the state in the areas it controls (Cammet 2014) in a somewhat paradoxical play of who was there first (the state is not there because Hizbullah is, Hizbullah is there because the state is not). Hizbullah, as the para-state in the areas it dominates, today controls the machinery of tobacco as it does other domains, such as education, health care, security, and culture. The reconfigured logic of tobacco, like other institutions of (state, capitalist) power, was wrested from the hands of the old elites and became a medium and instrument of the new powers that be. Many who are employed in the production and trade sectors of the tobacco industry are affiliated with Amal or Hizbullah (this is not a unique phenomenon; it follows the absolutely standardized sectarian clientelist logic of public-sector employment in Lebanon). But tobacco cultivation, although largely Shi'a (because they are largest sectarian demographic in the South), involves all the sectarian communities residing in South Lebanon, because everyone there, *"fellah* or doctor or engineer," as they like to say, plants tobacco.

George, the mayor of a pretty, Christian frontline village, is as clear-eyed about the southerners' relationship with tobacco as he is about their relationship with Hizbullah (regardless of sectarian affiliation):

> It is called the "bitter crop" because it is hard work. Each phase is harder than the next. It is menial work, not mechanized: we work it with our hands and in our homes. But here in the [border] strip there is nothing—no factories, no employment. There is no state! And as long as there is no state and no stability here we will remain floating in this nowhere land. In the meanwhile, we farm tobacco. The Hizb help out—they compensated all the damages in our village [after the July War] and donated a bobcat and digger.

"I am not saying this because I have to," he adds, preemptively deflecting those who would cynically dismiss the brutal pragmatism of such alliances as serving political (and self) interests. "I always think in terms of what is good for my village and for that I appreciate their cooperation and their help." In places of war such pragmatism is absolutely necessary to survival and often overrides the identities and alliances prescribed by politics. Political allegiances that serve the interests of the political class inform the social landscape of the borderland, but up to a certain point. As I will describe in chapter 6, the politics of resistance and survival over-writes a prevalent politics serving the interests of distant and powerful others. Local collaborations count and mean much more and sometimes go against the grain of mainstream politics. Such is the attachment to tobacco, a "profane" cash crop that thrives in this warzone and that locals have partnered with to survive.

The Lebanese state, a complex and confounding (and incorrigibly, audaciously, tragically corrupt) configuration (Leenders 2012), is a central yet haunting presence in the business of tobacco: the two are deeply enmeshed, and their relationship comes into focus at different moments and in different affective registers. Spectrally almost, through the tobacco monopoly, the Lebanese state maintains a consistent and reliable (if extractive and exploitative) presence in the lives of some of its most disenfranchised and battered citizens. But almost no one sees it this way. Rather than the state, which is constantly (and accurately) vilified as absent, neglectful, and exploitative, it is the tobacco plant itself that gets the bitter praise. "Tobacco makes us live," "tobacco taught us," "tobacco is all we have," "there is nothing here but tobacco," "our life is tobacco"—these are statements made all the time by the war-seasoned tobacco-farmers of the borderland. Tobacco is perceived to be on the side of life; the state, on the other hand, is not. As hajj Abbas, the mayor of a major tobacco-farming (Shi'a) frontline village matter-of-factly told me: "We [tobacco farmers] have only two enemies: a bad season and the state." George, the mayor of the Christian village, who also works as an "expert" in the Régie, was even more dismissive: "Where is the state? There is no state!" So the state is and is not there at the frayed edges of its realm. It is an enemy and it is neglectful, and yet it hovers behind the stability of tobacco—everyone knows that. Still, as everyone also knows, the state monopoly subsidizes tobacco for its own political and economic gain: it takes everything and gives very little (but in such worlds, that little is a lot). Tobacco, the "bitter crop," embodies this asymmetrical and yet vital relationship.

"THE WORKING HAND IS FEMALE"

Tobacco is domestic labor. It is female labor, and often that of children (IWFCL 2002). The villages and towns of the borderland are largely inhabited by individuals who do not or cannot enter the wage-labor market (or fight): the elderly, women (daughters, sisters, wives), and children, those who hold onto place while their kin make money (or war) elsewhere. Tobacco income is the baseline for families who remain in the villages, holding down the fort, so to speak. Across the cultivating households of South Lebanon tobacco is the work of the vulnerable and dependent.[8] But it empowers them and roots them in place. It is largely women and chil-

Figure 9. "The working hand is female." Sisters working tobacco in the courtyard of their home.

dren who continue to work the land, keeping agriculture alive and villages semipopulated.[9] Khawla says: "I would like to point out that all the [tobacco] workers in the village are girls and women, *banet wa niswan.* Here we live with our father, but it is we, the girls, who work the tobacco. A boy works tobacco until he is ten or eleven, and then he either goes to continue his education in Beirut or travels abroad for work. *Al yadd al-'amleh untha,* The working hand is female."

As I sit and thread with the sisters, they share with me in words, feelings and actions their life with tobacco. This is clearly an ecology of care (Bellacasa 2012; Reisman 2021). Khawla, the eldest, the most outgoing and talkative, and my closest friend among the three sisters, takes the lead. In her mid-forties, small and compact with an intelligent round face, light eyes, and small, deft hands, she has worked tobacco her whole life. Tobacco, she feels, is her life. She is not married to a human. "I am married to tobacco!" she laughs. Indeed, she is bound up in its life and labor, its care and cultivation. Khawla expresses this entanglement as *marbuta,* tied, to tobacco—and hence rooted in the place where tobacco is grown. She describes her relationship with this plant in phrases and postures such as bearing responsibility, caring for, nurturing, cultivating, bringing to life, growing-up. And in a manner of a mother complaining about her children, she complains about tobacco: it is labor intensive,[10] it is tiresome, it cannot be left alone, it is a heavy responsibility, it ties her down, it is getting more expensive to plant and less profitable to sell. But for all her complaints it is clear: tobacco—in addition to its status as a base cash crop—is an affective ecology (Yildirim 2021; Langwick 2018; Archambault 2016) and a (counterintuitive) practice of care that both generates and grounds, sustains and saturates life in a warzone. Beyond ensuring her survival in a deadly world, tobacco gives Khawla's life purpose, a sense of independence, and ongoing, annually renewed meaning.

Because of the ever-returning waves of war, inhabitants of this rural region (like elsewhere) double down on reliable agricultural processes (Geertz 1963) requiring minimal risk, investment, and infrastructure and offering fast turnover. As Khawla puts it, "The nature of life here—you know there are circumstances since 1948, every little while there is a war or a catastrophe, *kil fatra fi harb fi nakbi*." Thanks to its natural capacities as a hardy dryland crop that can be planted almost anywhere in the uneven and rocky topography of the southern highlands, its reliance on domestic labor, and its makeshift curing and flexible storage, as well as its peculiar political economy that coheres with available domestic labor while also serving vested interests, tobacco fits local configurations (and constraints) beautifully. As a cash crop with a selling price fixed by the Lebanese government independent of market fluctuations, tobacco's reliability as a source of income is the magic formula the inhabitants of this regional battlefield need. Khawla calls tobacco *malja*, "a refuge." In South Lebanon there are no bomb-shelters, but there is tobacco! Farmers who tighten their belts and rely on subsistence farming for survival remind me: "You can't eat tobacco!" And more and more they plant it.[11] Through many decades of war (and other unfortunate events), tobacco has proven itself a stalwart companion of the suffering humans inhabiting these difficult quarters. Still, tobacco farmers are neither duped nor bedazzled by the shrub's saving graces; they acknowledge their relationship to tobacco as a hard marriage of convenience; they recognize the dire existential need that binds them to tobacco and its bitter toil in a warzone. And still they farm it, even as they dream of better lives.

Khawla says: "Here in the frontline villages, tobacco is the only means of livelihood, and hence people have to depend on it. Otherwise anyone would look for an alternative! The work is tiresome and takes so much time, and we get paid not very much and only once a year." To illustrate this, Khawla tells me about a guy in the village who won the "big prize" in the Lotto, the Lebanese public lottery. "You know what he did with the money?" she asks. "He planted fruit trees!" Fruit trees are a luxury. They take a long time to grow and bear fruit, their irrigation in the arid highlands costs money—digging a well and investing in diesel-fueled pumps and other irrigation infrastructure is beyond the means of most. This is nothing an average farmer inhabiting a frontline village oft-visited by war would sink meager resources into or dream of relying on as a source of livelihood, especially since trees, as "guerrilla cover," are explicitly and consistently targeted and destroyed by the Israeli war machine. The destruction of this livelihood would be an unsustainable loss to the average villager, who much more readily invests already available domestic labor in tobacco cultivation and can guarantee the sale of the crop every year to the Régie. And thus it would take the unlikely windfall of actually winning the lottery to do something so coveted and crazy, so frivolous and indulgent of just-out-of-reach dreams, as planting a fruit orchard. Casting her eyes greenly over the next hill at the leafy orchards *just there* across an uncrossable border and an entire world apart, Khawla says bitterly, "Look at the orchards in Israel just over there! Apples and peaches and pears! How we would love to plant those. But there is no water here, no infrastructure, no support, no alternative! The only viable crop is tobacco." And once again comes the refrain: "It is what makes us live."

THE "BITTER CROP"

The life cycle of the tobacco plant, a hardy vegetal being, begins in February when the powdery seeds harvested from the dried flower at the end of last season are scattered on the awakening red earth and sprinkled with water and left to sprout under protective nylon sheets (called *maskab* or *mashtal*) close to the village home. After fifteen days under the soft springtime sun, the shoots begin to show. After twenty days, soil is sprinkled over the budding sprouts, which get sturdier as they grow. When school is out in April during the Easter holidays, a time of rebirth celebrated by the many Christian communities of the borderland (who wrap eggs in wildflowers and boil them with red onion peels to imprint upon them the shapes of nature's rebirth and gift them to neighbors and kin, along with sugar-dusted, pistachio-stuffed *maamoul* cookies) families across the South gather in their village homes (many traveling from the cities where they reside) for the *zre'* (planting) to transfer tobacco sprouts from the tents to the thrice-ploughed fields. The young plants grow up in the fields nourished by the soft sun and gentle rains of April. Khawla's family pays a neighbor to plough their fields with a horse or mule-drawn plough, as Bou Sahel is now too old to do this strenuous work that is not easily mechanized because of the tight, terraced, and irregular surfaces of the borderland where tobacco grows. By mid-May, the earth has exhaled the last of its spring moisture and the rainy season has ended. In the highlands of South Lebanon, the warm summer air is humid and mornings are cool, and the tobacco plants draw their sustenance from the morning dew, needing no irrigation once they have taken root in the fields. By late May, the harvesting, *qtifi*, that busies the hot summer months of June, July, and August begins. Spring and summer are also the seasons of war. But tobacco does not fear war. Along with its cultivators, it has learned to inhabit and thus resist war's space-times and rhythms.

The tobacco plant stands about a meter off the ground, a bright green stalk with twenty-odd leaves stacked along the stem. The leaves are harvested at dawn throughout the summer. Five types of leaves are collected in harvesting "rounds," bottom to top (*tik'ibi*, heel; *thanwi*, second; *saleeb*, cross; *raqabi*, neck; and *tarbuni*, head) with the value and nicotine content of the leaf increasing as one proceeds up the body of the plant. The *tarbuni*, the topmost leaf, is the smallest and most tender; it is thick with syrupy black tar and has the highest nicotine content. Khawla says:

> With each picking you can tell from the thickness of the tar left on your hands, each picking leaves more. With the first picking nothing sticks to your hands, and that is why the monopoly considers it worthless. The higher up you go on the plant the more quality tobacco you get. The highest leaf is

Figure 10. Kboosh hanging like tinsel from on the terrace of a home near a faded poster of Hizbullah secretary general Hassan Nasrallah.

the *tarbuni*—it's the best quality and the leaf that gives a good price. After the *tarbuni* all that is left is the tobacco flower, *al zihri*. The flower you leave on the plant, and once you are done with the *tarbuni* the petals soak up the plant's nutrients. And it is from this flower that you take the seeds at the very end of the season: a flower with a beautiful color at the end of the tobacco stalk.

The fresh green leaves are sorted by size and threaded immediately after plucking and then hung out on drying lines, *thaqqali*, in the sun outside the home in eye-pleasing horizontal series that look like suspended furrows or waves, with successive harvests expressing a spectrum from green to gold. After about fifteen days, the strands of dried tobacco leaves, now copper, rust, and gold, are removed from the drying lines and hung in groups of seven strings looped in bunches called *kboosh* in protected areas in or around the family home. They dangle like tinsel from ceilings and rafters, on roofs and patios, terraces and garages, and there they remain above the heads of the tobacco-planting households, shedding invisible, sweet tobacco dust on everyone and everything until the end of harvesting and drying season.

In September begins the deft art of packing that varies in name and style from village to village: the *kboosh* are brought down and taken off the thread and resorted according to color (blonde, honey color is ideal). Khawla explains the "deceptive" art of sorting: "You have the leaves in crates beside you sorted according to color, and you pick the pretty blonde leaves and you face them outwards to cover up the burned and crumpled leaves." The leaves are thus packed into square wooden frames and then bound in burlap. Each bale cannot exceed 30 kilograms in weight. Most bales weigh 20–25 kilograms, as that makes it easier for the tobacco farmer to calculate the amount permitted for them to sell as limited by their license for four *dunums* of planted land. There are "tricks" at every stage, as Khawla explains: "The farmer tries to trick the monopoly, and the monopoly tries to trick the farmer. But in the end everyone is looking out for their own survival, because that is what we have toiled for!" Each *dunum* of land produces 100 kilograms of tobacco, and that is quartered into four bales, as each license permits the sale of 400 kilograms of tobacco per holder. As *zeitoun*, olive, season takes over in October and November, the tobacco tasks have been completed and the packed bales are piled up in a dry and dark place in the household awaiting the time of "giving up," *tasleem*, which begins around Christmas and continues into the New Year. Once the bales are given up, in the words of Khawla, "they line them up, one, two, three, four, and it is no longer your business." And just like that, a resistant ecology of care and a landscape of bitter life is alienated into commodity form.

Tobacco is an affective and vitalizing ecology that roots lifeworlds around the daily tasks, spaces, temporalities, and relationships that grow around it; it is resistant for the staying-power that this capitalist cottage industry enables. It is necessary to keep in mind however, that the care and cultivation of tobacco, for all of its affective nature and vitalizing capacities, is fueled by an exploitative capitalist industry that lines the coffers of the Lebanese state (more precisely, like anything in this kleptocracy, the pockets of its political elite and their cronies and clients) as well as those of the multinational companies that do business with it. Thus the feeling of being vitally bound to tobacco is also a stuck place of no easy exit, a dimension of enduring structural violence that for the past seventy years has been consistently punctuated by seasons of war.

TASLEEM/GIVING UP

It is a cold, bright morning and the start of another long day of tobacco-selling, or *tasleem* (literally, "giving up"),[12] in a dusty warehouse, an otherwise unused cement and corrugated-iron structure where tobacco farmers are bringing in their bales to sell back to the monopoly, the Régie. It is early in the year, January or February, the usual time for the Régie to collect its property from those who grow it and to issue its yearly payouts. It is also the beginning of Lent. In the Maronite Christian village where the warehouse is located and where the farmers from surrounding villages are gathering as the morning brightens, I observe deeply grooved faces that speak of toil in the sun, faces the same color and texture as the freshly ploughed earth in the fields outside. Some of the farmers have ash crosses on their foreheads, others not; but no matter, their sectarian difference is muddied by the undertow of shared labor upon this harsh and giving earth.

Hassan, the young engineer who works for the monopoly, says something that I often hear echoed across the tobacco-planting South, where in the 1960s and '70s a class-based political consciousness was cultivated that started to gain momentum before it was fractured by the events of the Lebanese civil war into sectarian enclaves herded by their respective overlords ruling the enduring vertical power structures of the Lebanese state. Hassan says to me: "In the city it is easy to tell Christian from Muslim, but here all growers of tobacco look the same. We look like the earth." By virtue of a license possessed by a named person for the duration of a life, farmers are yoked to this giving earth through the brief life and long toil of tobacco.

Ali, a tobacco farmer, recounted how his mother was getting too old to work the tobacco herself. He told her, "Come on *yamma* [mother] give me your license!" She shook her head and said sternly "Son, I am not dead yet." When tobacco planting is over, so is life, it appears. Another farmer was being jokingly chastised by the regional representative of the Régie for packing his bales with lowly pickings and he protested, laughing, "Sir, I have ten children and I love them all equally. Would you have it that I treat some better than others? It is the same with my tobacco!" As always, themes of family, life, love, pulse through the affective lifeworld of tobacco.

Here at the warehouse each burlap-wrapped bale handled by strapping young men is heaved onto a low arched wooden platform for the old inspector—the *khabeer*, or "expert"—to price.[13] Farmers mill nervously about as a bale of densely packed tobacco leaves weighing 20–30 kilograms is selected from the pile towering to the ceiling and dumped at the feet of Abu Fawzi, the old *khabeer*. The bale lands with a puff of glimmering tobacco dust that curls and sparkles in the cold winter light oozing in from a glassless window. The owner of the bale, a woman, is summoned in booming tones by Abu Fawzi's assistant. She comes and stands behind Abu Fawzi's right shoulder, hands folded demurely, head bowed, awaiting fate's decree, a barely suppressed expression of eagerness on her face anticipates the imminent, long-awaited rustle of money the end of this transaction will bring. Abu Fawzi, handling a smooth wooden paddle (*al-ma'liqa*, the spoon) to separate the densely packed golden-brown leaves, bends over the bale to inspect their quality, picking out small stacks here and there, caressing the powdery gold stuff between his fingers like the money it will soon become, smelling them, holding them up like gems to the light from the window that illuminates his freckled, cheery face.

The *khabeer* evaluates the tobacco leaves according to a depreciating price scale, from excellent, medium, low, to worthless, which is deemed of no value. In a calculation involving percentages, the *khabeer*'s assistant combines these values in a single bale and multiplies them by the total number of bales to come up with an average price for all the tobacco sold by one person/license-holder. The assistant then tallies up the numbers and prints out a paper with the breakdown of the assessment and the total price, which is now read out to the license-owner, to their pleasure or chagrin. When the price is proclaimed and the paper is printed and stamped and delivered to the farmer, so ends and begins another "tobacco year." The farmer, deflated, meekly takes her crumpled paper and shuffles off to the makeshift office next door to receive the money. Then the bales are placed in piles around the warehouse according to their quality. Each bale contains a year of toil in the form of tasks, times, care, concerns, affects, and anticipations

Figure 11. Tobacco dries in a *thaqqali* in undulating rows, expressing a spectrum from green to gold.

that compose the thrum of life in tobacco-growing country. As those dry leaves change hands, the crop that will be dead and sold a year hence is already greenly sprouting in the tobacco nurseries across the fields of the borderland. The tobacco tasks unfold upon the earth that brings the bitter crop forth with the steady round of seasons (Olwig 2005) and the agricultural rhythms that fulfill the promise of money, and with it a secured livelihood, once a year. This is the landscape of (bitter) life in this war-seasoned borderland.

Outside the warehouse, whose towering ceilings, dusky corners, and cold stone walls remind me of a church, the farmers huddle in murmuring, restless, hunched, smoky clusters of barely smothered disaffection, which they resolutely hide from the old *khabeer*, to whom they present their best face and pray for the best price. But once the price is declared, tempers can flare. One farmer, who had just received 4.4 million lira for his 400 kilograms of tobacco (an average price) spoke up: "I have six kids—I can't support them, *'ayyishon* [literally, "make them live"], with this money!" So I ask him, "Why do you plant tobacco?" and he looks at me blankly, as unable to grasp the very premise of my question. A few seconds pass as he gathers his wits and then answers: "Not plant tobacco? How can I not plant tobacco? There is nothing else!" He shakes his head at my stupidity, turning away. Tobacco—of course!—bridges the existential abyss between this life—and nothing.

"Experts," like Abu Fawzi here today, are the human interface between the Lebanese state-owned tobacco monopoly and the farmers in the field who plant the commodity that is later bartered on the global market by the Régie. The *khabeer* Abu Fawzi has been working this job for eighteen years, since the end of the Lebanese civil war in 1990 and long before the end of the Israeli occupation of South Lebanon in 2000. I sit with him daily during his fifteen-day stint in this village, after which he will rotate to another. Every day for hours I sit by his side as he picks through more than two hundred bales and prices them. As he does so I inhale with him and with everyone else the dizzyingly sweet tobacco dust as it puffs and swirls in the creamy light. Suddenly, a farmer who had just "handed over" many bales bursts out, shouting: "This is unfair! We pay 50,000 [LBP] for chemicals! This is impossible! The prices have never been so low! Just take them all for free and don't humiliate us!" Abu Fawzi flinches, his back to the angry shouter, but he does not stop smiling. It seems his face is made that way: ruddy, freckled, smiling, and kindly. He is used to this. The shouter continues: "You are pricing others better than us! Just because they have connections!" Sectarian logic colors all social and political expression in Lebanon, and so this statement is clearly a sectarian accusation—that those counted as part of the constituencies of the Shi'a politicians (the majority in the borderland) will get better treatment than Christian farmers. As the outburst subsides, Abu Fawzi, who is Shi'a but not from the borderland, responds to the angry farmer in calm, avuncular tones: "I price the tobacco for what it is worth. Give me good tobacco and I give you a good price." "Have pity! Poor us!" the farmer, suddenly docile, beseeches him, arms extended, hands open, palms up. Abu Joseph, Abu Fawzi's assistant, is a Christian inhabitant of this village and himself a tobacco farmer who has sold 1,000 kilograms of tobacco from nine *dunums* to the Régie. He watches the scene impassively, ever so slightly shakes his head, then lowers his eyes to the ledgers. Abu Joseph's stifled gesture is heartbreakingly poignant. Both sympathetic and dismissive, it describes the difficulty of inhabiting a rapacious and relentless political system that preys on its citizens—*everyone* must hustle to survive. In such a world, where survival hinges on the meagre scraps snatched from the table of the political class, who luxuriously thrive on the desperate insecurity of their clients and constituents, solidarity is a difficult—at times a seemingly impossible—path.

Turning to me after expertly managing this difficult scene (that happens every few minutes, every day, across the tobacco borderlands in selling season), Abu Fawzi meets my eyes with a secret and troubled look. He admits that his job is a thankless one. He—like the farmers, like Abu Joseph, like everyone not in the upper echelons of power—is caught between a rock and a hard place. "I feel for the farmers, I love them, I do. I try to help them within the limits of possibility—but I cannot do anything out of line." He pauses a moment, looking down at yet another bale he has to price that has just landed at his feet, directing his distress at it for a moment. And then, looking up, he buoyantly resumes his cheery disposition. "I don't love them more than I love myself!" he declares with a mischievous smile and a twinkle in his eye. His assistant Abu Joseph tells me, "We are the human front of the Régie, the institution that is the ministry of finance and the state! The price of tobacco has not risen since 1994, but the price of living keeps going up. I know it's not fair, but what can we do?" This scene poignantly illuminates the moral ambiguities and ordinary struggles of inhabiting a structurally violent and predatory system.

THE RÉGIE

I heard so much about the Régie. It was quoted by everyone and referred to constantly: Régie this, Régie that. It appeared as a kind of omnipresent, anthropomorphized institutional presence across the tobacco-farming South representing an authority (and reliable source of cash), the state, Beirut, international markets, an elsewhere. The southerners refer to it as *al hasr*, the monopoly, or as Régie, but in their pronunciation it sounds more like the French pronunciation of the name "Roger," taking on even more anthropomorphic tones. I went to meet Roger myself. The Régie headquarters is housed in a behemoth of brutalist architecture in Hadath, a Christian suburb of Beirut, and to get permission to speak to any representative of this institution is no easy matter. But eventually I got written permission to go, and I did. There, I was introduced to the director of the Régie's South Lebanon branch, Jaafar, a kind, helpful, and insightful person who was my guide to this enduring and labyrinthine institution.

The following week, I visited Jaafar in the regional headquarters building and factory in Ghaziyeh near Saida's southern exit, and he took me on a tour of the premises where all the bales of tobacco that are "given up" in South Lebanon converge. And here they are split, dumped, and resorted in an assembly-line operation worked entirely by women. Tobacco work is almost entirely the work of women, from seed to plant to market commodity. And yet it is largely men who earn the money at the levels of the village and the employees of the Régie's overstaffed administration (which like all public institutions in Lebanon is staffed in return for political allegiance, as per the state's clientelist logic). It is remarkable and illustrative how this system dominated by men depends almost entirely on the labor of women. And upon closer scrutiny, one notices that it is not a singular story of alienated labor and dispossession by patriarchy and capitalism and war. Resistant life makes its ways into the cracks. In the southern villages, men are often elsewhere—working or warring—and tobacco has become a supplemental income that underwrites the continued survival of domestic units in this borderland and warzone. The income generated may be meager, and the labor may be hard, but tobacco sustains women-led households in this warzone, saving them from a life of further abjection and keeping the borderland populated. Tobacco is the landscape of life here, binding people to the land, holding down the fort, guarding the frontlines.

At the factory I got a quick lesson from a resident *khabeer* who, dressed in a lab coat the color of a dry tobacco leaf, explained to me the art and science of tobacco-leaf drying, preservation, and sorting. Not a shred of tobacco goes to waste here. The women working the belts first dispose of all extraneous material, stuffing that is hidden in the bales for "free" weight, junk that has nothing to do with tobacco. Then the line workers sort the leaves from highest to lowest quality and market value. Further along the belts the leaves get smaller and smaller. In the end there is nothing but crushed tobacco dust—and even this is collected for resale! Nothing is discarded. It occurred to me while I observed these women hard at work in the factory that they were in effect working against the toil of those doing the growing and packing—their job was to undo the work of sorting and packing that takes place in the household tobacco "production units" in the villages at the end of the land.

In his cluttered office furnished with a big glass-topped desk and metal lockers overflowing with piles upon piles of papers, Jaafar explained, the Régie operates under the authority of the ministry of finance and is technically a part of the Lebanese state; its administration and finances are under the supervision of the ministry. Through its international trade in tobacco it generates money for the Lebanese state (the state does not spend money on the Régie). The Régie covers its expenses by operating in three distinct spheres: trade, production, and agriculture. The agricultural sector operates at a loss, the production sector (which produces local cigarettes named Cedars, smoked only by those who cannot afford anything else) breaks even, and the trade sector makes a (huge) profit. The profits from trade cover the costs of production and agriculture. The Régie subsidizes 13,000–14,000 tobacco farmers at an expense of $20–$30 million per year. According to Jaafar, tobacco is bought from the farmers at more than double the international market price of around $4 per kilogram. This differs from other countries in the region that farm tobacco, like Turkey and Bulgaria, where farmers sell their tobacco for the market price. "Before the Liberation, tobacco farming was a defiant nationalist project, as 45 percent of Lebanon's tobacco was still being grown in the occupied strip and sold to the Régie. It was a practice of resistance! Now it is mainly a supplementary income that women and children work while husbands and sons work elsewhere—but the Régie wants to change this," says Jaafar. He hopes to see tobacco as more than just a supplementary household income and more of a large-scale industry supporting many farming households and invigorating the depressed economy across the rural South.

The trade side of the equation is premised upon an international barter regime. International tobacco companies like Philip Morris and British American Tobacco and others who want to secure a segment of the Lebanese cigarette market have to buy a percentage of the Lebanese tobacco crop equivalent to that segment. The Régie profits from the sales of the cigarettes and the Lebanese state profits from the taxes on the cigarettes. A fraction of the profits generated finance the agricultural and production sectors of the monopoly. At the end of the day what it comes down to is this: the Lebanese smoker who purchases and smokes imported cigarettes finances the whole industry (Chaaban, Naamani, and Salti 2010).

And what do these tobacco multinationals do with the Lebanese tobacco crop? A crop that is worked by families across the Lebanese South, constituting incomes, livelihoods, task-scapes, landscapes, lifeworlds, resistance, and survival? Many—those who work it—assert, hand on heart and with conviction, that Lebanese tobacco is among the best in the world. But the moment they hand over the fruits of their intensive labor the tobacco is no longer their concern, as they have been paid in cash and are already preparing for the next agricultural cycle. But an employee of a multinational tobacco company that buys around 30 percent of the Lebanese crop (and thus corners 30 percent of the cigarette market) told me something strange. He said that the Lebanese tobacco crop is simply too uneven, of inferior quality due to a lack of systemic support to the farmer by the Lebanese government (and no nongovernmental organization will touch tobacco to make it "better"). Its fate is one of the absurdities of capitalism: Lebanese tobacco is bought up by the multinational tobacco companies for a corresponding percentage of the Lebanese cigarette market and is subsequently destroyed.[14] The paradox of tobacco casts a strange light on the whole industry in Lebanon and underlines how this enterprise and lifeworld cannot be understood in mere market terms. It is one of the absurdities and contradictions of the Lebanese system writ large and one that in many ways defies analytical logic—and it lumbers along in increasingly unbearable ways.

This rather absurd fate of the painstakingly grown, dried, and packed Lebanese tobacco crop as it is transformed into a commodity (and possibly destroyed) underlines the existential importance of tobacco farming in Lebanon. This cash crop that is produced by thousands of farmers along the poor margins of the country provides livelihoods and allows continued presence in place in a war-ridden periphery, making the landscape in times and tasks, rhythms and patterns of life ongoing, a resistant ecology of practice in a landscape of war. As I have already described, the tobacco subsidy is the vestige of a brief moment in early 1970s when the state was pressured by a strong labor movement to redistribute the privileges of the *zu'ama*, the political elite. The subsidy was extended during the Israeli occupation for reasons of Lebanese national resistance and remains in place today thanks to the ongoing grammar of clientelist politics in the post–civil war era. In a tensive space opened up between politics and capitalist profit blossoms a kind of life upon a thin topsoil and fractured, war-seasoned terrain. Premised upon a more-than-human assemblage of kinship and labor, terrain and makeshift infrastructure, and a hardy crop with a fleeting but vital presence, life goes on amidst the ongoing wreckage of war, nation-state, and capitalism.

MARJ, MONEY, MONOCULTURE

One silvery February day, as the earth is waking up from its winter repose, I accompany Khawla and her sister Zahra to a family-owned plot that they farm that lay fallow for two decades during the Israeli occupation due to its proximity to the border and front. We climb up a hillside to reach the slip of farmland clinging to a steep slope on a narrow terrace of blood-red rocky soil near the crest of a ridge, which is sliced straight across by the border. The only way to access this piece of land is by foot, and so we follow a narrow path up the hill. As we continue, some villagers on the road down below spot us and call up half-joking: "Where are you going? The Israelis are up there!" Khawla answers, laughing, "What do we care? It's our land!" The women feel safe venturing up the slope this close to the borderline because it is their land and they assume the Israelis know that. They say reassuringly, "We are often up here, so they [the Israelis] won't think it amiss." I nod and go with the flow. "Sometimes during the time of the [tobacco] planting, we are working up here and the Israeli planes spraying pesticide on the fruit trees on their side of the border spray us too!" Zahra tells me. It is a continuous and lush landscape scored and riven through and through by the wounds of war. We are ascending in the direction of Israel, and soon we arrive at a narrow terrace that is encircled by an old hand-hewn stone wall. The dusty border track, where Israeli armored personnel carriers patrol, is a little removed from the technical fence up here, and instead wild greenery clamors across the barbed wire from the other side, innocent and heedless of the absolute segregation imposed by human political enmity. Above the trees rises a spindly aerial stabbing at the sky. "This is our land!" Khawla tells me, pointing towards the aerial. The Israelis planted that thing in the middle of our land and then ate it up!" As we near the freshly-ploughed plot, the sisters show me a stone trough and well carved into the bedrock. "Our grandfather made this to gather the rainwater that sluices down the hill . . . from Palestine!" says Khawla. She stops for a moment with a wistful expression to consider what Lebanon and Palestine share and chuckles. Indeed, as the crest of the hill is beyond the border fence she is correct. "Our grandfather—and father, but not during the occupation because this land was off-limits to us then—would use the water collected here to irrigate the crops and rehydrate the beast doing the ploughing." Water heeds no human borders—ecologies of life remain resistantly whole despite the desperate and dividing human histories of warfare. This tiny plot at the very end of the land has been recently ploughed in preparation for its tobacco crop. It has evolved with the conditions that have changed around it and the immediate needs of the people who farm it. The plot used to be planted with fruit trees, which were chopped down to make way for tobacco, whose fast temporal clip and elastic, rhizomic (Deleuze and Guattari 1987) spatial dimensions are much better attuned to the demands of this warzone. Trees need care and time and space—they embody continuous presence but diminishing returns—their fruits are not easily converted to social security. Rooted in place, their sheltering branches are targeted by Israelis as partisans in the resistance. These days villagers prefer the easy money of tobacco. Tobacco hedges its bets and guarantees an income. It is the crop of resistance and survival.[15]

I settle down with Khawla and Zahra on the side of the hill overlooking their village, a jumble of single-story homes huddling together cheek by jowl. The *marj*, a flat fertile plain abutting the village, is a watery mirror, a temporary winter pond, a shrinking water clock that reflects on its silvery surface the pastel colors of the village homes, blurred like an impressionist painting. The *marj* used to be the village commons and was planted with a whole variety of subsistence crops that changed with the seasons. It is now parceled up into privately owned plots that are used to plant tobacco for the monopoly. The sisters tell me:

You see the *marj*? The *marj* is our village. There is not a single person in our village who does not have a piece of the *marj*. That's because it used to be a commons for all the village people, and it was where we planted kitchen vegetables, grapes, sunflowers, tomatoes, wild cucumbers, chickpeas, and in winter green beans, cabbage, zucchini, all of it! But now we only plant tobacco. That is because we need the money. We cannot afford to not plant tobacco. Water lasts throughout the season; we don't irrigate here and that is why this agriculture is called *ba'l* [from Baal, the sun god].

I think to myself as I gaze at the scene, listen to the girls, and nibble on the wild dandelion pastries that they brought with them, that the *marj* is a physical reflection of the growing dependence of the inhabitants of Lebanon's southern frontier on the monoculture of tobacco. As the earth warms, the water-face contracts, the reflected houses disappear, the red earth is ploughed, and soon completely taken over by the electric green of tobacco.

Tobacco is the resilient homegrown crop, the crop of warspace and wartime, an ecology of survival. Because of this, it is taking over the borderland, uprooting more diverse forms of agriculture and becoming a monoculture. As Federici (2012) observes, "War . . . reclaims the land for capitalist use, boosting the production of cash crops and export-oriented agriculture" (79). Tobacco unifies the dependence of those it sustains on its munificence, narrowing the diverse base of subsistence farming that has also contributed to the staying power of those inhabiting the borderland. Tobacco's success as a crop of survival is creating potential precarities as more people come to be more dependent on it and a monetized economy. For example, in 2018, most of the tobacco planted in South Lebanon was afflicted by a virus caused by climate change that severely impacted the livelihood of farmers who, due to their increasing dependence on this usually reliable monocrop, have fewer options for securing their subsistence. Still, in the presence of continuous war and the absence of real initiatives addressing rural livelihoods, tobacco, the bitter crop, will continue to thrive. "Subsidies to tobacco-farmers are a relatively easy way for the government to engage with farmers without having to invest in designing and implementing serious rural development policies that could help farmers improve their livelihoods," writes Hamade (2014, 45). And the Lebanese state, which is perfectly content with the status quo as it continues to reap rewarding profits off the labor of its most vulnerable citizens, will not initiate change. The farmers, too, will not budge; they cannot let go of their only stable source of income. They have, as they constantly put it, "no alternative."

RESISTANT ECOLOGY, BITTER LIFE

Sahel says to me:

> Here people are living with two faces. The first face, and that is the reality of the people here, is that they do not care a radish about Israel or the whole world who wants to protect Israel. And the second face is that when people here find themselves displaced or dying seven deaths then they prefer to die here standing on their own feet. This is what keeps people here! If people didn't identify with this geography and with this land they would not stay here an hour! Life here is not different from slow death in any way. Life here comprises suffering at the level of agriculture. For example, tobacco this year didn't work out because the state will not send anyone to advise the farmers what chemicals to use, what fertilizers. In this way people continue to live, despite themselves.

Tobacco cultivation in South Lebanon is a counterintuitive flourishing in a broken, ravaged world. Its contradictions embody the predicament of life in trapped and precarious places. Palestine, breathing under a similar set of unlivable conditions and in close contact with the same vicious adversary (Meneley 2014; Tesdell et al. 2019), has witnessed a boom in unregulated tobacco cultivation (Shuttleworth 2015; Melhem 2015; Palestine Economic Policy Research Institute 2016). To many in South Lebanon, the only way out of the wretchedness of life here is to leave, and indeed the borderland is severely depopulated. But the resistant life that remains is inevitably linked to tobacco. In the villages where tobacco flourishes, many remain: presence, *life*, and tobacco are always copresent. To those who cannot or do not leave, tobacco remains a lifeline of last recourse. In many cases, it is creatively combined with other modes of making a living to enable frontline village households to survive. By tracing the tangle of tobacco cultivation in South Lebanon, I have shown how survival in such worlds is crafted within overlapping violent processes along vitalizing but also destructive relations and practices that nevertheless knit together the possibility of life in catastrophic quarters. Instead of seeking redemptive spaces of wholesome alterity to capitalism's extractive and war's destructive logics, I illuminate instead an agricultural process in a landscape of war to describe a resistant ecology that thrives in the very midst of ongoing industrial-military wreckage.

In South Lebanon tobacco farming, which remains the labor of the poor, has been turned into a somewhat nourishing local lifeway. Female labor shapes a resistant ecology and a practiced politics of care in a world structured by extractive capitalism and military destruction. From tender seedling to dried and packed commodity, tobacco is worked by women's hands. Men, of course, dominate the institutional and transactional sectors of the industry. But the care and labor connected to the plant are female. Tobacco work enables a generally dependent and vulnerable demographic in a deeply patriarchal system and in a warzone to be relatively self-reliant; it enables its cultivators to remain in their homes and to plant their land amidst layers of difficulties. In many ways, the *longue durée* of war is lived by those perceived as its most vulnerable subjects as active agents of resistance and survival. The tobacco farmed, the homesteads kept, the kitchen gardens cultivated, the bread baked, and the provisions pickled and preserved by women inhabiting frontline villages reflect vital practices of (military) resistance and survival through seasons of war. In South Lebanon, the resistant ecology of tobacco farming that is worked almost entirely by women is an unexpected source of life in a wretched landscape of capitalist exploitation and ongoing warfare.

The life that grows around tobacco cannot be explained entirely in economic terms. Likewise, the deep commitment to tobacco's care and labor is not only driven by poverty and desperation (although that is a large part of it). Tobacco cultivation grounds and structures the lives of frontline villagers in this warzone. And although tobacco cultivation is grueling, the work that it extracts from its cultivators is more than alienated labor. In thinking about tobacco, I try to not subsume its labor entirely to the rationale of capital (Chakrabarty 2008), for the lifeworld of tobacco is too complex and contradictory to be explained away thus. Abu Gebran, a lifelong communist and inhabitant of a frontline village explained to me that the work of tobacco is like the household industry of small electronic parts in China: alienating assembly-line work, but in a domestic setting. I

Figure 12. The "expert" Abu Fawzi uses a *ma'liqa* to inspect a tobacco bale before pricing while farmers look nervously on.

appreciate the comparison, but I think the vital qualities of tobacco, its rootedness in the history and geography and topsoil of this place, carries with it something vital beyond than an economic explanation can contain. Despite its capitalist profanity, this relational economy is something more: it is an ecology, and a resistant one at that.

There are two apparently irreconcilable ways of understanding tobacco: as a grueling, laborious, embittering cash crop that serves ascendant political interests and as a valiant crop of resistance and steadfastness that has provided the only consistent lifeline to the impoverished inhabitants of Lebanon's war-battered southern borderland. These contradictory understandings are both true—one does not exclude the other, and a kind of life flourishes in this difficult contradiction and tensive opening. The bitterness of the life that is held onto and not easily let go of speaks of the fraught existential climate within which dwellers of warzones and other difficult worlds survive. The enduring nature of tobacco farming is not reducible to a singular logic, for it is at the same time a laborious and extractive cash crop and a lifeline (and lifeworld) to many. As Bernal (1994) has shown for cotton farmers in the Sudan, singular narratives cannot account for the entire story: "Neither the assumption that peasants operate on noncapitalist principles, nor the assumption that peasant households operate like capitalist enterprises is able to account for what we actually observe" (793). This is where affect comes in, the practice of care that maintains and sustains living landscapes and landscapes of living. Although the multispecies human-tobacco alliance can be seen as an example of resistant "human-plant solidarity" (Myers 2017), this "solidarity" does not sit easily with the desire in some more-than-human approaches to celebrate the wholesome, redemptive, anticapitalist side of multispecies collaboration. Bitterly thriving in the midst of rapacious capitalism and endless war, the human-tobacco relationship making life possible in this warzone is held in place by violent structures. And yet one cannot disregard its resistant life-making powers here in this wretched corner of the planet.

A conversation between Khawla and her father (and myself) illustrates the vital and passionate contradictions tobacco holds:

BOU SAHEL: So in the South, the coastal area from Naqura to Saida, you have orchards and you have water [irrigation], but coming from Nabatiyyeh towards here on the mountain [the highland plain of Jabal 'Amil] there is no water, so there is tobacco and grain agriculture, but grain didn't work.[16] Tobacco, when they first started, in each village there were only a handful of licenses per village [owned by the landlords]. But the Régie strengthened tobacco farming by allowing more people to have licenses. Now about 80 percent of the South—if it weren't for tobacco they wouldn't live here. What would they do? [He smacks his hands together in a gesture indicating "Nothing! It's all over."]

KHAWLA: But it could be that they [the state] are committing people [through this agriculture] to sacrifice them along the border, to keep the area weak—it is not just a matter of water.

BOU SAHEL: No! that is not true!

KHAWLA: This area stays weak and people who don't have anything will do anything to continue to fight Israel from their hunger.

BOU SAHEL [SHOUTING]:   If they cut off tobacco how could we stay here an hour! [His voice vibrates with emotion. The very prospect of leaving this place is devastating to him.]

KHAWLA: The way they have done plantations [in Israel] let them [the Lebanese state] make plantations here as well! It is a conspiracy of the state against the people!

BOU SAHEL: Plantations of what?! You don't have enough land here! Say someone wants to plant a *dunum* of *bamiyeh* [okra]—what would that *dunum* of okra do for him? You will need to plant 40 *dunums*! [He is making a point about the lack of wide expanses of land for largescale agriculture in South Lebanon and how tobacco is just fine with that, as opposed to other cash crops.]

ME: So you think tobacco is good for southerners?

BOU SAHEL: Tobacco is the most basic thing. It is sustaining and keeping southerners alive. There is no alternative.

During the 2006 war, the tobacco crop, as the source of southern life, was heavily targeted by the Israeli war machine. The Israelis burned fields and peppered them with cluster bombs in the month-long conflagration that took place during tobacco's harvest season. Khawla says: "We are committed to our daily routines, yet if you think in longer terms then you will become anxious and you will begin to live in worry and say, goodness, if anything happens the tobacco will go! But you can't think that way!" In the aftermath of the 2006 war, some "with connections" got recompensed for their lost tobacco crop, but most tobacco farmers "got themselves out of the hole one way or another." Khawla says to me with confidence: "As long as we have our health and our land we can plant tobacco again and we will live."

Tobacco cultivation is an ecology of practice (a resistant ecology in a landscape of war) that enables those it ensnares to somewhat resist hopeless poverty, displacement, and endless, destructive war. At the same time, we must recognize that the persistence and ubiquity of tobacco farming is generated and fueled by the harsh conditions created by war, capitalism, and the predatory nation-state. The life that thrives around tobacco cultivation, an ecology of resistance and survival in an often unlivable world, holds the tension between deadliness and vitality. The tension does not resolve. It remains suspended as bitter life.

4 How to Live (and Die) in an Explosive Landscape

Across the lush southern landscape, cheek by jowl with planted fields, snuggled up to olive groves, blooming in picturesque valleys, and nestled at the foot of majestic mountains, are signs warning of deadly things. Angry red triangles emblazoned with skull and crossbones warn: "Danger Mines!" Other signs elaborate the threat: "Dangerous Area! Mines . . . Suspicious objects . . . Unexploded bombs . . . Danger to your life . . . And to the life of your family! Don't get close! Don't touch!" And a UNIFIL-sponsored poster campaign across borderland municipalities begs: "Don't pick the wrong fruit! Unexploded cluster bombs kill!" These ubiquitous markers of doom are mostly scoffed at by locals, who sometimes pilfer them to hilariously decorate their tractors or to provocatively include them in an "objects of war" display at home. Mainly though, they are ignored for a more serious reason: staying alive.

This chapter describes a rather peculiar resistant ecology prevalent across the South Lebanon borderland that merges life-making pathways with enduring technologies of death in an artful and resistant pas de deux that (like most things) is nevertheless not infallible. Here, I illuminate the everyday precarity of living in militarized worlds where those who must carry on do so amidst recurrent bouts of war and the "slow violence"

Figure 13. Tractor with a "Danger Mines" sign. Somewhere in a minefield, a sign is missing.

(Nixon 2013) of those wars' enduring remains (Navaro-Yashin 2009; Henig 2019; Kim 2016). In South Lebanon, humans and goats form multispecies assemblages that enliven a landscape peppered with deadly unexploded ordnance such as mines and cluster bombs. These nestled explosives intentionally target "the hybrid forms of human and nonhuman coexistence and encloses them within the interior world of the war machine" (Shaw 2016, 14). Naturally, residents are perfectly aware of the bombs planted in the earth and dangling from branches, and they resist them by pursuing their lifeways all the same. "Daughter! Death is in human livelihood!" 'Am Dawud reminds me, as if it is just crazy that I could overlook such a crucial and yet mundane detail. In a warzone, navigation, habitation, and domestication are creative everyday acts[1] that reclaim a place of war for life. As the authors of "The Geography of Warscape" (Korf et al. 2010) write, "Navigating in perilous and life-threatening warscapes demands actors to redraw trajectories, strategies and tactics of agency. With increasing navigation experience, these tactics and strategies become ingrained in specific everyday praxis" (389). If war is a condition that targets the living environment (Sloterdijk 2009), then resistant ecologies are the life-making relations that bind humans, animals, plants, and minerals, as well as spirits, into hardy and durable "survival collectives" (Tsing 2015) that are resistantly able to continue to live in such deadly worlds. Resistant ecologies are life-making practices that through war's *longue durée* "become with" (Haraway 2016) the death lurking in the everyday pursuit of living.

In this chapter, I depict the practiced (if not failsafe) arts of living amidst the explosive remnants of war. By insisting on an approach to war that does not fixate solely upon war's violent dimensions but also actively recognizes the vitalizing relationships and dynamic pathways that are forged amidst war's lethal objects and technologies, I formulate a decolonized and ecologized approach to war. Not unlike denizens of other disastrous sites of industrial modernity and environmental destruction, those who have no choice but to live in deadly warzones strive to make and hold onto life in these worlds. Indeed in war, too, "Humans become only one of many participants making livability" (Tsing 2015, 263). And war as a lethal environment must be resisted by its dwellers "through the worlding labor of a multiplicity of beings of which humans are only one kind" (Govindrajan 2018, 19). Through careful attention to the agency and life-making strategies innovated by those who have no choice but to continue to live in such deadly worlds we recognize that living in a warzone, like other deadly environments of the Anthropocene, is also a multispecies affair.

·   ·   ·   ·   ·

Before the advent of the border/front and wars to South Lebanon, inhabitants of Jabal 'Amil and Galilee relied on various kinds of livestock: camels, mules, donkeys, horses, cattle, and goats. The use of pack animals declined with the fixing of borders and the rise of motorized transport. Since the beginning of war in the area, cattle have become a liability (too expensive to buy and feed, too difficult to protect and maintain in times of active war), yet goats have continued to thrive. Goat herding continues to be practiced across the borderland, and goats remain the most viable and

Figure 14. Inquisitive goats at home in the explosive landscape.

lucrative livestock in this warzone, because of their compatibility with wartime environments and unexploded ordnance. Goats are flexible and movable and can survive periods of scarcity during active war, occupations, or invasions by foraging for food and eating almost anything. Most crucially, goats are small and light and can graze in the borderland's many minefields without setting off the hidden explosives that are designed to kill humans, who are not as light-footed. So the mine-neutralizing qualities of goats are well known among locals, who send their nimble beasts to nutritious (because fallow or grown wild) mined pastures. In this way, an explosive military technology that endures in lived worlds long after conflict is over, is reoccupied and resisted by a homegrown, antimine survival collective. These beings—humans and otherwise—have no choice but to live in such deadly places, and these bombs are a part of their ordinary worlds. When technologies of death become a part of the world as lived they must be depicted as such. This is not a naturalizing move, but an ethnographic one that compels us to think of war not as an event, but as a structure, an environment, a landscape where life creatively resists death.

"Goats have persisted while other animals faltered," writes Penny Johnson in *Companions in Conflict: Animals in Occupied Palestine* (2019, 57). "Goats can survive in scrubland and continue to produce milk even when the land's deeply rooted weeds, twigs, and dry grasses are the only food available" (ibid.). Hardy, light, relatively inexpensive, reproducible, replaceable, and moveable, are some of the qualities that have allowed goats to flourish in this seasoned battlefield. One of the primary reasons goats thrive in the South Lebanon borderland is that they are too light to spring mines and can forage, nibble, and graze to their hearts' content in the borderland's many minefields where delicious grasses grow throughout the long dry season. As a result, the humans who also need to continue to live here have aligned their lifeways with the resistant qualities of those clever beasts (who are sources of milk, meat, and manure), and together humans and goats find a way to inhabit and in this way resist the explosive landscape. But making-live by tricking mines is by no means an easy art or an accurate science, and the threat of death-in-livelihood remains. Among other things, goatherds are frequently abducted by the Israeli Army on border patrol and taken in for questioning. Their flocks are confiscated; they are regularly accused of covering up for or aiding and abetting guerrillas; and they are shot at if they wander too close to the border fence. One goatherd put it to me thus: "Because of the places we frequent, we are distrusted by everyone." And needless to say, and despite their goats' adeptness at not triggering mines, humans continue to stumble upon explosives, setting them off (cluster bombs are another kind of explosive prevalent in South Lebanon that are more erratic and hence harder to live with than mines). It is a hard and deadly life, but a life nonetheless.

THE LANDSCAPE AS WEAPON

During the 2006 July War between Israel and Lebanon, Israel rained, *poured*, on South Lebanon—villages, towns, roads, valleys, fields, orchards, gardens, homes—4.6 million cluster bombs,[2] seeding the earth with deadly explosives. The cluster bombs used by Israel in Lebanon are largely leftover stock from the munitions used by the US in Vietnam that were given to Israel by the US. Because they are old, a disproportionate number of the bomblets did not explode upon impact and remained where they landed, transforming into de facto mines, "a deadly legacy of unexploded duds that continue to kill and injure civilians on a daily basis and impede efforts to rebuild lives and livelihoods in the wake of conflict"(HRW 2008). TeKimiti Gilbert is a mines-clearance expert heading the United Nations Mine Action and Coordination Center (UNMACC) who I met in 2009 in Naqura at the highly fortified UNIFIL headquarters surrounded by blast walls and metal watchtowers. UNMACC's offices were located in several prefab structures within the camp, and there I spent several hours talking to Gilbert, who, like most of those working in de-mining, is a former military man with strong opinions about the gratuitous lethality and excessive nature of unexploded ordnance across South Lebanon. Gilbert said:

> If you listen to the Israelis, they will tell you they were targeting Hizbullah sites and Hizbullah positions. That is what they tell us is the reasoning behind where they strike. However, if you look at the ground, there are a lot of areas that you can tell there were no Hizbullah positions there.
> To be fair there were a lot of rockets, Katyushas, being fired from orchards, although I don't think that explains everything. Obviously, there was a balance; yes the Israelis were targeting Hizbullah sites, however the cluster bombs came in the last three days. So up until then, there was a lot of fighting, a lot of bombs, a lot of naval gunfire, a lot of ground fire, ground fighting especially in Maroun al Ras and Bint Jbeil. And up until then, there was very limited use of cluster bombs. But in the last few days there was a curfew imposed by the Israelis saying that anyone out on the streets is a target so stay in your homes, don't move—and so people weren't moving anywhere. And the cluster bombs came in the last few days. Given the contamination we experienced afterwards, I find it very unlikely that these cluster bombs were targeting only Hizbullah. My personal opinion is that there were three days left, the [UN] Security Council agreed [that] on August 4th, 8 pm local time fighting stops. So both sides were taking the opportunity to inflict as much damage and destruction as they could before the ceasefire.
> I think the Israelis held off using cluster bombs until the end because they weren't sure whether they were going to have their own forces moving

into these areas. However, once the ceasefire had been agreed to they knew that things are going to stop. So they knew that okay, three days to go. Let's just saturate the country with cluster bombs. They pointed their guns in the direction of Lebanon and then—fire!

"What we did was monstrous, we covered entire towns in cluster-bombs," an Israeli soldier heading a rocket unit said to *Haaretz* (September 12, 2006). In a report for Landmine Action entitled "Foreseeable Harm: The Use and Impact of Cluster Munitions in Lebanon, 2006," Nash (2006) writes that Israel's "excessive" cluster bombing of South Lebanon did "not appear to have had any significant impact toward the military aims stated by Israel during the war. The massive and widespread use of cluster munitions across South Lebanon doesn't seem to accord with any recognizable military strategy." When I spoke with Claus Nielsen, head of the Danish de-mining outfit Dan Church Aid, he described Israel's use of cluster munitions as "excessive": "There is no strategic pattern to cluster contamination. It is pure contamination, pure obstruction of land. When you block the land, you block the farmer's livelihood." A former military man, Nielsen insisted that this cluster bombing of landscape exceeded any military purposes. "It is pure terror what the Israelis have done, the resistance [Hizbullah] was not in such huge areas. It is pure terror to block access to the land that is so important. A farmer's field or orchard is not a battle tank! *Everything* is contaminated."[3]

This is the logic of "terror" that has been deployed by (imperial) militaries since the dawn of industrial warfare. As Sloterdijk writes in *Terror from the Air* (2009): "The 20th century will be remembered as the age whose essential thought consisted in targeting no longer the body, but the enemy's environment. This is the basic idea of terrorism in the more explicit sense" (14). Rob Nixon (2007) observes, "when, in defiance of the Geneva conventions, American, British, Israeli and Russian forces have fired cluster bombs into populated areas, the failed offspring of those bombs become, long term and en masse, 'situational obstacles' to life itself" (167). It is what Sloterdijk (2009) describe as "the ecologization of warfare" (53), drawing our attention to the way in which modern warfare targets the atmosphere, the very living environment of the organism and in this way destroys its capacity to live. Applying the logic of "atmoterrorism" (ibid.), or environmental warfare, Israel targeted the landscape to disrupt the living ecologies it contains and sustains.[4] By flooding the landscape with explosives, Israel in South Lebanon sought to transform the environment of the borderland into a deadly weapon. Thus the "flooding" or "seeding" of southern land with bombs was intended to disrupt ecologies of living across the southern borderland. "Terrorism, from an environmental perspective, voids the distinction between violence against people and violence against things: it comprises a form of violence against the very human-ambient "things" without which people cannot remain people" (Sloterdijk 2009, 25). The "things" targeted by the Israeli war machine in South Lebanon are the ecologies, landscapes, and lifeworlds described in this book that resist by finding ways to stay alive in Israel's explicitly ecocidal wars. When the target of war is life, to insist on living is to resist.

After the July war, more than forty people were killed and around three hundred injured by landmines and unexploded cluster bombs. A fog of fear clung to the landscape, the source of life but now a place of death and danger. "The land is scary now," villagers would say. Describing the long and too often invisible aftermath of militarized conflict, Nixon (2013) writes, "Whole provinces inhabit a twilight realm in which everyday life remains semimilitarized and in which the earth itself must be treated with permanent suspicion, as armed and dangerous" (169). In the July 2006 war's immediate aftermath, a humanitarian campaign was launched in South Lebanon to clear away the cluster bombs, and about 200,000 were removed. Since then, the clearing effort has petered out due to lack of funding (humanitarian relief has a short attention span as Didier Fassin [2012] points out). Another season of war may have blown over, but the cluster bombs remain, adding another layer of lethality to that already presented by the minefields across the borderland. Says Gilbert:

> We know there are around a thousand minefields along the Blue Line, which equates to around 357,000 mines along the Blue Line, based on records. And we know because we can clearly see the minefields down there, there is a fence there and there is a minefield fence and a technical fence, so in between the two, there are mines. And to be honest we don't need the records because we know where the minefields are. So the situation we have

now is that there are still cluster bombs in the South and there's a lot less than when we first started back in 2006, and it's been almost three years now of clearance and there's been a lot of clearance conducted, a lot of money has gone into this. Around 190,000 cluster bombs that we know about that have been located and destroyed, which is a joint effort from the Lebanese Army, the UNIFIL teams, and the civilian organizations that we have working here. The job isn't finished, there's still work to be done. But like everything else, Lebanon is now falling off the world's attention. Until the next conflict, whenever it happens. And that's the reality. The international community loses interest. In 2007, at the height of mine clearance activity, we had 61 cluster teams, in 2008 they dropped to 44, and in 2009 at the start of this year, we started with 40 and we've now dropped down to around 27 teams now, so it's a third of the team we had back in 2007.

More than a million cluster bombs and 357,000 landmines remain planted in the earth of South Lebanon. And they are not going away any time soon. They are a part of the environment that the inhabitants of the borderland must live with. According to Gilbert, relatively speaking and despite its "postage stamp" size, Lebanon is the country worst affected by cluster bombs in terms of contamination density. Cluster bombs and mines as physical remnants of war entangle with the lives and livelihoods of the borderland's inhabitants in ways that extend into periods when wartime violence is not acute (Touhouliotis 2018). It is clear, though, that dwellers of the southern borderland must contend with the deadly nature of the land to continue to live there. As has been observed in other bomb-infested landscapes (Zani 2019; Kim 2016; Henig 2019), bombs do not deter farmers from using the land.

Gilbert stressed that mines and cluster bombs become a problem when people use the land. He says:

Up until May 2000 the mines weren't a really big problem. Because [of the Israeli occupation] people weren't using the land extensively; relatively speaking there was less agriculture going on. . . . However, after the withdrawal, as you can imagine, there was a lot of happiness and people . . . came flooding back to the South, and they were confronted by these minefields. And there were a lot of accidents that occurred just after the withdrawal, because people were unaware of the mines and people were desperate to cultivate the land and get their livelihoods restarted again. [Because of the ongoing state of war] the Lebanese government excluded a number of areas [from mine clearance]: the Blue Line and minefields north of the Litani

river. The people who are suffering are the [frontline] villages on the Blue
Line, because during the occupation they were denied their land. The
Israelis left nine years ago now, and still nine years later, they are still in the
same situation as when the Israelis were occupying the South. The villagers
can't use their land, and land is valuable in the South and not only for agriculture but also for grazing. So every meter of land for them is of use and
value. If we could clear that land of minefields and release the land back to
the people it would be so much better for them.

The inhabitants of the farming villages of the southern borderland who
have been living through wars for generations and do not have many alternatives are taking matters into their own hands, because they cannot pas-
sively accept the deadly weaponization of the landscape, the major source
of their livelihoods.[5] And although there are risks involved, they choose to
pursue their livelihoods amidst militarized ecologies, joining forces with
other life-forms (goats, tobacco, olives) to resist the technologies that seek
to disrupt their lifeways. They will seek (creatively, desperately) to reverse
the impositions of the deadly technology making their living environments unlivable. "Mines can function effectively as area-denial weapons
when their existence is discovered, most tragically after someone has been
killed or injured. . . . Yet the ability of mines to deter human trespass is
also viewed as a form of social control, surveillance and dispossession,
which some villagers resist, especially as they are loath to let perfectly
good land remain uncultivated" (Kim 2016, 177–78).

Gilbert shows me a mine and explains to me how it works—most inter-
estingly, how it works against humans (or cows) but not against goats.

GILBERT: I will show you an example of a mine here. This is a number 4 anti-
personnel mine, Israeli-made. That's all it is: a plastic casing. This
used to be a live mine but the explosives have been taken out—200
grams of explosives connected with a fuse. As you can see here it has
a lid, a collar. The collar sits on the firing pin, and it is laid under the
ground like this, around two to three inches below the surface, and
the pressure of a person standing on that pushes the lid down,
which pushes the collar away which lets the firing pin go forward
and it explodes—and it all happens within a flash. A millisecond.

ME: It's so small huh?

GILBERT: Yeah but it is powerful. 200 grams of explosives is enough to take
your leg off. But goats, because goats are relatively light compared

to a person, these things can often take five to seven kilograms of weight but that depends on the depth of the mine, how deep it has been laid. So generally, goats are not heavy enough to set off one of these mines, and the farmers know this. And they also know that the good grazing land is inside the minefield fencing. The grass there is a lot better, and so they let the goats go inside and then, taking the risk that, you know, these goats aren't heavy enough. However, every now and then cows get inside, and cows set things off. So, we had a number of accidents with cows losing their legs, and then they're sitting in the minefield and the farmer goes into the minefield to get the cow and gets killed.

The interactive agency of explosives and humans—and beasts in the South Lebanon setting—is productive of resistant, more-than-human ecologies and landscapes that refuse the military impositions of military technology aiming to enforce limits and control on life and movement. These explosives do not germinate and grow, but these bombs do grow worlds (times, spaces, horizons, possibilities) that are actively inhabited by those who must. Henig (2019) notes the ways in which "indeterminacy" and "fear" force Bosnians to "revalue" their relationship to land contaminated with postwar military waste. But what I observed among the (human and nonhuman) inhabitants of the bomb-infested borderlands of South Lebanon was not fear. It was an insistence on turning tragedy into opportunity, an irreverence and gumption that saps the hold of fear, creating instead attitudes and actions of vitalizing resistance in the face of such ordinary, embedded dangers. Such resistant attitudes to adversity enable denizen of war, those with little wiggle room, to reoccupy and reclaim the unavoidably deadly terrain of their lives.

In her work on the minefields along the Korean DMZ, Eleana Kim (2016) captures the dynamic, "intra-active" nature of the (potentially explosive) relationship of humans, nonhumans, and mines. She writes, "To think of landmines through a relational ontology means refuting the notion that either mine or human are ontologically pre-given. Rather, landmines, which were emplaced as an articulation of sovereign power, become, over time, unpredictable and deterritorialized through their ecological entanglements and evolving relations with humans and nonhumans" (164–65). Calling the mines "rogue infrastructure," Kim describes "the multiplicity of mines in their intra-actions with humans as area-denial weapons, indiscriminate and antihumanitarian political agents, military property, useless waste, and valuable natural resources" (166). Pushing past their reductive framing as tools of sovereign power and imperial geopolitics and "area-denial weapons," Kim explores the ways that mines can "exceed [their] expected technological and political determinations" (ibid.). I especially agree with Kim's observation that in addition to their destructive capacities, landmines "produce environments."

To those inhabiting the crossfire of national and imperial wars, mines are more than "military waste." Inhabitants of such worlds resist the intended political and military outcome of such deadly technologies by finding a way (however imperfect) to live with them. Rather than negative, abject, and melancholic framings (despite the tragic conditions), in South Lebanon I also favor an approach that shows how uninhabitable worlds are actively, collaboratively inhabited. I ethnographically describe how the deadly technology planted in the soil of life is inhabited, occupied, countered, and vitally resisted. Indeed, a farmer's field or orchard is not a battle tank, but the ability of the southern farmer to continue to exist in this enduring battlefield is a critical dimension of the resistant (if also deadly) nature of life across seasons of militarized conflict in South Lebanon. This is how war as environment is lived when it is not going away and when nobody else can or will help you.

'AM DAWUD'S COW

Along the northern slope of a ridge defining the borderline, where bristling Israeli outposts squat behind lines of cypresses, patches of tobacco and groves of olives intermingle with wild meadows, and little houses surrounded by little gardens line a road that ends in a small watering hole. The house of 'Am Dawud is the last cottage before the pond at the foot of the hill. His home is in the shadow of an Israeli outpost at the end of a dirt road that cuts a vertical line up to the top of the hill and the end of the land. This road is used by farmers to access their lands on the slopes of this rise, but it is also a military road many a tank has lumbered down in times of war. 'Am Dawud lives here with his wife and son; their daughters are married and live nearby. The house is a single-level cream-and-brick painted cement structure that, like many village homes, is built around the vestiges of his father's stone cottage. His father and mother are buried at the base of a tall pine tree shading the front yard, where his wife plants a vegetable garden and he keeps some bees. 'Am Dawud has a small herd of goats who live at the back of the house in an enclosure built against its southern wall. Beneath the Israeli outpost at the top of the ridge, the land falls steeply away and then levels out slightly, and there is an olive grove that 'Am Dawud lovingly tends. The borderland is mined, and sometimes with the rains the mines slip down the slope. 'Am Dawud is old and tired, but there is fire in him still. We sit on his patio in the shade surrounded by the hum and buzz of insects in the summer air. All the time we talk the Israeli outpost glowers on the hill above us. As is usual in the flow of such conversations, we begin by talking about life on the land, but as always what we are talking about is life in war. Mines have an agency of their own, and their actions shape the actions and the choices of the humans and beasts who must cohabit with them. 'Am Dawud says, sighing deeply:

> They [the mines] enter the village, and where they end up God knows. They come disguised in soil and enter a person's land, and you don't know anything about them until one of them explodes. . . . You cannot know. Our land is dangerous! Death is in our livelihood! But I work the land, *walla* I do. All the olives and the tobacco, I dug the earth and I planted them. Do you think it is only in my land? The whole border strip from the sea to Mtulleh is like this, do you understand? From Naqura to the last place on earth! They [the Israelis] have wired, bordered, and mined Lebanese land. Don't tell me, *khalas*, what can you do? I plant tobacco, lentils, beans, olives, all the goodness of God's earth, *al hamdulillah*. The most important thing is for a person to find a place of calm, *yihda balo*, and to live.

Through my conversations with 'Am Dawud I came to understand how the dwellers of this landscape of war allow the militarized realities they are unable to overcome shape their vital ecologies. 'Am Dawud's main concern is his livelihood, his family's and animals' and crops' well-being; war as event and as enduring condition enters into his *rizq*, his life and livelihood, as an inescapable reality that must be minimized and managed. His livelihood is deeply dependent upon the land and it is upon this source of life, also the place of war, that he must rely and return. There is always death in livelihood, as 'Am Dawud tells us:

Now when all the people left this place during the [July] war, we—all the strip—were displaced. We went a little down the road and stayed there. We took our cows with us to the UNIFIL [base] and they stayed there two or three days. But the beast, where she is broken she will return. So . . . there was no water. Nobody gave them water! So where was she broken? Here! So the beast found her way back here and there was nobody home. So she went up to the *birkeh*, pond. The mines are right next to the water; barely a few meters from the water there are mines, on the *qibla*, southern, side. And she stepped on a mine and died. I found her blown up and rotting when I returned after the war was over. And my goats were scattered but alive and I gathered them.

The sad story of 'Am Dawud's cow, who trod a practiced path known to nurture and replenish suddenly turned deadly, illuminates the reality of death in livelihood. It shows how those dependent on a livelihood that intersects with war's lethal infrastructure must adjust their life-making practices to the impositions of war by shifting to proven resistant alliances and ecologies. It is a relational ontology, as noted by Kim (2016). Those who live and labor in a warzone must be attuned to its demands and align their survival practices with its lethal limits in order to live. Since 2006 'Am Dawud no longer keeps cows. Cows are too cumbersome to be relied on by those who inhabit war. Goats, on the other hand, showed their resourcefulness, survivability, and mettle in the last war and have proven to be resistant. They are reliable, survivable. They are steadfast allies in the fight for life here. Like many along the borderline, 'Am Dawud and his family now rely on goats and tobacco and olives as well as subsistence farming to stay alive. His words about finding a place of calm amidst the storms of life and war have stayed with me long after he spoke them. Indeed, this may be the goal in any endeavor: to find a point of calm in any storm and to find a way to live. Because life is always precarious (Butler 2009), and we can never expect the sun to rise tomorrow.

HYENAS, BOARS, AND BOMBS

We walk in a deep valley enclosing freshwater springs and "health fortify-ing" forests, following the footpath that sinks down in a green zigzag between two level plateaus facing each other on either side of sheer cliffs north and south. The valley transforms into a defensive trench during times of active war as it gashes across the north-south trajectory of offensive and defensive warfare: shallow and wide along the coast to the west, it narrows as it cuts east and then widens again as it approaches a village nestled in a crook at the head of the rift. The plateaus on either side increase in elevation as they march away from the coast. During the Israeli occupation, this valley formed the border of the occupation zone. So for twenty-two years it was abuzz with resistance activity—surveillance, reconnaissance, and infiltration—and UNIFIL activity—observation and obstruction—and constant Israeli bombardment. Due to its geography and location during the occupation, this leafy valley was off-limits to the inhabitants of the nearby villages, as a place of wilderness and warfare. Since the occupation ended in 2000, villagers have reclaimed parts of it, especially where the freshwater spring bubbles out of the ground. But after the 2006 war, the valley once again became a place of danger and death, as the Israeli air force generously peppered it with cluster bombs to discourage villagers as much as fighters from frequenting it. But the inhabitants of the surrounding villages will not stay away. Families picnic, swim, and wash in the stream, and some—out of necessity—venture farther into the lush woodland, literally taking the valley's explosive nature into their stride.

Following a dusty dirt track leading past a chalk quarry on our left, we soon come upon villagers cooling off by the rock-pools to our right, families with small children sit and play in and around the green water. We continue along the dirt path, cleaving to a passage on a ledge against the sheer northern face of the valley wall, plunging deeper into the undergrowth crowding upon us in a friendly, pushy way from either side. Soon we realize that we have stumbled across a network of foxholes, bunkers, and dugouts—active or abandoned? Not clear, but most likely the latter. The ones we recognize seem to be in a state of disrepair. Plastic pipes stick out in odd places from under the earth. Under canopies of bouncy greenery, wooden planks reinforce an underground trench, and discarded pieces of olive-colored ammunition boxes are strewn here and there. Soon the path ends in a pile of rocks across the way, and the undergrowth surges past us, indicating the way forward—but not for us. A rash of oleander brightens the forested foot of the valley following where the water runs and where we can only go with our eyes. We look upward toward the lip of the gorge and the sky and note along the way several black cave mouths silenced with twigs and branches like fingers lifted to mouths: *shhhhhh.*

This explosive valley is the everyday haunt of goatherds and their flocks of nimble goats. Beginning at the entrance of the valley, at dawn the goats and their human companions wander, *israh*, slowly up the valley along the water source, spreading out to browse and graze along the flanks of the gorge as it deepens. Goats and goatherds spread across the hills and together encounter the war objects nestled in the woodland maquis. The valley is an ideal grazing ground: due to heightened military presence and sensitivity it is uncultivated, wild, and overgrown. And since it is not private property, the grazing of the goats can proceed without trespass.

At the beginning of the valley, in the clearing by the rock pools, I meet Abu Bilal, a Bedouin goatherd with his goats. Sun-wizened, spare, and wiry, and bent at the hip in a perpetual upward gait, he resembles the goats he spends his days and life with. A bit of twine pokes out of his grubby shirt between the buttons, and he holds a black nylon bundle in the crook of his arm—lunch. Every morning as the sun makes its way up the dome of the sky he and his twenty goats and ten cows make their eastward way up the valley from a village in the west. The cows stay near the water in the lower levels of the valley to cool off as the day warms, and goatherd and goats continue along the steep flanks of the valley. Like his goats, Abu Bilal has inhabited these hillsides for all of his life, and thus he has an intuitive sense and practiced knowledge of its characteristics, features, flora, and fauna. He intimately (Raffles 2002) knows the terrain with its many hidden dangers. He explains to me: the wild boars stay in the foot of the valley and only emerge at night; the hyenas remain high up near the craggy peaks; he does not fear them. Holding a finger skywards, Abu Bilal, who is *bedu*, loudly proclaims, with a finger pointing upwards for emphasis:

> We 'Arab, we *bedu*, are history and geography because we have been living for generations in this land. And the son of the wilderness, *ibn al-barr*, doesn't fear, he stays brave, *bajiss*. He walks in the night and he walks in the day and he doesn't fear. I walk in the night and my step is sure. I submit to nobody except God who created me. The brave man is not shaken, not by wind and not by a mountain. I am courageous! I don't fear the wilderness or anything in it . . . except sometimes those.

Figure 15. The goatherd Abu Bilal strikes a defiant pose next to a familiar object: a cluster bomb, at his feet.

He points his finger downwards, and sure enough at his feet near a pink oleander is a small, perfectly spherical cluster bomb. The bomb has been surrounded by rocks and marked with blue spray paint by de-mining crews. Abu Bilal says that he is always on the lookout for bomblets while wandering with his goats, and although they are dangerous and unpredictable they do not entirely cramp his style. As with the hyenas and the boars, he has learned their ways and can deal with them. "They are all over the *wa'ar* [wilderness]. When I find one, I surround it with rocks and cover it with a bigger rock so that we don't trip on it." He crouches down close to the small spherical object, unfazed by its deadly qualities, to demonstrate—I instinctively take a step back. Straightening up and smirking somewhat at my wariness of silly bombs, he continues, "The goats and I try to remember the location of the bombs we have encountered, to avoid bumping into them as we walk. We are pretty good at it together!" Their combined method is surely not infallible, but it does not hinder them from venturing forth, and so far they seem to be doing ok. Plus, "The best greenery is where they have thrown the most bombs!" For those who inhabit this geography and depend on it for a living, the bombs—as much as hyenas and wild boars —*must* be accommodated, navigated.

Because the uncultivated land is low priority in terms of de-mining, there is little chance that it will ever be cleared, and the cluster bombs remain hidden there year after year as deadly secrets in the underbrush and soil, and in the meantime Abu Bilal and his goats have little choice but to continue to walk this explosive landscape. The multispecies relationship to this lush valley and its hidden explosives takes in stride the danger of the bombs present. And so despite the bombs, Abu Bilal's feet and his goats' nimble hooves continue to tread their daily pathways together. "With such a close, centaurian synergy of human and beast, it is difficult to assign agency unequivocally to one side or the other" (Vergunst and Ingold 2008, 12). These resistant ecologies encompass "human-animal hybrids whose combined feet and hooves move in unison and whose perception is attuned to features of the world of common concern to such compound beings" (ibid.) Goats are nimble, intelligent, yet "anarchistic and whimsical" (Gooch 2008, 70) creatures who browse the landscape for edibles, climbing up rocks, cliffs, and even trees to grab a nibble. They communicate with their human companions as they alternately follow

Figure 16. Goats and goatherd, a resistant, antimine assemblage, *israh* in the mined hills along the borderline.

and lead them through the landscape. Goats and goatherd form a war-resistant antimine assemblage that must remain alive to the presence of the bombs in the landscape they daily traverse. By navigating bombs, these multispecies survival collectives draw explosives into the realm of the ordinary hazards that goats and humans encounter. Like poisonous plants, hyenas, and wild boars, the explosives are also generative of their daily geographies, lifeways, landscapes.

The practice of herding is a key landscape practice tying people to place (Gray 1999; Olwig 2008) and one that becomes more complicated as relationships to land, in particular regarding access, transform as political landscapes are imposed (Gooch 2008). In the case of South Lebanon, the limits on movement are less about the enclosing and delimiting of private property and more about the lethal presence of unexploded mines and cluster bombs in pasturelands. Land that has become off-limits due to cluster bombs and mines becomes more attractive to goats and goatherds, who traverse at their own risk. Counterintuitively though, the bombs (and the enduring state of war) have staved off other kinds of use (construction, development, privatization, etc.) and kept the land accessible (if you dare) and wild and juicy (Kim 2014). (The "wilderness" also aids and abets gue-rilla warfare, and the proliferation of "nature reserves" across the southern borderland attest to that). Abu Bilal and his goats—and other multispe-cies survival collectives like them—adapted their pastoral pathways to accommodate the deadly remnants in the land, resistantly reclaiming a deadly landscape. So far so good. They have still not stumbled. For Abu Bilal and his goats, the landscape of war remains navigable. Their encoun-ters with bombs in the landscape tame the explosives, domesticate them, bring them into their shared, practiced lifeworld. But goat herding along the Lebanese-Israeli border remains a precarious practice, and many are not as fortunate as Abu Bilal has been thus far.

THE HANDS OF FATIMA

The hands of Fatima are stained black. She sits in the heat of a July morn-ing in a pool of bright shade under a makeshift canopy outside her home in a village in South Lebanon, one year after the last war, threading tobacco. On July 12, 2006, Fatima was sitting where she is sitting now, like every morning at this time of the year, when suddenly, the air was pierced by the blaring of the village mosque loudspeakers. Fatima thought to herself, as she continued threading, that they were going to announce the results of the state school exams. Instead, it was a proclamation of that morning's capture by Hizbullah of two Israeli soldiers, the event that sparked what is now known as *harb tammuz*, the July War. Soon after, bombs began to rain down as the Israeli air force took to the skies. Fatima's husband Hussein was at pasture with his goats, like all mornings, when all of a sudden, he found himself lying on the ground, his animals scattered. Picking himself up, he gathered his herd and returned home, only then realizing that his hand pained him. Washing the soot off his blackened limb, he found a small piercing in the skin that continued to burn his flesh even after he had cleaned it. Hussein and his goats at pasture had been hit by a white phos-phorous bomb, familiar to locals as *harraq*, the burner, a weapon that is banned by the Geneva Convention for use in civilian areas. Despite his peculiar injury and the bombs that continued to fall, Hussein and Fatima did not leave their home. Fatima could not leave her tobacco plants, which were in high season and required daily picking and threading, and Hussein would not leave his fifty-five goats, who needed his pastoral care. The couple had weathered many war-storms before, having lived in the village all their lives, farming tobacco and keeping goats while bringing up six sons. The lively pull of their homestead that formed the entire basis of their livelihood outweighed the push of the deadly violence that had just reappeared in their lives. And so, like so many across the borderland once again turned battlefield, they remained where they were, weathering another war.

There are no bomb shelters across the South, despite decades of recurrent Israeli aerial bombardment, and so like everyone else, Fatima and Hussein sheltered from the shelling in their single-level, flat-roofed village home, which, like many structures in places of gentle climate, is built to embrace the environment. Since it was a white phosphorous wound, the hole in Hussein's hand continued to smolder and only ceased consuming him when he held it under water. The couple cowered in their home under the constant shelling. "Every bomb that fell, we couldn't see or breathe from the smoke and dust. We didn't have any windows or doors left to close! We crouched behind the cracked walls of our home as the war went on outside. Divine power is what kept us," Fatima recalls, pausing a moment in her threading to point with a tar-blackened finger straight up toward the heavens and lifting her eyes skywards. "There was no light, no food, or water. It was sweltering summer, mosquitos ate us alive, and we were unable to step one step outside. By the end of the second week of war, we were soaking semolina and tea from our larder in cold water from the well and drinking it to stay alive." During a brief lull in the fighting on July 23, the couple left their home in search of medical help for Hussein, who was in constant desperate pain and getting weaker. By now, the tobacco was withering on the stalk and the goats would just have to fend for themselves. "We left thinking we were dead," says Fatima. Indeed, it was only when they had given up on life itself that Fatima and Hussein took the decision to abandon their plants and animals—their sources of life. The old couple walked along blasted roads and eventually reached the nearest hospital, where they found that the white phosphorous had burnt

Hussein's arm down to the blackened bone. "His body was poisoned, and after a few days he died. His time was up," Fatima sighs deeply, with unfathomable sadness. She is very tiny, and her black-socked feet look like those of a child. Her face is smooth and almost expressionless, yet it is suffused with a mixture of resignation and sorrow.

In thirty-four days of violent conflict, with land fighting, mortars, and aerial bombardment, Fatima's village was reduced to rubble. As the final ceasefire was finally agreed, the Israeli air force dropped more than four million cluster bombs across the agricultural and residential landscapes of South Lebanon. The de-mining crews came to Fatima's village and began to clear the land by priority: first the village proper and the homes, then the agricultural land. The woodland and other such areas were deemed of low priority and were not cleared. But bombs remain in the land: "The de-miners keep coming back!" says Fatima, "They say this piece of land is now 'clean,' and then someone finds a bomb, and so they return. Fifteen times they have cleared the same piece of land, but it will never get clean—the bombs are hidden in the earth! And in order to plant tobacco one has to dig into the soil, so one never knows. . . . The land is dangerous now! Most of the land is dangerous now!" But that doesn't stop the farmers. Fatima has seen many wars, but she says this one was the worst, because its prime target was the land that contained the entangled sources of her very being: "This war was much worse than when they reached Beirut!" she says, referring to the 1982 Israeli invasion. "Before, they mainly killed people, but now they target the land, which is far, far worse!" This time, it is clear, the Israeli war machine was set on destroying the very ecologies that made life here possible. But war did not stop those left alive. Fatima found two bomblets hanging from her apricot tree and harvested them herself, with her own bare hands. A strange and deadly crop, but Fatima did not hesitate and did not fear. "Who still has life will not die," she says with quiet conviction, her head bowed over her tobacco. "We, people of the South, whatever happens we hold on to the land," she says clenching her blackened fingers into a fist. "We don't have anything else."

Fatima is not talking merely in terms of livelihood. There is a powerful sense of existential communion, too, for these practices and their rhythms constitute her lifeworld: "You need to just sleep one night here and breathe the air here, and you will understand," she says to me with the glimmer of smile. Military logic often misjudges the power of existential sources of village life and their relationship to both civilian and military resistance. According to Shaw, "Many believed that the U.S. military lost the Vietnam War because of how it routinely misunderstood the importance of village life as both a wellspring of identity and insurgency" (Shaw 2016, 9).

Today, a year after the last war, in which she lost husband, flock, and field, Fatima is threading tobacco. In fact, within hours of the final cease-fire she was back in her home, removing bombs from her garden and nursing her dusty and shaken fruit trees back to life. As she describes their return to health, her hands momentarily leave off from threading to describe the movement of supple young branches swaying in the wind and her face lights up briefly. When her husband died, she sold the goats, and now her life—like the lives of many across this borderland—is centered entirely upon tobacco. It will keep her here and keep her alive. And although that source of living has been made more difficult, the difficulties are—evidently—neither unnavigable nor insurmountable. One could say that Fatima has found a way to continue to live with and through seasonal gusts of war, always yoked to the swift, practiced time and steady income of tobacco.

Now it is one summer after the war, and Fatima is back to working tobacco like all the summers of her life, through wars and wars. During the three-month tobacco harvest, she gets up before the first light to collect the pickings of the day while the leaves are still tender with dew. Back home, she sits on the ground to thread until noon. Fatima makes a net profit of about half of what the Régie pays her for her tobacco at the end of the year, and this is what she lives from. But since it is only herself she needs to support these days, she remains mostly self-reliant. The whole time we were talking, she did not miss a single beat with the *maybar*, the long, flat threading needle stabbing at the rubbery leaves. And as I take my leave, she continues, leaf after leaf, thread after thread, year after year, war after war, until her time is up.

Fatima's unheroic and ordinary struggle to stay alive—to care for her only home in the world and her fruit trees that sometimes bear apricots and sometimes explosives and to continue to plant tobacco in the bomb-sprinkled earth—is a resistant ecology of survival in a landscape of war and devastation. Fatima and her tobacco embody a resistant ecology, a human-plant alliance, a multispecies partnership that quietly defies the destructive nature of the wars that have made their shared world.

OF MINES AND MEN

It is Sunday in this small border village, the day when families, dispersed across the generations, gather. Abu Nimr sits in the courtyard of his home in the midst of many: his grown children and their spouses and children. Yet he looks lost, forlorn, and quite alone, despite the cheerful hubbub all around him. The low buildings around the central space are an eclectic mix of old and new, used and abandoned, ruined and maintained. The older structures were used as enclosures for a flock of hundreds of goats, but today there is no trace of their former inhabitants apart from the empty troughs lining the sides of one wall, carved into the mud plaster. These structures are now filled with golden loops of tobacco hanging from the wooden rafters. I sat and spoke for a long time with the *tarrash*, the old goatherd, who had finally sold his entire flock—the last animal just two months ago—and given up his lifelong practice after the death of his son Ali four years ago, in 2005.

Ali was Abu Nimr's fifth child and the only one among his ten siblings who left school and instead learned from his father (and their goats) how to walk the warscape. "Ali had it in him," the old man says, rubbing his reddening eyes, which makes the blue of the irises stand out even more brightly, "Ali was interested in the work. The moment he learned how to walk he was walking with me with the *ma'za*, goats. Ali learned to communicate with the beasts and he had the stamina to be out in the *wa'ar*, wilderness, under the sun all day." Ali continued to accompany his father and their flock of more than five hundred goats through the borderland pastures in the landscape around their village; they would often run into trouble. More than once they were shot at. The old man took a bullet in his arm and was detained and taken in for questioning by the Israelis on numerous occasions.

Abu Nimr found that his goats' temperament and lightfootedness worked well in the militarizing landscape. Together they—human and animals—adapted to the militarizing realities of their habitat. "Goats sense danger before humans do; they would always tell me when something was not right—whether it was a snake in the bushes or Israeli infiltrators or guerrillas," he says with a smile. Abu Nimr continued goat herding during the difficult years of the Palestinian guerrilla war along the border, beginning in the 1960s and until the 1978 Israeli invasion. After the 1982 Israeli invasion had barreled over the hill and through their village and by the time the Israeli occupation had entrenched itself in the borderland, things unexpectedly became easier for Abu Nimr and his goats, as the lines of battle settled farther away from their village and pastures, north of the borderline that ran all along the southern edge of the village. "During the occupation, there were clear limits as to where we could go and when we could be at pasture," Abu Nimr says. During this time, his eldest son served as soldier in the South Lebanon Army (SLA), the Israeli proxy militia. This necessary sacrifice allowed the family some breathing room to continue to live within the occupation. As the rest of his sons neared adulthood they left to Beirut to avoid conscription, and there one became a policeman, another a schoolteacher, and another a journalist. Abu Nimr, Ali, and the goats continued to walk the borderland. After the end of the occupation Ali and his father continued to walk with their goats, selling lambs, their manure, their milk, occasionally their meat. It was a decent living, bringing in around 25 million lira (around $16,000) a year. Yet the warscape shifted once again when the Israelis suddenly withdrew from the occupation zone in May 2000. New realities came to define the geography, the border between Lebanon and Israel was once again a front slicing along the southern edge of their village.

On the day he died, Ali was walking along the main strip of road (which runs parallel to and barely twenty meters removed from the Lebanese-Israeli borderline); this would have been impossible during the time of occupation, when movement on the main road, which was priority access for the Israeli military and their allies, was strictly circumscribed and often violently controlled. In the wake of the Israeli withdrawal, new freedoms and new restrictions emerged (and new dangers). There was a period of uncertainty and trial and error as people gingerly came to get a feel for this new ground. Having inhabited the occupation since he was six, Ali was familiar with its dimensions, dangers, and limits; it was his habitat and home. It was in the more unfamiliar (if relatively less encumbered and less controlled) period that followed that he lost his footing and stumbled upon a mine the occupiers had left behind—upon the new reality that was over-writing, shuffling, blending, replacing, the older occupation order.

As his father greyed, Ali began to take over more and more of the stren-uous work. One bright cold day in November 2005, Ali was heading back home alone with the flock after a long day at pasture. The goats swarmed along the main road leading toward the village that runs adjacent to a well-known minefield. Heading east with the setting sun at his back Ali came up behind as the goats fanned out to the left of the road where the land rose into a gentle slope. To the right, where the minefield snaked along accompanying the goatherd and his flock, the land fell steeply into a shallow plain beyond which the technical fence defining the northern lim-its of Israel bluntly truncated the landscape. Suddenly, a pregnant goat lost her footing and stumbled down the short ledge to the shallow grass-land that hid mines. Although there were no markings that it was a mine-field, Ali knew what this stretch of earth concealed and moved quickly to help the goat back onto the road. Ali's instinct for danger was correct but he acted in haste. Stepping off the asphalt he stepped on the mine that the goat probably trod on and did not trigger. In his instinctive rush to protect a life, Ali met his death. He was thirty-three years old. He left behind a wife, two young children, and an unborn child.

Ali's widow sits in a drift of tobacco as Abu Nimr tells the story. She is dressed in black from head to toe. Her daughters, who are now five and three, help with the work of *shakk*, threading the leaves, and the boy, who is around seven, hangs around listening to his grandfather tell the story he knows too well. Since Ali's early death, Abu Nimr tried to take up goat herding again, but he could not manage. After he fell and broke his arm, his wife and children urged him to give it up, and soon he had no choice but to give in. His body was no longer able. Little by little he sold his flock of several hundred, and now, after lifetimes and generations, this family's goat herding practice has come to an end. "I am left alone without my son, without my goats," Abu Nimr laments. Although Abu Nimr continues to exist here on earth, there is something hollow, lifeless in his demeanor, movements, and presence. In fact, the old man does look lost. He wanders over to thread some tobacco with the women and children, but he does it half-heartedly and soon drops the thread and begins to cry. His

Figure 17. The goatherd Abu Nimr cries surrounded by his grandchildren and widowed daughter-in-law as they thread tobacco.

grandchildren clamber around him, accustomed (but not oblivious) to his painful affect. He lights another cigarette.

None of Abu Nimr's descendants will walk with goats along the southern borders of Lebanon again. His living sons are employed and live in the cities, and apart from the eldest, have established lives away from the village. Generally speaking, once someone leaves the village and the rural way of life, there is no turning back. Formal education, employment, and urban dwelling are considered a step up in social standing and ease of life, and hence very few take the step "back" to the land-based life of toil. These days Abu Nimr spends most of his time sitting in the village square with other old men, smoking hand-chopped tobacco from their own fields. The income lost by the end of his flock is now gained by leaning more heavily on the tobacco that the women (wives of sons, granddaughters) of his household work; he sometimes helps the women and children in threading, nothing a man otherwise able would consider doing. So, although years have passed since a mine ended his brief life, this old man cannot stop mourning the death of his son: for Ali's death is at once the end of a short human life and of a long tradition and practice, a significant liveli-hood—a lifeworld and landscape.

Bereft of his son and his flock, his lifeways and lifeworld, Abu Nimr has nothing more to say to me today. His city-dwelling sons, visiting for the weekend, take up the thread of the conversation when their father stops. They have set up a memorial and shrine to their lost brother in the *dar* of their home. They take me up there to have a look. As I gaze into the pho-tographed face of Ali, a spare young man with the fair complexion, bony face, and light eyes of his father, I think about how as different rural liveli-hoods become harder to maintain, tobacco, the bright green cash crop, almost always takes their place. As people let go of enduring traditions of practice in the face of insurmountable war-related obstacles, tobacco is often all that remains.

POSTSCRIPT

Sometimes life is stranger than fiction. On July 5, 2017, Abu Nimr, now in his eighties and after decades of nimbly tricking technologies of death, stepped on a mine while herding his beloved goats. He had returned to goat herding soon after I last saw him in 2009. His wife and children had eventually relented and allowed him to reestablish a smaller, more man-ageable herd when they saw that he truly could not live without his beloved beasts. On the day he died, a kid had wandered away from the flock and into the minefield. Like his son before him, he impulsively followed her and in doing so stepped on a mine that the kid did not trigger, and died. When I heard the news, I couldn't believe it at first. Such an ending struck me as almost scripted, stranger than fiction. But there was nothing scripted, strange, or fictional about it: mines are real, enduring, violent legacies of war that constitute and shape the local geographies and lifeways of those who must live with them and that continue to kill and maim.

Goat herding in a militarized landscape is a practice that shows us how human-animal collaborators—survival collectives or resistant ecologies—

Figure 18. Resistant ecologies: tobacco drying lines and an inquisitive goat peeking over the fence of its enclosure.

find ways to overcome the deadly limitations on life that the human-centered violence of war and weaponry impose. Military technologies of death, such as landmines and cluster bombs, are area-denying weapons. "Thus, although landmines are precisely designed for human triggers, once emplaced, their ontological instability creates opportunities for the reterritorialization and deterritorialization of space" (Kim 2016, 178). So the areas denied can be reverse-occupied by clever multispecies assemblages that can trick death machines designed to kill humans and transform now-deadly landscapes into once-again lively ones. But, as I have shown, making-live by tricking bombs is by no means an easy art or an accurate science, and the threat of death-in-livelihood is ever-present. Not unlike tobacco, goat herding is simultaneously enlivening and lethal—a bitter lot. In the summer of 2019, I visited the village and drank sweet hot tea and ate cold watermelon slices with Abu Nimr's eldest son, Nimr, the one who had served in the SLA militia and now owns a grocery store on the main road. Ali's son is now a tall, sweet-faced teenager who helps his uncle at the store. He has his father's and grandfather's light eyes. As I took my leave, I mentioned that I would visit the wife and mother of the dead goatherds and belatedly pay my condolences. "Don't," Nimr urged me, his light eyes clouding with concern, "leave her be."

This chapter ends on a tragic note as a reminder that war and its lethal remains are relentlessly deadly. Still, I show how creative life-making practices or resistant ecologies constitute the possibility of life in unlivable quarters, giving ethnographic presence to the resistant life that goes on in war, a condition that not many can imagine, let alone inhabit. The daily practices of those inhabiting wars are dominated by the fight for life every day. Some may lose this war, but some hold on until the bitter end. And that is not nothing.

5 *Maskun,* or Nature's Resistance

This land where we are standing contains ancient olives and oaks and almond and pistachio trees. There are uncountable numbers of plants and trees here grown wild. Look at the hawthorn—when it comes into season you should taste it! This area has been neglected because of Israel and has grown wild. But this is Galilee, and Galilee is a piece of heaven here on earth! Its nature and its winds and its climate, ya Allah! This here is *tayyun,* sage. It is medicinal and bees love it—there are a lot of bees in the hills among the rocks. This deep valley here is called *'imyani,* blindness, and at the very top of that hill there is a sacred place. In Galilee on the top of every hill there lives a prophet.

—Sahel

TWO TREES

There is a tree in South Lebanon very close to the front line and border with Israel. It is an old tree, an oak called *sindian* that has been twisted and hollowed by long time. The tree is *maskun,* in it lives a spirit, or *ruh,* who the locals call *saleh,* good. The tree and its spirit dwell, entwined, on a hilltop in a semiruined hamlet on the outskirts of a small tobacco-farming and goat-herding village; they keep each other company in a violent yet verdant landscape unfurling all around. Enclosed by national borders and buffeted by seasons of war, this living landscape anchors and contains "natural histories of destruction" (Sebald 2004). The spirit has given its name to the surrounding landscape, but not many people recognize it anymore.

Figure 19. This ancient oak is *maskun* by a good spirit.

There is another old tree on another hilltop—also in South Lebanon, but along an erstwhile border and former front: that of the occupation zone that was liberated in 2000. This ancient oak lives on in the midst of a museumized military topography, the "Resistance Tourism Landmark," and lends its blessings, *baraka*, to Mleeta, the cultural landscape project innovated and designed by Hizbullah, the Islamic resistance that ultimately liberated South Lebanon from Israeli occupation. This ancient oak would not be uprooted as the bulldozers first broke earth to build the landmark, its sylvan steadfastness signaling to the architects of the landmark, as they narrate it, the immanence of the divine here, the resistance of nature's sacred forces that protect this land and those who fought here and were victorious. The natural landscape has long contained spirits, and hence Mleeta simultaneously naturalizes, sacralizes, and materializes Hizbullah's message, drawing its blessings from the landscape that contains enduring spirits of nature.

This chapter explores in ethnographic counterpoint these two hilltops, crowned by two trees that materially and spectrally, sacredly and mundanely, bind lifeworlds and landscapes of war. One hilltop is a crinkled collective, a heterogeneous assemblage of resistant residues that silently embody the ebb and flow of social worlds, the various movements of space-time, multiple life-forms, histories of destruction and regeneration. This hilltop is a "patchy landscape" that collects "multiple temporalities and shifting assemblages of humans and nonhumans" (Tsing 2015, 20); it is a border-land and battlefield, a liminal space and interstice (Navaro 2017, 211) that gathers life ongoing in a tangle of goats, unruly rubble, spirits, and trees into a prickly constellation (Gordillo 2014) not easily contained by fences, borders, or ideologies. These heterogeneous elements, each with its own way of being, compose this landscape and serendipitously resist political regimes seeking to pull them into docile orbit.[1]

Such as the other hilltop, which has been resurrected as the spiritual and symbolic stronghold of a political and military regime currently hold-ing sway in South Lebanon, that of Hizbullah. Mleeta, the Resistance landmark, is a carefully curated and cultivated communal space of politi-cal pedagogy for contemplating and celebrating the victorious history and geography of the Islamic resistance, its political, communitarian, and sec-tarian goals in the present and future. Mleeta narrates and memorializes the military resistance of Hizbullah through landscape, a medium that is always simultaneously natural and cultural and the most important ally of defensive warfare (Pearson 2008; Gregory 2016; F. Hoffman 2007). Mleeta is built upon a former battleground, but nearby linger all-but-for-gotten shrines, and all around, sacred affect ripples through the landscape, giving the Resistance landmark power and presence, meaning and depth. The old tree channels this affect, and as a potent form of blessed nature, it is placed close to the symbolic, narrative, and pedagogical heart of the landmark. Condensing and embodying an authority and affect salvaged from the surrounding hillside, which has a long but waning history of sacred presences and practices, Mleeta sources fading heterodox, com-munal, rural beliefs and practices to authorize and empower an exclusive sectarian project in the present. Mleeta simultaneously preserves and overwrites other worlds.

Both these landscapes, one cultivated, one abandoned, are grafts of natural-sacred sediments and military remains that have grown together and continue to proliferate. In an agricultural rural landscape smothered by all kinds of violence, "plant-thinking" enables a verdant yet grounded approach (Marder 2013), and trees are particularly good at sheltering and rooting ethnography and analysis (Rival 1998; Jones and Cloke 2002; Makhzoumi 1997; Meneley 2020). Even when they do not house spirits, trees are wonders in the warscape of South Lebanon. Consistently targeted in warfare for their guerrilla-sheltering qualities, their slow time and unmoving presence disrupt the technical ease of offensive warfare. Ingold (1993) writes: "The tree bridges the gap between the apparently fixed and invariant forms of the landscape and the mobile and transient forms of animal life, visible proof that all of these forms, from the most permanent to the most ephemeral, are dynamically linked under transformation within the movement of becoming of the world as a whole" (168). In South Lebanon, trees anchor affective auras and other times; they mark presence on terrain and of course are always places of shelter and shade— community—to all kinds of beings and relations. Trees are beings that cooperate nicely as ethnographic portals, and hence I root this chapter with them.

"WHERE THE EARTH SPEAKS TO THE HEAVENS"

I visit the Mleeta landmark on a bright day soon after its inauguration on May 25, 2010, on the tenth anniversary of the liberation of the borderland.[2] Driving through the twisty roads and tiny villages of Iqlim al Tuffah ("region of apples") in the hills above Saida, I spy a large brown sign spanning the road pointing the way towards the "Resistance Tourism Landmark." Crowning the hilltop, the landmark lies sparkling new in the bright spring sunlight: geometric, minimalist, sharp-edged, low-slung buildings of unadorned cement and glass. I park in the immense lot, pay the entry fee, collect my brochures (one can select Arabic, English, or Farsi), and enter the iron gates.

Most of the visitors are families, here to combine an outing in nature with a sound dose of culture. Other visitors are school groups, Hizbullah-sponsored women's groups, tour groups from Iran, the odd anthropologist, and a handful of curious, nonaffiliated visitors. The atmosphere is one of leisure (Deeb and Harb 2013), with various groups making use of the nature setting to stretch their legs and *shimm-il-hawa*, breathe the air. Here and there, male figures in black caps are seen lecturing to knots of attentive listeners. I am soon adopted by one who immediately takes me to behold the ancient oak that would not be uprooted as the bulldozers first broke earth to build the landmark. The tree, gnarled, squat, and unperturbed, continues its long life in an unobtrusive spot. This oak, the guide says, embodies the steadfast *resistance of nature*. It embodies the spiritual and physical connection of the resistance to nature, of the earth and sky to the divine and earthly success of the resistance. This connection is expressed in the slogan of the landmark: "Where the Land Speaks to the Heavens."

Walking up the manicured, neatly cobbled promenade, I stop to contemplate the landmark's plan. It is clear, and the order of consumption is indicated by numbers. The layout is a large cross with a central field called, like many village squares, the square, *al saha*, where a large circular pool reflects the sky, a form quoting the rain-collecting pools at the center of many southern villages. Curling off from the main quadrant and down the precipitous decline of the hill is a long and twisty footpath that eventually, by way of deep into the earth, brings you back to the center of the landmark. I follow the prescribed order of business.

The first stop is in the plush, air-conditioned screening-room of the multipurpose hall to watch a short film presenting Mleeta's central narrative. We are welcomed to Mleeta by the secretary general of Hizbullah, Hassan Nasrallah, who addresses us, his audience, directly. Then, floating on the rousing crescendo of operatic music, the long and bloody history of the Israeli-Lebanese wars is unfolded in dates, sound bites, and gut-wrenching images soaked in pathos and tragedy. The 1982 invasion—tanks rolling through tobacco fields as villagers stand by helplessly and watch; endless Israeli attacks; explosion upon explosion upon explosion; dead and bloodied children; the beginnings of resistance with the November 1982 suicide bombing in Sur. Early Hizbullah leaders who met violent deaths at the hands of Israel are shown speaking rousing words of angry defiance. Soon the music ascends in urgency as the resistance gains momentum and the tables begin to turn. Fighting in village streets and explosions in orchards. Hassan Nasrallah takes the helm of the Resistance, a younger black-haired man of thirty-four. As the Resistance come into its own and makes the occupation a losing game for the Israelis and their henchmen, Nasrallah declares in his now signature style of address "a Resistance, honorable and magnificent and up to the challenge; no one can defeat it and it will be victorious by the grace of God!" Israeli soldiers are seen scrambling, an image is flashed of the assassinated South Lebanon Army (SLA) commander Aql Hashem. Finally Israel withdraws from the borderland and locks up the gate behind it. The prisoners languishing in the detention camp of Khiam are freed with desperate, scrabbling bare hands against rusted metal grates, and people stream back in euphoria to their liberated villages: old women throwing rice, and young men kissing their grandfathers. Then comes the 2006 war as a testament to the al-*wa'ad al-sadeq*, the "true promise," and Israeli soldiers are shown running, scattered, injured, dying, and in coffins. Thanks to the *nasr min Allah*, the "divine victory" scored by Hizbullah in this conflict, Israel releases the remaining Lebanese prisoners in its jails, and they are personally welcomed and embraced by Nasrallah amidst a sea of yellow flags in the immense bombed-out square where the dense heart of *dahiyeh* used to be. Standing defiantly exposed under the night sky beside the freed prisoners,[3] Nasrallah famously pledges that "the time of defeats is over and the time of victories has begun." A new chapter begins. Nasrallah appears on the screen shaking a warning finger as if at naughty children: "If you bomb Rafiq Hariri International Airport in Beirut we will bomb Ben-Gurion Airport in Tel Aviv, if you bomb our ports we will bomb your ports, if you bomb our factories we will bomb your factories," in his famous "eye for an eye" speech from 2008. The feeling is one of ascending might, good over evil. The war is not over (it is "to be continued"), but the clip must end, and it does with a taste of what is to come: the late Abbas al Musawi, assassinated in 1992 by Israel from the air as he traveled by car in South Lebanon with his wife and infant son, raises his finger and turns to the camera. His pale skin is in stark contrast to the blackness of his beard, and his thick-framed glasses serve to enhance the intensity of his already electric gaze. All background music stops as he calmly and matter-of-factly states: *Isra'eel saqatat*, Israel has fallen. The staccato and sober pronunciation of these final words reverberates powerfully throughout the room. This eerie pronouncement from beyond the grave is in the past tense. The unsettling conviction with which it is spoken, the calm assuredness of the long-dead man's demeanor, his direct address and the pastness of the statement impart an uncanny sense of an *alternate present*. The room is hushed as we contemplate this possibility, this *reality*. Suddenly, jarring us out of our reverie, the soundtrack resumes, and Hizbullah's militant and pumping anthem *Ruwwad al ard*, "Pioneers of the earth," jerks us back to where we are in the here and now, as we are visually swept out of this particular history with universal claims and into the spaces of the landmark, down into "the abyss" and along the winding path. . . . *This* place here is the site of (this) history's "continual" presence and unfolding.

Our feet follow the righteous path. Emerging charged with appropriate emotion into the bright light of day I move along with the rest of the visiting families toward "the exhibit," *al ma'arad*, where sundry objects captured from Israeli soldiers over years of violent encounters are on display. Everything from arms to fatigues and helmets, field supplies and rations, canned food and drink, radios, hand grenades, medic kits, and the various odds and ends that a squadron carries with it on a mission into enemy territory are exhibited in glass cases, strewn around carelessly, haphazardly. The collected junk of war looks oddly familiar, homely even, as these objects address the basic human needs for sustenance, apparel, and shelter from the elements.

Warring gets inserted into this "ordinary" category through its scattered, discarded objects, as Navaro-Yashin (2009) has shown.[4] The feeling—and the message—they evoke is palpable: *These boys (the supposedly formidable enemy) are mortal, vulnerable, bungling. Look how we can take their toys from them just like candy from a baby!* A couple with two girls and two boys all dressed up for the outing as identical pairs in pink and blue direct their children to pose for a photograph in front of a case with captured Israeli guns and rocket launchers. The children obediently hug each other and smile at the camera. This is the (naturalized) political environment of their upbringing. The walls of the exhibition hall are covered with slick murals and dioramas painstakingly detailing the command-structure of the "undefeatable" Israel Army, maps of military installations juxtaposed with salient excerpts from Nasrallah's "eye for an eye" speech. These convey a single and unequivocal message: we know our enemy! From their canned beef to the finest details of their intelligence structure and hidden weapon caches. Of course: knowledge is power.

On the Warpath

Beyond the peaceful "village square," *al saha*, and upon emerging from the exhibition hall, I enter "the abyss," *al hawiya*, where destroyed Israeli tanks and armored personnel carriers are sunk haphazardly into a massive, circular cement pit with scattered letters spelling out in Hebrew TZAHAL, the acronym for the Israel Defense Forces (IDF). The abyss is designed to be viewed from above: it is a message to the Israeli jets and MK unmanned drones that continue to pierce the skies of Lebanon. Scattered letters spell out in Hebrew "the Lebanese quagmire" around the sunken vehicles, to complete the picture for those who read Hebrew and care to have a look (and shudder in memory or in anticipation). The Merkava 4 is Israel's "invincible" tank, and the ones on display here with the muzzles of their guns cartoonishly tied up in knots were lost in the 2006 battles in Wadi Saluqi and Wadi Hujeir, where an entire Israeli tank column was destroyed by resistance guerrillas hidden in the undergrowth as the tanks blundered along the foot of a narrow valley towards the Litani River with the inexplicable (because tactically irrelevant if symbolically charged) goal of crossing it. These tanks are Hizbullah's biggest booty (and Israeli's biggest loss) of the 2006 war and represent one of the resistance's great military victories, and here they are on jeering, nose-thumbing display. The museum path winds us around and around the abyss. I, along with the rest of the landmark's visitors, stop and take pictures and point and remember the well-known episode.[5]

Leaving the abyss I enter "the path," *al masar*. A sign positioned among the undergrowth reads:

> This is a rugged and bushy area where thousands of mujahedin had positions during the years of occupation. From there, they launched hundreds of jihadi operations against facing enemy outposts as well as inside the occupied security zone.
>
> "Standing up to" is a weapon.

Figure 20. The "Sayyid Abbas barricade," a spirited spot in Mleeta, the Resistance landmark.

From 1948 until Lebanon's invasion in 1982, the Israeli enemy imposed on Lebanon and the region one choice: surrender, defeat and submission. On 11-11-1982, a martyrdom seeker named Ahmad Qassir blew himself up at the Israeli ruler stronghold in Tyr [Sur] to announce the birth of a different choice, the Islamic Resistance, another new course with its slogan, "Never to Submit," and its method, "O ye who believe! If ye will aid (the cause of) God, He will aid you and plant your feet firmly."

A rough-hewn footpath under a protective canopy of dancing trees making dappled shadows on the ground takes us steeply down the scrub-covered hillside, where I almost expect to see families barbecuing on a Sunday outing but instead encounter scenes of war-making in a nature setting: from camouflaged rocket launchers and makeshift field hospitals to protective natural shrines like the "Sayyid Abbas barricade," where Abbas al-Musawi, the martyred secretary-general of the party, prayed when he visited "the boys," *al shabab*, on the front. His prayer spot, a leafy

alcove, has been transformed into a natural shrine, like those of the proph-
ets that dot the countryside, testament to his continued spiritual guidance
and presence among the fighters despite his violent and early death: his
voice wafts through hidden speakers and envelopes the visitor, who is
invited to pray upon the reed mat covering the dirt floor beneath his picture beside a casually propped Kalashnikov. This space is an enchanted
portal, a place of sacred affect that is inhabited by a lingering spirit. It
quotes the widespread presence of good spirits in nature. But here and
now it directs the worshiper's attention to a specific spiritual presence:
Hizbullah, the Resistance.

Familiar nature sounds—birdsong, crickets, and the rustling trees—and
smells of warmed earth and vegetation—dust, thyme, and resin—envelope
our senses as we crunch along the dappled nature trail sheltered from the
open blue sky by the protective woodland. Occasional placards inform us
as we stroll deeper into the woods about the arts of guerrilla warfare.

MISSILE POWER, AL QIWA AL SARUKHIYYA

This military unit is commissioned with short, medium, and long-range
surface-to-surface missiles whose aim is to deter the enemy from targeting
Lebanese civilians and infrastructure.

MARTYRDOM SEEKERS, AL ISTISHADIYUN

This unit takes direct orders from the supreme leadership of the Resistance.
It numbers hundreds of trained and equipped volunteers ready to sacrifice
their lives.

The end of the pathway delivers us into the pièce de résistance of the
landmark, "the cave," *al mghara*, and "the tunnel," *al nafaq*. The sign outside reads:

This is a rocky bunker that the Resistance militants constructed when
they used Mleeta as their stronghold. Initially this cave was merely a
1-square-meter gap that the Resistance militants used as a refuge against
the Israeli enemy bombardment and to protect themselves from the harsh
weather elements. It was later transformed into a 200-meter-long tunnel
over the course of three years, in excess of 1,000 men dug and prepared in
rotation, excavating over 350 square meters of rocks and soil. The weight of
almost 1,000 tons of excavation was disposed under trees to cover an area
of more than 4,000 square meters in a camouflaged manner that made it

difficult for the enemy air observation to discover. After completion, Mleeta cave was transformed into a military integral base dubbed by Resistance fighters as "the Point," which formed several parts and rooms. Moreover it was linked to a water supply for drinking and other purposes and was equipped with electricity, safety devices, and ventilation, allowing more than 7,000 Resistance militants to use it as a barracks and main base to resist the enemy in the area.

"The tunnel" takes us through the dark and stony heart of the mountain and to the ideological and pedagogic core of Hizbullah's landscape project: naturalizing the holy struggle, fusing its otherworldly goals with the materials of this earth, the long arc of the eternal struggle with the shorter but ever-replenished cycle of life. Deep underground I breathe into my lungs the damp, close air, and once my eyes have adjusted to the gloom, I view there between cold, sweating walls the technologically cutting-edge operations room, where a massive detailed area map is laid out on a tabletop and illuminated with a basic oil lamp while an IBM laptop flickers nearby. Jagged, staticky, urgent radio communications are piped through the sound system and echo tinnily in the gloom: "Haidar, Haidar, Haidar. I read you Ali, Ali, Ali." The constant night and cramped darkness of the underworld is experienced in stark contrast with the bright airiness of outside. Here one is cocooned in an earthly grave and must face the harsh realities of war and the inevitable finality of death alone in the depths of the mountain. Along the tunnel walls, piles of Kalashnikovs, *kleshen,* the beloved and familiar Russian-made AK-47 machine gun, loyal companion of guerrilla fighters everywhere, are on (somewhat Warholian) display in glass panels built into the walls of the snug passageway. I enter the barracks—bare stone walls, thin mattresses, a prayer mat, a small battery radio, tinned goods on a shelf, a braid of onions (a staple in any southern larder), and the writing on the wall: *Silahi wa ruhi taw'aman,* "My weapons and my soul are twins." *'Alayna takween mujtama' al-harb li muwajahat isra'eel,* "It is upon us to create a war society to fight Israel," another poster reminds us, a famous call to arms by Ragheb Harb, an early (assassinated, naturally) leader of the party. In the heart of the mountain we are made to feel the spiritual and physical communion of the earth and its beings, nature and (holy) war. The medium is the message. Being *there* where *they* were between the same walls of stone is thrilling. A communion is taking place;

if not exactly a shared ideology, then a deep, almost primal, affect is roused from its bodily slumber deep in this (resisting) earth.

Emerging from the ever-night darkness of the dank tunnel into dazzling daylight half way up the hill, we fall blinking and disoriented out onto "the outlook," *al matall.* It is breathtaking, like flying in place as a bird of prey suspended in midair above a cascading valley dotted with miniature, toylike villages. Hizbullah fighters have no control of the air; the earth is their element (see F. Hoffman 2007). But with the help of the topography of their home turf they can acquire strategic advantages like this position here. The wind is sharp and whips us, and the Lebanese and Hizbullah flags flap and snap insistently over our heads. The tunnel has regurgitated us halfway up the hill. After our exhilarating encounter with heights, we turn and continue our ascent on the surface of the earth through the thickly wooded hillside among the embedded heavy guns of the resistance along "the line of fire," *khatt al nar,* and thus proceed through a progressive, enacted, embedded, and embodied history of Hizbullah's kind of warfare.

THE LINE OF FIRE, KHATT AL NAR

The Resistance developed its military structure since 1982, hence inventing a unique military concept blending the classical and the nonclassical guerrilla tactics. It also obtained a system of different weapons constituting the modern with the ancient military techniques and specializations, which it professionally utilized on both tactical and on maneuvering fields.

I continue perusing the arsenal deployed to fight the enemy, with some dug into the ground and some concealed by trees, as we struggle uphill. Figures of guerrillas are inserted in the undergrowth and among the trees. These model "the special forces," *al qiwa al khassa,* "a highly trained, fully equipped special force." Dressed in camouflaged fatigues, the dummies are barely discernable among the bushes, and when glimpsed suddenly can startle.[6] I take in with interest the various types of mines that can be encountered in the southern wilderness, like an amateur botanist browsing an exhibit of the different native species of wild mushroom. Waiting my turn among excited families, I pose with and gleefully manipulate some of the missile launchers and antiaircraft guns, like the Doshka, a staple in any guerrilla war, where lightness of foot and mobility are key.

Placing War: Military Objects and Affective Places

The (war) objects on display throughout the landmark are carefully placed in an affective landscape that is the habitat and life-source of the rural communities from whence Hizbullah emerged and continues to draw its power. This is also the landscape that generates Hizbullah's kind of warfare and offers the geography that enables its military advantage. There is an explicit awareness here of the power of place and its ability to hold memory and stories. Mleeta mobilizes the sacred natures and auras of *ard al janub,* southern earth, and grafts them with military materiel into a singular, powerful assemblage. The natural-setting of the landmark is a hilly maquis landscape identical to many across the Mediterranean, but it is subtly altered: in Mleeta, a landscape of war is reconfigured and brought home. The exhibitionary form (Mitchell 1991) and its disciplinary purpose expose the landmark as a technology of (para)state power. But beyond this disciplinary purpose lies the affective power of place and the unnamed, heterogeneous forces harnessed towards a singular goal here. The power of place was underlined by one of the museum's architects when I met him one day in his office in the southern suburbs of Beirut. He put the idea behind the project and its location thus:

> We could have chosen a location for our museum in Beirut, and it would have been easily accessible to everyone, but *it did not have the memory that is stored in the place.* Therefore we decided to locate it in a place that witnessed live Resistance activity, and the village of Mleeta, which is now liberated, was at one time on the front line on Sujud hill. Before 2000, this valley was the connection and interface between Israel and the Resistance. We chose this location for its natural beauty, but there is also a cave that is located in it and is an important position that remained active. Resistance fighters used its underground tunnels up until the 2006 war. (emphasis added)

Mleeta draws on the "gathering" power of place (Casey 1996). It is where the community of the Resistance goes to find itself. In *Wisdom Sits in Places* (Basso 1996) Dudley Patterson, Keith Basso's Apache interlocutor, explains to him, "Wisdom sits in places. It's like water that never dries up. You need water to stay alive, don't you? Well you also need to drink from places. You must remember everything about them. You must learn their names. You must remember what happened at them long ago. You must think about it and keep on thinking about it" (70). Mleeta is named after the village in which it was built. According to the architect, *Mleeta* is an Aramaic word that comes close in meaning to the Arabic word for "to fill, become full; fullness or repletion." The architect said that the name stems from the plethora of water sources in the area. "We thought of giving it another name but decided to preserve its historic name, in line with the landmark's spirit of preservation." The name alludes to the fullness and fecundity of this earth—as *the* source of this community.

Often in villages, I would be taken to places to be told stories; it was as if those places held (and generated) the stories. I was once pestering Abu Jalil to tell me a story about the village. We were far away from the place he was speaking of. He was usually eloquent and forthcoming, but this time his language was stilted, his sentences came out cropped, stunted, wilted, dry. He said "I would be able to tell you this better when we are both there in place, *bil makan.*" It was as if the place could not be narrated, made present in words, unless one were physically there; unless it were underfoot, all around. It is as if the landscape itself were the source and storage of the stories that it collects and that, when tapped, gush forth from it. In Arabic the word for "story" is *riwaya,* and "to narrate" is *yirwa/tirwa,* from *rawa*—this is the same root—the same word—for "to water, irrigate." To narrate is to irrigate, to draw from the earth the water held within it and sprinkle it upon its surface and thus grow the stories, that it brings forth to life.

Winded, hot, and dusty, I am finally back at the top of the hill. This is the freedom field," *maydan al tahrir.* Here I stroll through an exhibition of Hizbullah's heavy arms, antitank missiles, and other more technologically advanced weaponry, as compared to the basic artillery and guns encountered in the woodland. Here the Kornet-E, Malyutka, and Fagot are installed: antitank guided missiles whose innovative use was key in getting the upper hand in the pitched battles of the 2006 war, like that of Wadi Saluqi, where the IDF tank column was demolished. These weapon systems are on display in a cheery rambling rose garden where children run amok among the missiles and flowers. A young boy, too young to have (yet) lived through any war, rides on his father's shoulders and asks him about the weapons, and his father takes time to explain them to him: "Listen *habibi* my love . . ." In the "freedom field," *maydan al tahrir,* there is a wall that serves as a *mihrab*, or prayer corner, that is inscribed with excerpts of Hassan Nasrallah's speeches from the 2006 war. Praying is a way of exiting the shell of the self; it is a bodily enactment of communion (Mahmood 2001). To stand here and pray here is to spiritually connect with the collective taking shape, to participate in its principles and to support its victorious trajectory in this natural place of war.

The last stop of our tour through the war-laced countryside and "natural museum" is "the hill," *al talleh,* a geographic form found in any village (often both a militarily strategic location and the enshrined dwelling of a local prophet), the rounded mighty buttress that presides on the highest ground of the landmark. It evokes at once the crusader castles that dot the southern landscape across its highest points and the many military fortifications that the Israelis built on top of them (as well as those crouching along the border at regular intervals).[7] The gigantic height when approached from below makes one feel small, earth-ridden, vulnerable, mortal, a little akin to what one feels like when under bombardment. Upon this highpoint is the "martyrs' garden," *rawdat al shuhada.* I ascend a wide and steep and very long stairway. As I climb the stairs I get tired, weighed down by the pull of the earth's gravity and unsheltered from the already mean rays of the early summer sun high in a bare blue sky. As I stop to catch my breath, my sense of overwhelming physical exhaustion allows me to connect bodily with the effort, *juhd,* pain, and sacrifice of the mujahideen. The pinnacle exposes the hilly southern landscape that had been occupied by Israel until 2000 and beyond. Standing here, we appreciate the military value of this strategic position and participate bodily in its posture of empowerment. The scene that the eye takes in, in full surround, is all about (military) power and its culmination in absolute victory, but also about the culmination of the spirit's journey in martyrdom and its eternal reward in heaven, *janna,* Paradise.

"ON EVERY HILLTOP THERE LIVES A PROPHET"

Sujud hill, where the landmark is located, takes its name from a Jewish prophet[8] whose *baraka* is still faintly recognized by the inhabitants of the region (who today are mostly Muslim, mostly Shi'a).[9] The shrine of Nabi

Figure 21. "On every hill there lives a prophet." The sun sets behind the spirited hilltops of Galilee.

Sujud was a place of pilgrimage for the different religious groups of the region (Jews, Muslims, and Christians; Abou Hodeib 2015). The shrine was a multicommunal node in a landscape of hardening borders and wars and occupation. Entrapped in a riven landscape of war, the shrine and its resident spirit fell out of practice, and only a subtle glimmer of other-worldly presence remained. For example, the guide who showed me the spirit tree recounted, gesturing to a nearby hilltop, the presence of a prophet, who he was unable to identify. Nevertheless, he still heartily invoked him to underline the holy nature of this place and project.

Across the Lebanese South (and beyond) linger sacred nature spots where spirits reside (Albera and Couroucli 2012; Henig 2012; Thubron 2008; Bowman 2013a, 1993, 2013b, 1986). Spirited, or *maskun*, caves, springs, trees, or hilltops were for centuries sites of contemplation and sup-plication where people came to ask for divine intervention in earthly mat-ters.[10] Such sacred spaces in the landscape illuminate a communitarian topography shaping sociality, a "jinneaolgy" (Taneja 2018) crosshatching and connecting the different communities of the borderland. Places of vernacular worship contain an increasingly abandoned yet still resonant tradition of intercommunal belief and practice that cuts across the riven political landscape.[11] It is such repositories of traditional rural practices, where people worship good spirits in "nature," that a "natural museum" such as Mleeta affectively and materially mimics and mines. A more-than-human sensibility including spirits—as well as other beings—opens up the possibilities of another politics in the present (de Cadena 2015; Hage 2015; Viveiros de Castro 2016; Blaser 2016; Povinelli 2012).

Sujud hill became an active front where the Resistance fought for more than twenty years, where the fighters enrolled the landscape in their fight against the Israeli occupation. One of the architects of the landmark described the alliance of the fighters and the landscape as a spiritual one. This is why, he told me, that during the design process he had insisted upon an aesthetic and form for Mleeta that reflected the "natural habitat" of the Resistance fighter and that made explicit the deep spiritual connection between the fighters and the earth upon which they fight.

> We considered and thought through many options before we decided on a plan of construction. . . . We wanted to make something that stems from resistance, *muqawama*, and that resonates with it. We could have made something like Centre Pompidou, but that does not resemble us and is not native to the land. So we said that we would build it according to the Resistance fighter. . . . Our first concern was to cooperate with nature, because we consider that there is an organic connection between the Resistance fighter, *muqawim*, and the oak tree. This is the tree that protected the *muqawim*, in addition to its natural qualities of purifying the air. We consider it a strategic connection, so we attempted to preserve the area as a natural reserve. We are extremely mindful of protecting the site's natural surroundings and working with them. Let me tell you a story that happened during the occupation. Israel was extremely bothered by the *hirsh* the uncultivated woodland that has the oak, *sindian*, trees, and so they burned it all via helicopters that poured napalm over the trees and ignited them, but the wind blew the fire away from the trees to an area that has no trees! And the trees were spared. This is another example of the kindness of God [to the Resistance].

The communion of the fighter with the earth is at once spiritual and military. The protective arm nature extends to shield the fighters taking refuge in the earth and utilizing its natural formations for strategic and tactical gain in warfare is explicitly celebrated in Mleeta (and elsewhere) as a recognition of the divine sanction of the Resistance's cause. Nature mobilizes its forces and beings on behalf of the Resistance.[12] Yet the alliance and affect summoned here for a particular military and political project in the present is sourced from deep and diverse vernacular beliefs and practices still half alive across the rural communities of the Mediterranean, where spirits are known to reside in nature.

In Mleeta, Hizbullah, the Resistance, utilizes the potent medium of landscape to claim, narrate, domesticate, and naturalize war. War becomes a dominant trope of a certain cultural narrative as it is used to craft a "war society." Mleeta places desiring subjects and affective objects together in a landscape of war, positioning them within a teleology and spatiotemporality of existential, ordinary warfare. By making the earth tell a particular story, Hizbullah both claims the southern landscape as a source of ongoing cultural and moral identity and cohesive community and enshrines the landscape itself as the site and source of its political and military strength and ultimate "divine victory"—a resistant ecology. As Harb and Deeb (2011) write, "In Mleeta, the tree, rock, flower, bird, sky, cloud, and mountain are each (and all) symbol(s) or Hizballah's resistance which is equated with (one) history, which is associated with (this) nature, (this) land, which forms (our) culture, and these correspondences are made to be incontestably right, or righteous" (29). Hizbullah's landmark thus reconfigures the manifold histories and presences of Sujud hill into a Resistance landscape.

INTO ENCHANTED WILD MARGINS

Sacred landscapes thrive in borderlands. They are "traditionally situated on frontiers, on territorial boundaries where conversions and conflict have taken place" (Albera and Couroucli 2012, 4). The southern landscape thrums with reverberating presences in "caves, fountains, or sacred trees where the holy men [and women] can manifest themselves, chthonian spirits living in the underworld" (6). Many of these enchanted spaces— caves and hilltops in particular—transformed into militarized geography during the wars and occupations of the borderland. In South Lebanon, sacred nature and material remnants of war blend together into a peculiar formation: a charged affective geography that Navaro-Yashin (2009) refers to as ruination: "the material remains or artefacts of destruction and violation, but also to the subjectivities and residual affects that linger, like a hangover, in the aftermath of war or violence" (5). As wars erupt and subside, remains of war and spirits and nature tangle with regenerating greenery and the lives of humans and animals and fuse into a resonant topography, as in this ruined and enchanted hilltop at the very edge of Lebanon's nation-space. This hilltop was what the locals referred to dismissively as a *khirbeh*, ruin. But the place beckoned to me. Something stirred there that was not immediately apparent.

The sacred-natural landscape upon which Mleeta is premised and draws is sourced from such deeply resonant places; the landmark reconfigures these resistant residues, tames them and shapes them into a singular, legible landscape of Resistance. Off the manicured museum path and into the jumble of village life and surrounding countryside, one encounters multiple, layered, unscripted sediments that thrive in abandon/ment. The landscape we enter now unfurls around a *maskun* tree and expresses in its resonant material "the ruptured multiplicity that is constitutive of all geographies as they are produced, destroyed and made" (Gordillo 2014, 2).

The hilltop is a snug plateau that gives a comforting sense of elevation from the surrounding landscape and embodies strategic geography: it overlooks the mined borderline and bristling militarized border-fence that runs west to east from the sea inland, slashing through a cascade of gently sloping hills a few hundred meters to the south of this place; to the north, the hilltop guards a deep and narrow valley that falls away suddenly, bifurcating the geography. The hilltop is crowned by the spirit-tree at whose roots lie a collection of graves. Nearby huddles a burnt-out stone cottage containing a hearth; a wooden wardrobe on its side, some broken chairs, charred walls, and some graffiti complete the scene of reckless use and dank abandonment. A fig tree bearing fat fruit for nobody hugs the outer wall of the abandoned abode, and a thick vine twists around the collapsed rubble, green grapes mingling with the dirt. There is an out-of-use stone olive press, next to which a seasonal goat enclosure has been cobbled together. On the southwestern edge of the hilltop, overlooking the border and front, are a few shallow terraces where tobacco has been planted around some ancient olive trees, and on the southeastern approach, where the rutted dirt path from the village ends, stands a clump of trees encircling a deep hollow gorge. Since the end of the occupation, the inhabitants of the nearby village have reclaimed the hilltop as an extension of their everyday lifeways. It is a popular picnic spot, where villagers congregate, forage for wild herbs, and grill under the trees. This is a heterogeneous space that continues to vividly and vitally express the various pasts and the ongoing lifeworlds that it enfolds and unfolds. The spirit-tree dominates its surroundings, collecting both the tangible and intangible beings and remains of this place around its massive twisted branches and deep gnarled roots.

Upon my first encounter with this place I take in its beautiful and thrilling topography, exclaiming at the view, shuddering at the closeness of the border (so close and yet so far), the vista of the landscape sliced by a front on one side and a precipitous rocky natural trench on the other. Sahel, my companion draws my attention to the military and agricultural topography, the mined border, the settlement in Israel beyond, the fertile red earth below, the quarried white earth yonder, the remains of the former Israeli outpost on a nearby hill (that was the last outpost to be abandoned during the Israeli withdrawal in 2000). He points out the spirit-tree and speaks of a delicious nut that it occasionally bears. He underlines to me the advantage that local fighters have in such terrain, since they are intimate—and hence intimately allied—with the landscape. He makes no mention of a spirit.

I note some litter on the ground attesting to recent picnickers, pet an inquisitive goat, eat the sweet fig that Sahel offers me. The ramshackle piles of rubble, the big hollow tree, the lonely graves at its roots, the air of devastation that clings to the ruined stone structures give off an affect that catches my senses. Later, we sit together in the blueness of the deepening twilight with his family, and I ask about the ruin on the hill, the graves under the tree, and a deep silence falls. Soon, someone mutters: "The tree is *maskun*. A good spirit lives there." And some stories are dislodged, unfurl, that until now were silently coiled up in the rubble.

In times now vanished, the tree was a node of local pilgrimage and was visited by all the nearby communities, a diverse lot: Christians, Shi'a, and the *bedu*, the pastoral nomads of the Galilee who would accompany their

beasts to their summertime settlement upon the hill. Pilgrims and sup-
plicants at the tree would make offerings and vows, tying knots of cloth
torn from their clothes to its branches or pouring libations of water—
gathered at a freshwater spring deep in the valley and lugged all the way
up the hill—at its roots, while asking the spirit of the tree for healing, for
fertility, for love, or to resolve conflicts, among other things. For a long
time the spirit-tree was a lively participant in local affairs, centering a
landscape and life-world, maintaining a commonality of practice and
familiarity, a multisectarian, cross-border, local network that has almost,
but not entirely, vanished.

I am told: the tree lights up on blessed nights and glitters with shim-
mery sacred light that is echoed by a luminous halo around another tree,
on a neighboring hilltop. "God forgive those who say they have seen it if it's
not true!" murmurs Khawla. Despite being skeptical, she will not flatly
deny this well-known and apparently oft observed phenomenon. Another
more pedestrian and slapstick story from the life of the spirit-tree bubbles
up from the gathering as night falls: a young boy from the village accompanied his mother to make a vow at the tree and he put the water bucket
used to carry the water offering to the tree upon his head. This was pun-
ished by the spirit. The bucket stuck to the head of the boy and would not
dislodge until the boy's mother took her irreverent son to the tree and
made a pledge, by way of apology or appeasement, on his behalf to the
spirit, who finally relented, and released the boy. This boy's misfortune
became a comedic ditty that is still sung by the villagers. The young boy is
now an old man.

In 1948, the tree was there as Palestine became Israel. Palestinian refugees escaping the genocidal violence in their villages flowed across the
border and settled under this and other trees on the Lebanese side of the
border, awaiting the war to subside so they could return to their hastily
abandoned homes just over those hills. But war took hold, and the porous
border between Lebanon and now occupied Palestine/Israel hardened
into a dangerous front. The summer of 1948 became winter and then
spring and summer again and again, and the refugees did not return home
but instead were rounded up by the Lebanese Army and resettled in refugee camps on the outskirts of the major coastal cities of Lebanon, where

their descendants remain today. The spirit-tree, a deciduous oak, faith-fully kept the seasons as the borderland became a battlefield, and when the Palestinians returned as guerrillas to liberate Palestine from South Lebanon. It was there war transformed the hilltop and Bedouin campsite into strategic military geography that exposed enemy country across the nearby border and front that was more and more intensively mined. Nomadic life was no longer viable in this wartime environment, yet the *bedu* found new uses for their old intimate knowledge of terrain; their familiarity with its nature was an invaluable asset to the guerrillas who were unfamiliar with this landscape. A real-life encounter of nomadology versus the war machine (Deleuze and Guattari 1987) unfolded as the *bedu* under the cover of night expertly piloted guerrillas into enemy terri-tory, evading advanced military technology through deeply genealogical, sensory, and organic means. The campsite on the hill was overtaken by guerrillas and their nomadic shepherds, and the spirit-tree was there. Some of the young *bedu* were killed during this time and are buried at the roots of the tree, in their old camping grounds, their names and dates of death scrawled in petrified wet cement: 1949, 1968.

The hamlet's last human residents, an old couple who lived there all their lives, are also buried, alongside the two *bedu,* under the spirit-tree, which lives on. Date of death according to gravestones: July 1983. Only the fruitful fig tree, now grown wild outside their front door, really knows how they died, but the villagers whisper about a grenade (thrown by *who knows*) that exploded as the couple sat down to an untouched dinner. These were the days of the Israeli occupation when the occupiers were establishing new military configurations on the ground to wrest control of the borderland and hilltops from its long-term dwellers—and from the emerging (grassroots and multiple) resistance that was forming in response. Hilltops exposing surrounding country were permanently cleared, "secured," by the Israeli occupiers (Weizman 2007). The old cou-ple living on in their home and tending their tobacco and olives and vine and fig could no longer be there. After their death, the hamlet's stone dwellings became military barracks, first for the Israelis and then for their local allies and militia, the SLA, which was recruited from among the vil-lages across the border strip. The stone structures absorbed waves of

destruction, melting into the hillside as the forces of nature and war battered them collaboratively. The mosque remained in occasional use by
Israel-allied local militiamen until it was destroyed in the last war to blow
over the area in 2006; each smashed wall frames life-size rural scenes.
The stopped clock on the wall points uncannily to a moment of ruin now
past. This is no place for chronological time, but the spirit-tree and its
vegetal companions—the grapevine, fig, olives and, others—enrolled as
protective cover for military elements and also perhaps for good blessings,
continue to proliferate and steadily keep the seasons.

In May 2000, after years of persistent homegrown resistance that was
gradually taken over, perfected, and monopolized by Hizbullah, the Israeli
occupation of South Lebanon collapsed, and the first wave of the present
order under the military dominance of Hizbullah—the last and most successful of the resistors and the ones who were victorious—came to reign
over the borderland and hamlet. Inhabitants of the nearby village, who
were not allowed to move freely during the time of military rule, returned
to hilltops that had been off limits to them, walking paths, traversing
meadows, picnicking under trees, tending olives, keeping goats in the
tumbledown stone dwellings, and planting tobacco in any accessible flat
space with some soil cover.

Things have changed in the borderland—namely nation-states and
borders and wars and capitalist extraction have divided and destroyed—
but not entirely. The *bedu* who remain now reside in neighboring villages,
and many ended up across the now uncrossable border in Israel, relocated
to settlements away from the militarized border (that also slashed through
families) so as not to unsettle its absolutely controlling and dividing reality and logic. These days the *bedu* are no longer pastoral nomads; they, like
most of the inhabitants of Lebanon's southern borderland, are poor farmers who grow tobacco for the state-owned monopoly and also keep livestock. They do not visit this tree anymore. Today the main identifying
quality of *bedu*, like all of the communities that inhabit the borderland
(and all citizens of Lebanon), is their sectarian identity; this determines
and shapes them as social and political subjects and places them within
the acrimonious and sectarian logic of the Lebanese political system. All
of the communities that inhabit the borderland (and the rest of the land)
are claimed and cultivated by sectarian political formations and currents

that are often starkly opposed; a shared way of being premised upon communities of land-based livelihood and shared spiritual practices around sacred natural places is fading fast. Military sediments pepper the earth like deeply embedded shrapnel, and borders cleave it, but the tree still stands as a resistant being disrupting the flattened, encompassing, saturating, forms of landscape, momentarily unsettling them.

Here in this hamlet—and across the land—remnants of ongoing entanglements with different formations of power, not all modern—Roman, Crusader, Ottoman, French, Lebanese or Israeli, and others—remain, and these are shallowly interred in the landscape. This hamlet is one among a myriad of places across the Mediterranean landscape that reverberate (Navaro-Yashin et al. 2021) with presences that do not tamely fit the flat and homogeneous present of the nation-state and its hegemonic political projects. The affect that lingers in these places is *maskun,* inhabited by otherworldly presences, haunted. Off the beaten path, such places are well-known among locals at a remove from centers of power and can be experienced when one obliquely enters the hidden landscapes of the ordinary, which emerge from "the other side of silence" (Wood 2017).

This landscape is multiple (Rodman 1992). It is a gathering ongoing. It cannot be fenced in, trapped in a single heritage site or ideological project, or even just ignored. War and seasons of destruction have shaped it, as have cycles and seasons of life, and together they unfold. The landscape is not protected from the violence of the cadaster, capitalism, agribusiness, quarries, or wars. Recently I was told by a young villager that I need to revisit the hilltop. "They have fixed it up and made it really nice!" she exclaimed excitedly. I feared what I would find upon my next visit—or more precisely what I would *not* find, and I did not ask if the resistant spirit of the place remains steadfast in the tree, or if the violent forces of the present have prevailed.

Like the tree in the Brueghel painting *The Harvesters* that Ingold (1993) dwells on in "The Temporality of the Landscape," this tree centers this place as a living being—upright, rooted and old. But at the same time, and due to its inhabitation by spirits, the tree, rooted, vertical, and strong, also unsettles the insistence of the world that we currently inhabit. The tree's material presence is encountered in the here and now, its resonance as a house of spirits and good magic is an echo from awareness that creeps like a guerrilla in the maquis into our world. We can hardly grasp it with our feet firmly planted in the here and now, but we sense it (Santner 2006). Here the hamlet on the hill, unlike the carefully scripted narrative of the memorial or landmark that we are made to consume as docile political subjects, these *other* places contain resonant matter that unsettles the scripted landscapes of the political present. Taussig (2006) writes, "a monument . . . may center and fix this landscape, but that spell is broken by the even greater spell of the landscape" (28).

The villagers call the tree with the spirit *maskun*, and this refers to all forms of spirit-dwelling in nature. A spirit *dwells. Maskun* is an Arabic word describing the recognized presence of "spirits" in nature (and other forms). Rooted in the three letters *s-k-n*, meaning silence, and simultaneously evoking silence and presence, habitation and hauntedness, *maskun* describes the power of landscape to unsettle predatory present orders.

NATURE'S RESISTANCE (OR TWO RETURNS AND AN ENDING)

It is a cold clear day, and the wind cuts sharply across the elevation and into us as the sun sets, transforming the greenery around us into shades of lustrous ochre and copper. Everything is shimmering. I am exhilarated to be back here, but I am also somewhat disturbed, for it has only been a handful of years since I was here last, and the place has drastically changed in the meanwhile, as was cheerfully reported to me by the youngster. I had heard that "exciting" things had been happening—a place that when I came to know it right after the July War of 2006 was a pile of radiant rubble, a semi-abandoned place of late afternoon outings, some tobacco fields, a few ancient olives, a destroyed mosque, a jumble of abandoned stone houses, goats in the wintertime, and an unruly tangle of stories. The landscape still gathered around the trees; some stood in a circle around a deep hole, and one—the spirit tree—stood apart, twisted and gnarled and protective of a collection of graves at its feet, as before. Now, the sun was disappearing over the next hill, a shaft of golden light stretched across the land, illuminating the scenery as if from within. The families there were bundling up to go home as the shadows fell and the wind picked up. Everyone was getting a bit cold. Standing by the circular clump of trees and wondering about the stones and concrete that had been thrown in the deep gorge around which these trees had always stood, I noticed that the floor was densely littered with acorns that glittered like gold in the sun's setting rays. I bent down and impulsively gathered a few and stood there observing them shining in the palm of my hand. "Oh no, no, don't do that! Put them back!" Munya my companion admonished me urgently. "Why?" I asked. "Because you should never take anything from those trees unless you plan to give back something in return. This place is *maskun* you know." I hesitated, weighing her words while holding the warm, gleaming acorns in my hand. "I shouldn't take them?" I ask again. "No," was the unequivocal answer—"leave them right here." I reluctantly let the magical drops of gold fall back to the ground.

· · · · ·

The enchanted hilltop that I love and knew is all but dead. The spirit tree is half burnt, its spirit gone. Now the whole hilltop has a completely exposed feel to it, and I can barely find my bearings. The place is littered with garbage, and most distressing of all, a road has been cut through it that links it to the valley below and to the coast. The "state" has done this, the villagers tell me. Indeed. Nothing irrevocably alters a place of nature like a slick, paved road. The municipality, along with the Hizb, under the rubric of a nongovernmental organization called Green on the Borders, *akhdar 'al hudūd* (there is a placard advertising this), has taken over the hilltop. The mosque has been entirely rebuilt, unrecognizable from the resonant pile of rubble it once was, and adjacent to it, where the old stone dwellings used to be, there is now a cement block where the young men of the Hizb man the lookout. They eye me suspiciously. If only they knew how deeply I know and love this place, what in the decade or so of coming here I have experienced, encountered and learned. The villagers with me today, Munya and Ghida and her daughter who was in her belly on the day of the Liberation, regale me with variations of stories that I have heard already, and I smile and nod and occasionally fill in the blanks. They call with laughter in their voices to the young men, "She's one of us!" I smile wanly at the stern youths in camo. They glower back. Theirs is a dead serious mission. My smile is sad.

The Resistance has—for now—overpowered the resistant spirits of nature.

6 The Gray Zone

This chapter is about limens, borders, and gray zones; neighbors and enemies; life and loves. It illuminates the ambiguities of coherent, cohesive framings in smashed and broken worlds and, beyond that, the moral difficulties of collaboration as a mode of survival in places of war. Here, I collect together ethnographic fragments of a fragmented landscape. The scenes below describe affective and lived spaces of moral (and epistemic) murkiness (Taussig 2004). Like a *barzakh* between sunlight and shadow, life in this borderland unfolds in a gray zone where it is impossible to go to one side, *"for existence has no edges"* (Ibn al-Arabi, quoted in Pandolfo 1997). But modern power formations do. They are sharp and slicing. They feel a bit like razor wire. How does one reality bleed across the edges of another? In friendship and collaboration, violence and pain, uncanny affect. In something as ordinary and as haunting as the unbordered lives of butterflies, birds, and bees, the free flow of water, and of radio waves.[1]

We know: the closer we get to war, the harder it is to draw a clear picture of it.

ON EDGE

We stand on a desolate promontory overlooking another world as the light wanes. Blue-grey chases red-gold across the landscape as the sun withdraws behind us. Nearby stand a phalanx of young pines, a row of skinny legs with knobby knees under prickly green tufts, promising us bravely with the naïve eagerness of youth that when they grow up they will do their bordering job more convincingly. They whisper to us between giggles: "Jihad al-Bina' planted us here![2] To thumb our noses at the border! At the enemy! At war! When we grow up we'll shelter guerrillas! We're not scared!" To our right on a low hilltop squats an Israeli outpost. To our left on a higher hill lurks a camouflaged Lebanese Army position.[3] We stand in the middle of two warring worlds, and the cold wind bites into us. Puddles of mud lie across the red-earth track: should we go any further? I shiver—am I feeling vulnerable, mortal, and small . . . or just cold?

We look at the two outposts and then at the neat industrial-agricultural landscape through the impervious looking glass before our eyes. A geometric patchwork of fields, right up to the border, a dividing line composed of visible and invisible forces of enmity, socioeconomic difference, networks of connectedness, identification: rows of cypress trees, paved roads on which cars (from another universe!) drive, dense, irrigated fruit orchards, a geometric hilltop settlement,[4] refrigerated hangars for agricultural produce. Our side of the border/this side of the glass: a scrub-covered and prickly abandoned agricultural plain, faint traces of cultivation—years and years ago, mere seconds in geographic time—tattered dirt roads, desolation, silence. A fracture between South and North, desolation and wealth, worlds of resistance and survival, worlds of profit and possibility, US/Europe and the Middle East.

My companion, Rabih, wants to go further down the track, toward the extreme edge of the nation-space—the Blue Line, which he claims is a stick in the ground topped by an overturned tin can (or so I picture it in my mind's eye), but I hesitate, my throat tightens into a familiar somatic knot. It looks too deserted. This place looks like it has been left to fend for itself in any which way since the French and the British sliced up their colonial dominions in the wake of the First World War and the end of the Ottoman Empire. Why is no one around? Why are some points of this border mega-militarized and others so rudimentary, basic? I feel like we are the last people on earth. Why are we the only people here? And more to the point, *are* we the only people here? I bet we are in the sights of both military outposts. I bet the Israelis are aiming their guns at us. I think of my baby son. And I refuse to budge. Instead, I take some pictures to capture the scene and feeling (is that worse?). Finally we get in the car to get away from this terrifying desolation, and a BMW jeep rounds the top of the hill, casually driving in the direction of the border along the dirt track. It is populated by a few women and a baby out on an afternoon drive, it appears. We slow down to inquire about the nation-state's physical limits, but the driver pretends not to see us. When we finally get her attention she stops. We ask her how far we can go. She says, "To the *birkeh* [there is a small pond down the slope toward the Israeli outpost about fifty meters away] it's *okkeh*." "Do you go there?" we ask. "Sometimes, but right now it is all muddy." Hmm, so where *is* she going? This is a dead-end track that ends in Israel. She drives off and a few meters down the road stops and turns. Suddenly, over the ridge a Mercedes comes hurtling toward us at a mad speed. What on earth! The guy who is driving and another guy sitting next to him glare at us like mad. We keep driving and so do they—we check them out in our rearview mirror—they get a few meters past us and make a high-speed hairpin turn, the car half skidding off the road. They must have been dispatched to get us away from where we were standing (we think), but we had already moved and their speed ended up representing misplaced urgency. Maybe the Israelis sent a message via UNIFIL saying: find out who those two are or else! Were they coming for us? Were they speeding because we were in danger? Were we transgressing some invisible borders? Ignorantly flaunting the rules of war? Who knows.

After that we drive through Yarun, the village at whose edge we were standing. It is one of the few mixed villages in these parts. Today its Shi'a inhabitants are mostly in Panama and mostly very rich and mostly building massive and tasteless mansions on former agricultural land surrounding and overwhelming the tiny remains of the largely Christian old village, a few tangled streets and flat-roofed stone homes huddled on the hilltop around a church and a walled monastery. All the life we see is concentrated in a few scrawny cats, who stare at us with hungry eyes. We continue to Marun al Ras, a high bluff swooping down into a flat and wide yet fallow agricultural plain, continuous, indulgently undulant, and yet unforgivingly gashed in the middle by the border, an integral flat topographic surface divided between enemy worlds: Lebanon and Israel. The Lebanese side is an eroded, faded, dry, cracked, and brown mirror of the verdant and agriculturally productive Israeli side. The borderline running along the middle in a southwesterly direction is the looking glass.

As the sun sinks and the gloom rises, a few lights begin to glimmer across the uncrossable border, as impermeable (to us) as a mirror. Cars and trucks smoothly trace the paved streets, purring contentedly in another world. We bump along on the moonscape asphalt in my little blue car. My companion says that he feels like he is standing on Earth and gazing at Mars. The landscape is silent poetry.

Nahariya? Akka?! Mars!

On the way back to the familiar coast where we habitually dwell (we know where the sun sets there—into the sea), we lose the border for a spell and inadvertently take a diverging route down through Haneen and Dibl. Haneen, a sunken Shi'a hamlet sitting on the one road connecting the two Christian villages of Ain Ibl and Dibl. Here, in the trench out of sight of the glowing western horizon, an inky night prematurely gathers. Haneen ("longing" in Arabic) was razed to nonexistence in the 1970s during the formation and consolidation of the local pro-Israeli forces in the borderland. Dibl was the home of Colonel Aql Hashem, the second in command of the South Lebanon Army (SLA), who was blown up there in front of his home by a bomb set by Hizbullah in the waning days of the occupation. Dibl was known then as a lair of SLA thugs (Timur Göksel described it to me as among "the worst"). Its name (which in Arabic connotes wilted, rotten things) still carries notes of fear to the erstwhile inhabitants of the occupation zone. From the *New York Times*, January 31, 2000:

> Guerrillas fighting to oust Israeli troops from southern Lebanon killed the second-most-senior officer of the Israeli-backed militia there today with a bomb that exploded near his house.
>
> The Iranian-backed Hezbollah, or Party of God, took responsibility for killing the officer, Col. Akl Hashem, 47, who commanded the western brigade of the pro-Israeli militia, known as the South Lebanon Army.

Colonel Hashem, who was also the chief of the group's intelligence service in his area of command, was considered the likely successor for the 71-year-old militia commander, Gen. Antoine Lahd.

Reports from southern Lebanon said that Colonel Hashem, who had survived several previous attempts on his life, was killed instantly when a cluster of explosive charges went off in the yard of his farmhouse near the village of Dibl in southern Lebanon.

We drive up and down snug and curling village streets, as the blue hour turns black. Some shadowy figures of boys note our intrusion. Fruit trees in gardens and low stone walls accompany our directionless path. We lose our orientation in time and space. Is this Hashem's home here? I think I remember it from the grainy recordings of the moments of his death that were broadcast triumphantly, repeatedly on al-Manar, Hizbullah's television station. I hold these thoughts in my heart as my companion and I speak of other things (other wars). I am sure that this is the front yard where Hashem met his death near his big white jeep. Will we ever get out of here? We finally exit the village and drive along a level road that runs parallel to an elevated shelf on our left. As the shadows coalesce around us, we come across a car parked on the other side of the road facing us; its lights are switched off, but its trunk is open. Beyond the car, in the olive grove in a concealed ditch between the road and the ridge above, we note the movement of some men working with long cylindrical objects; we swivel our heads in their direction but keep driving. What are they doing? Preparing the ground for the next round? Laying irrigation pipes? At long last we reconnect with the border road by coming up a steep incline from the murky slump where Dibl and Haneen dwell. We are back on (the) edge.

Breathe out: orientation. Heading toward the still-distant sea, we pass through Rmeish, Aita al- Shaab, Ramia, and then Marwaheen. (In Aita, at a fork in the road we ask the way. A youth shouts, "This is the way to Sur, *this* way leads to Nahariya!"[5] He and his friends explode into peals of laughter). As we drive toward Marwaheen, we crawl up a spine that soars above the Israeli north. We see the first lights twinkling along the Israeli coastline, a continuation of ours, a world away, and then suddenly the image swells, spreads, glitters and shimmers, overwhelming us. "Is that Akka [Acre]?" we wonder aloud to each other. We *want* it to be Akka.

Look at how the coast curves! It must be a gulf, no it's not Nahariya, it *has* to be Akka (the sister city of my hometown Saida, entangled with it throughout history—and this is the first time I see it!). We stop, our hearts beating, the lights sparkling like stars in our eyes, our mouths open in wonder. To our left, grid streets, electricity, urban sprawl. To our right, dark hills and valleys, scrubland, a few half-hearted naked light bulbs, poverty, denuded tobacco fields, a scattering of poor villages. What a place! A very significant nowhere strung across the universe, across worlds! A fertile crescent truncated by the border then ravaged with wars and peppered with ordnance. All the youth are somewhere else, apart from those who are busy as bees in underground lairs preparing for the wars to come. Only old people, women, and children keep the farming and the villages alive. And those with no exit plans. And yet the dark houses insist on continuing to embody a kind of life: a lit and loved lifeworld that is theirs.

This book inhabits a liminal place, a gray zone, a borderline, a front, a point of contact and of division, a space rife with murky ambiguity, mystery, and magic. I stand at this thrilling and uncanny boundary and stare through the invisible air that sometimes feels like an enormous looking glass and sometimes like a bell jar. It is eternal and unmoving this land beneath my feet, from the perspective of my tiny human form and finite lifespan; and immense and whole, the implements of earthly power rending it appear so futile and fragile under the giant arc of the everlasting sky. It is also painfully, wearily beautiful, this place both raw and ravaged, constantly renewed and so very old. It affects me profoundly and speaks to me in ways I think I understand; more and more yet less and less, the more I dwell here and journey here and watch and listen and taste and smell and feel here.

Ideally, the inquiry should compose its object symmetrically through an investigation that embraces both sides of the borderline. But due to several factors relating to the painful physical realities of political enmity and national bordering, embodied in the mortal form of the researcher and its inalienable stamp of Lebanese citizenship, this study can explore only one side of the two-sided figure that unites at the line between shadow and sunlight, the Lebanon/Israel frontier. Israel in this account remains at a physical remove, wrapped in its protective cocoon (the "iron dome"), a defensive and paranoid ghetto from which I am physically, morally, politically excluded. In South Lebanon it is touchable only with my eyes, and yet it is everywhere. Here in South Lebanon Israel is the enemy, *al-'adu,* to be ceaselessly fought in an endless struggle that defines the basis of being and gives shape to time. But Israel is *also* the next-door neighbor, just over there (and often enough over here) beyond this crest, along my vegetable patch, behind my beehive, between those trees; an enemy and a neighbor that is daily encountered and prosaically related (to). Israel then is something both existentially and mundanely constitutive of this place: it inhabits (haunts, occupies) every utterance, movement, feeling, being, object, thought, and place.

THE INTIMACY OF ENMITY

Israel and the inhabitants of South Lebanon go way back. They simultaneously became neighbors and enemies at the moment of inception, when Israel burst forth upon the land of Palestine. Despite their professed hatred, these neighbors/enemies complement one another and in a strange way need each other. Often during my time in the South I heard Israel (*hinneh,* them) referred to in familiar, familial terms: "We *know* them, *mna'rifon*"; "We live with them, *ma'ayshinon.*" This indicates an exclusive, tight relationship, a deep knowledge of this special other. And their relationship, like many long-term affairs, is rife with ambiguity and contradiction: can't live with them, can't live without them. One man described his life with Israel as a marriage, a violent one, but a kinship, an intimate bond nonetheless. "What can we do?" he said. "We southerners are stuck in this violent affair, there is no escape—and so we make the best of it and get on with things." Although morally/politically speaking, enmity is the prescribed, preferred (possibly only nontaboo) mode of relating to this other, there are other orientations toward the enemy/neighbor that are more ambiguous. And not as muted or subtle or silenced as one would prefer/expect.

Jihad's Story: The Neighbor, the Enemy

Jihad has lived all his forty-something years in a town that saw among the worst of the fighting and destruction in the 2006 war (and has since crazily rebounded). He often, in my presence and in the presence of others (provocatively) expresses his affection and regard for Israel. During the Israeli occupation he worked as a "technician" in a hospital in northern Israel and earned a decent living. It is not that Jihad does not earn a good living now. Ever the opportunist, he cashed in on the post-2006 (re)building boom, investing a part of the cash compensation he received for his destroyed home in a building-supplies business and transforming a piece of land that his family no longer farms into a quarry. His businesses have profited and proliferated. He is well-off by village standards; he cultivates a belly, tells jokes, drinks nonalcoholic beer, drives a jeep, and has many children (his wife gave birth to two successive children during the time I was in the field in addition to the five they already had). His relatives grumble that he has gotten rich exploiting the need of others, but there could be a hint of envy in their pronouncements. Others who know him prefer not to be in his presence because of his "compromised" past. I found this antipathy strange, because there were others with an equally or more "compromised" past who were not thus shunned by the same people, and anyway in the former occupied zone dogmatically pursuing such principles is just not very practical. It eventually dawned on me that most of his critics look down on him mainly because he belongs to a small family with no auspicious pedigree, one which did not have any significant standing in the village. Which is why he had no choice but to grab fate by the horns each time it bore down on him.

Most villages are composed of two or three large families that, due to a combination of descent, numbers, connections, acquired wealth, and mobility, dominate village power structures.[6] These powerful families often occupy public positions like head of the municipality, or *mukhtar*, in a social logic that applies to the rest of the Lebanese political landscape, as Joseph (2011) has extensively documented. Yet today, unlike during the time of the *zu'ama*, those close to power do not see themselves as a separate social class from the villagers, as most villagers today are descended from peasant families, *fallaheen*. In the village scene, the smaller, weaker families are worse off and socially denigrated and often marginalized. It is well known—and pretty understandable—that such subaltern families were the most eager to throw their lot in with the occupiers. During the occupation, enabled through their association with the brute force of occupying power, they turned the tables and climbed to the top of the village molehill, and their ascent was sometimes ugly.

One day I was driving in a nearby village and my companions pointed out a house built in the shape of an airplane. "That is the house of a big collaborator," they told me. "He was feared and hated in our village." "Where is he now?" I asked. "In Israel, never to return," they said. "He did too many people too much wrong. There is no place for him here ever again." During the time the collaborator had inhabited the house he had painted it in blue and white, the colors of the Israeli flag. Today it is repainted in different colors, and his relatives live in it. There is a clothesline outside and children's toys strewn about. But not everyone who collaborated did so at such a level and with such dramatic repercussions. Most people just made do with the occupation and somehow muddled along (Allen 2008). And that is the muddied moral nature of the present in every single village in the former occupation zone. It is hard—impossible mainly—for those who are struggling to survive to be politically principled and ideologically pure in a place of constantly shifting power amidst the intensity of war. Still (and this is in itself a contradiction), many people are.

As hard as the reality of collaboration is to stomach to those of us who, like me, are actively committed to resisting occupation, war and empire for those caught up in these structures and struggling to make their lives, collaboration (also across enemy lines) is a modality of resistance and of survival. As Göksel, a lifelong observer of the occupation of South Lebanon bluntly puts it to me (and as both Levi [1989] and Maček [2011] have shown), anyone who thinks they can judge these choices from afar has no lived comprehension of the fraught pathways of survival in the "gray zones" of war. Of course, there are many shades of gray, various levels of collaboration, and I should point out that what I am exploring in this chapter remains on the more innocuous end. I am fully aware of how uncomfortable any discussion of this kind of collaboration (but not other kinds!) makes us all feel, yet I think a truthful account of life in war should

not gloss over this awkward aspect. The ethnographic reality of collaboration raises questions that our disciplinary celebrations of collaboration
across other kinds of divides are unable to adequately answer (Bond
2021).

Jihad did not join the SLA; his brother did. But his brother then spon-
sored him to work in Israel. The sponsorship cost a hundred and fifty dollars a month, which Jihad paid from his salary, which came to about five
hundred dollars. Many people, who out of opportunity or out of need or
coercion took these jobs, were bussed into Israel daily to work as "techni-
cians," builders, agricultural laborers, and in other menial jobs. The pay,
although low, was relatively generous for occupied Lebanon. Some think
that Jihad's modest background is the reason for his lack of "moral integrity," yet it is just as likely that it is also the source of his ambitious streak:
he does not have the luxury of safety nets to fall back on, and thus he
makes the best of what he has. Principles in such a space are hard to maintain. Jihad's business is booming these days; he can barely keep up with
demand. He works his eldest son from sunup to way past sundown on
orders and deliveries of building materials as he sits back and works his
cell phone.

The first time I visited him in his home, Jihad was renting an apart-
ment in the center of the village while he built a new house on the southeastern outskirts of the village, overlooking the thorny hills of Israeli/
Palestinian Galilee. We sit in his living room, my sister and I, among his
wife and many children. At the center of the room, taking pride of place,
sits a huge television that is crowned with a picture of a smiling Sayyid
Hassan Nasrallah, the secretary general of Hizbullah. We get to talking
and soon, after a few questions from me he lowers his guard. "Life was
better back then," he says, laughing mischievously. Jihad appreciates
Israeli orderliness, the cleanliness of their cities, their free schooling and
affordable healthcare, their "respect for people," and their "democracy and
freedom." He says, "people in Israel are judged on merit, unlike here where
it is all about *wasta*, connections, and which politician has your back." His
wife and kids pipe up with fond memories of daytrips to Israel during the
time Jihad worked there: "It's just like Europe!" they said (although they
have never been to Europe). All throughout this discussion and disclosure
Sayyid Hassan Nasrallah crinkled his eyes and smiled his sweet smile at us

from atop the television. Jihad deeply loves and respects the Sayyid, although he does blame Hizbullah for provoking the last ruinous war (which made him rich). Jihad is full of contradictions.

Truth be told, at first I did not comprehend Jihad's contradictory declarations and contrary orientations, especially since he is not by any means disenfranchised by the current Hizbullah-run order in the former zone. As a matter of fact, he thrives in it. As he spoke glowingly of Israeli democracy and freedom, I pointed out that "democracy and freedom" were not things Jewish Israeli citizens shared with non-Jewish Israeli citizens, let alone with captive, menial day laborers bussed in from occupation zones! He did not disagree but brushed my objections away with unflattering descriptions of the Lebanese state as distant, neglectful, beset by cronyism, and corrupt and of the current crowd in control of the southern villages as equally so. It struck me that Jihad's apparent appreciation of Israel was a critical commentary on the way things are in South Lebanon today. He continued, "Let me explain the situation here to you in simple terms: before, we were living under an Israeli occupation and now we are living under Iranian occupation, and really not much has changed, except that Israel is now off limits to us and Hizbullah provokes wars whenever they please that kill us all and turn our homes to rubble." Then he switched subjects and launched into a cloak-and-dagger story about the late Hajj Imad (Mughnieh, a venerated Hizbullah leader, now assassinated) coming over to his place to break his fast unannounced one inky moonless night in Ramadan . . .

This shifting, this flipping, this ambiguous, political sensibility evokes the compromised nature of the drive to survive in the face of brutal power described by Primo Levi (1989) in *The Drowned and the Saved* when he speaks of the "gray zone" of complicity that defines life in the Lager:

> It is a gray zone, poorly defined, where the two camps of masters and servants both diverge and converge. This gray zone possesses an incredibly complicated internal structure and contains within itself enough to confuse our need to judge. (42)

When I spoke with Timur Göksel, he repeatedly deflected the urge to impose clear moral categories upon the dwellers of such spaces. He pointed to the daily realities and micropractices of survival for people living under an occupying power, acts often deemed immoral by the prescriptive judgment of those in control. He insinuated that survival is a gray zone that cannot be easily judged. Göksel, a careful, empathetic, and involved observer throughout his long tenure as UNIFIL spokesman and beyond, described the actions of the subjects of the occupation who threw their lot in with the occupiers in no uncertain terms: "I simply call it survival."

Ivana Maček (2005, 2011), writing about life in Sarajevo during the siege, captures this gray zone well:

> [This is] one of the most interesting discoveries I made during my work in Sarajevo. The richer the firsthand experiences of war, the more ambivalent the moral positioning of the people that I met. And vice versa. Those who had a meagre firsthand experience were more prone to simplifications of . . . war. The confusion similar to the one that Primo Levi describes at the entrance into the "indecipherable" world of the Lager, was characteristic of the majority of war stories I heard in Sarajevo between 1994 and 1996, i.e., after more than two years of direct war experiences. The categories of "us" and "them" were blurred, . . . the aims and causes of the war were not clear any more, the justification of killing and destruction was not convincing, and consequently also the judgements of right and wrong were difficult and ambiguous. (71)

Jihad's perspectives and affections and political views that simply do not add up relate to the contradictions of dwelling with an enemy who is also a neighbor (Žižek, Reinhard, and Santner 2013; Anidjar 2003). These apparently opposed forms of relating are deeply related, simultaneously and constantly constituting and undermining one another: familiarity generates affection and identification, among other things (like knowledge or contempt), and thus the enemy/neighbor (other) is always already a part of the self. Only those who inhabit enmity at a remove can fully participate in the dream of pure ideology, pure love, or pure hate. Now Jihad's oddly combined perspectives and strangely jarring affections make better sense.

A noteworthy aspect of Jihad's story is that it has been lived entirely in place, in his village. He was able to stay there (remain steadfast). Unlike many in South Lebanon, he has neither historical connections to political

families to ease his way into this or that municipal, military, or governmental job, nor a kinship network in the metropole pulling him there, nor
relatives abroad sending back remittances or visa letters. Parentless and
poor, he and his siblings made-do with the changing power situation and
opportunities that presented themselves in their village at the end of the
possible earth, at the limits of morality, aligning themselves with the
Israelis, who emerged over that hill yonder, during the time they were
there and then shifting casually back into the Hizb-dominated village
scene after serving some symbolic time in jail for "collaboration" after the
occupation ended in 2000 (only his brother did, civilian collaborators
were not imprisoned). And who knows what comes next. In any case it is
the present moment that matters. Now Jihad expresses rhetorical disaffection for the present regime and nostalgia for the absent Israelis, but it
could also be a way of rationalizing past acts or simply criticizing a current
social order that does not support him or respect him as much as he wishes
it to, although he does pretty well on his own. And his sons—of course!—
are in the Resistance. In any case, he is one amongst many like him who
face up to the difficulties of life that come their way and manage to find a
way through. In a way, the most striking—and prosaic—aspect of his story
is his "steadfastness" (*sumud*, the slogan of the Hizb and the suffering
southerner who remains in place through wars and wars): he never left his
village and he is still there making a living through the rise and fall of different, antithetical, existentially opposed systems of power. And come
what may.

Later, Jihad took me around his village and the surrounding landscape.
We visited his sister, whose husband is an educated man and worked as an
engineer in Libya for a spell but then lost his job, and now they are all back
in the village. They live in a dank, windowless two-room structure with
their son and daughter on a dusty main street where the gloomy indoor
spaces are compartmentalized by hanging cloths. The women work the
tobacco, which they have planted at the back of their home. They were
threading the morning's picking when we arrived, and their hands were
coated with tar. Upon our arrival they deftly retied their headscarves,
shifting the knot from the nape of their necks to their throats, and ran to
the grubby kitchen sink to scrub off the black goo from their fingers and

then make us coffee. Tobacco is their only income in times of dearth, as it is for most southerners fallen on hard times. ("Tobacco keeps us alive" is the eternal refrain: *Al-dukhan ma'ayyashna* or *'Aysheen min wara al dukhan.*) The daughter who is pretty and smart and ambitious and wants to be a teacher helps her mother; her older brother, a youth who dresses up in flamboyant village fashion (stonewashed skin-tight jeans and garish faux-croc shoes) and gels his hair into an exaggerated pompadour, mainly loafs around. And his father wrings his hands and bemoans his son's costly fashion sense and his own bitter fate.

Jihad then takes me into the woodland, and we got off the beaten track and onto rocky dirt roads surrounded on all sides by scrubland and the occasional tobacco field. He wants to show me something. We head deeper into the *wa'ar,* the uncultivated wilderness; there is barely a footpath underneath as the overgrowth crowds in on us while we bump along in his jeep. "This is the village *hima,* a natural reserve. You see that whole hill? The Hizb are underneath it, but you can't see them and you can't know that." Down we dip and turn and finally stop. Jihad's jeep is nestled in some leafy bushes that embrace us protectively, swallowing us from sight. This is probably the exact position of the resistance fighters who lay in wait with their antitank rocket launchers for the Humvees to come around the sharp bend that July morning in 2006. "This is *khallet wardeh* [Rose Valley] where the kidnapping operation took place: right there in the turn of the road, see how steeply it curves? Do you see where that Israeli flag is? The 'boys' cut through the border fence there and camped on the other side for days before the ambush." It was thrilling to be so close to the site from which such a devastating war was sparked. And here is Jihad, despite all his proclaimed disaffection for the current political order along the southern marches, partaking in its glory.

Ten Years Later . . .

This is the third house I visit Jihad and his family in. This one is a single-level structure with a front patio and back garden (the interim house was gifted to his eldest son, who is about to get married). Along the side of the house is the *sahra,* or vegetable garden. At the back there is a shady terrace adjacent to a back garden, and a baby bird hangs in a cage underneath a child's summer hat. His youngest daughter loves the baby bird and feeds it mushed grain with a spoon. Birds of many kinds flutter and putter about in the cluttered and junk-jammed back garden. There are chickens and a rooster. Quails and pigeons. "I love birds," Jihad says, reminding me of Mahmoud Darwish's lines of poetry:

> Where should we go after the last frontier?
> Where should the birds fly after the last sky?
> Where should the plants sleep after the last breath of air?
> We will write our names with scarlet steam.
> We will cut off the hand of the song to be finished by our flesh.
> We will die here, here in the last passage.
> Here and here our blood will plant its olive tree.

We sat in the back terrace and ate a delicious southern lunch (a riot of fresh vegetables and a southern delicacy conjured in my honor: *kibbeh nayyi*, freshly slaughtered raw lamb pounded with bulghur and spices and drizzled in dark green olive oil). As we were eating and talking Jihad mentioned that someone once asked him to translate a word from Hebrew to Arabic, and so I asked him: "Do you speak Hebrew?" "Of course!" he said. So I asked him: "Do you still remember it?" He said with a defiant grin, "Of course! How can anyone forget his first love?" He throws his head back and laughs long and hard. He still makes comments like these. He still loves to declaim about his "love affair" with Israel.

Batoul, his wife, recounted a time they went to Israel[7] with their two older children (the other six were not yet born) and visited Yafa and Haifa and ate delicious falafel there. They were invited to the wedding of a Palestinian friend of Jihad's from the hospital where he worked. The wedding was held in a village in Galilee. She remembered how the wedding procession went through the town. And how much fun it was. She said, "Everyone thought that Jihad was Israeli. He's blond and wore sunglasses and spoke Hebrew. He easily passed for one of them!" While many might read this as a classical colonial dynamic manifesting the colonized's fascination with and desire for the colonizer, and of course there is something of that present, I am not sure this fully captures the ambivalences and ambiguities at play here—or the provocative nature of such declarations. What I find illuminating about these difficult-to-parse narratives and orientations, which are more common

Figure 22. Doves fly around their coop in their backyard, after the last sky.

than anyone cares to admit, is the light that they shed on the pragmatic strategies for survival practiced by those who inhabit war and other deadly worlds. To live in such worlds entails all kinds of collaborations—some acceptable and some not. The difficulty of theoretically and morally grasping these choices, the lack of place in our understanding for their confounding and morally incomprehensible nature, says something about our distance from these worlds. This is an ethnographic point and need not be a political one (although it often is). It is possible to simultaneously ethnographically recognize the complexities of resisting and surviving war while also and always fighting oppression, exploitation, degradation, occupation, injustice and insist on better worlds that do not compel people to such fraught survival strategies. How we can do this without perpetuating further conceptual and actual violence is the question.

Jihad tells me that today he wants to take me for a drive on a road that was held by Israel after 2006 and that is the closest point to the border that I will ever get. He says no one can go there, but *he* can take me there. Some people exclaim: what if they shoot us? He says, "So what if they do? We will start the next war!" And he laughs. We get in his dusty, dirty jeep with some of his children, two or three smart and pretty girls, and bump along roads that soon become dirt paths. We drive past the outskirts of the village. He takes us to a bizarre abandoned villa right on the border in sight of a UN Blue Line marker and an Israeli bulldozer doing some business on the other side. This place has two pools, which are empty. A rather absurd place to take off one's clothes and relax! We drive off, and there is a cement watchtower with mirrored windows, and he says that it is for Hizbullah. I snap a picture of it through the windshield of the car. He takes a left turn and drives towards the very close border, and soon we are deep in the underbrush; the jeep is crowded in on all sides by overgrowth, and we get closer and closer to the border. He pops a cassette of militant Hizbullah songs in the car's player—for atmosphere, I guess, or to show proper ideological credentials—and we bump along the dirt path, and he proudly says: "Only the army and the Resistance can come here, but I am bringing you here to see! This road was taken by Israel in 2006, but the Sayyid [Hassan Nasrallah] insisted it be returned to Lebanon." Indeed it hugs the border and front very close. No one could know of this road or even come here without this kind of escort. We pass very close to an Israeli outpost just on the other side. A Hizbullah flag flutters in its face on our side, a few meters across the way. The beautiful early summer meadow is mad all around us, pushing in at the windows and whipping at my arms as we drive past. I make him stop so I can nestle in the wildflowers for a moment and feel the weird border static. I stand with my back to Israel in the embrace of some very tall flowering shrubs, Queen Anne's Lace. It is so beautiful here and wild and strange. I love it deeply.

A rough road branches off. "The Lebanese army is down there," Jihad says. We continue bumping along the border road. He shows me what looks like a cairn of stones right on the border and says, "That's where the tunnel was that they destroyed" (*Haaretz* 2018; AP 2019).

He turns to me as we drive and says, "This won't be a very popular opinion, but the Jews were in Israel before the Palestinians! It's their land! Yes of course the Israelis are violent and aggressive and have done terrible things, but the Palestinians aren't innocent either!" I raise my eyebrows and take the bait and we proceed to heatedly argue about the proposed topic as we bump along the militarized borderline where war can break out at any second. Jihad's sons are in the Resistance. They go for periodic field training in Syria and Iraq. They are fully invested in the present political order along the borderline, and so is Jihad—deeply so. The contradictions that are contained in Jihad's words in light of his life now and that of his children appear stark but are not. In such fraught worlds, where survival is at stake, power is always approached pragmatically by ordinary people. The power that prevails becomes the environment within which life is waged. If we want people to make better choices, we must fight for better worlds.

This hill where we are driving is known to be a stronghold of the Resistance, as it commands a view of surrounding country. It is supposedly a no-go zone, but we go there anyway. As we drive back down a steep dirt track, a Hizbullah guy on a motocross bike comes up it. Jihad slows down and waves at him, but he barely pays us any attention and drives off. I wonder how okay it is for such borderline tourism to take place so casually, especially in the permanent climate of ongoing war. Jihad shrugs off the possibility of war: no way, Iran is just taunting America, and America will pay off the Saudis and all will be fine; there won't be any war.

He takes us to another border point, close by to minefields. Beyond the minefields is the border, and one can see a banana plantation covered in mesh and a vineyard across in Israel. I say, oops, there are mines here, and he scoffs at my urbane sensitivity to explosives and strikes off walking in the direction of the mines. He says, "Just don't get close to the signs—the mines are beyond there." He tells us a funny story of a "crazy" guy from the village who crossed the border there and got stuck, and the UNIFIL had to save him. They lowered a basket from a helicopter to pick him up. The next day this guy was found heading back in the same direction, and so they intercepted him and asked him where he was going. He said he was going back across the border because he lost one of his plastic slippers during the helicopter rescue! Some people have no regard for the dangers hidden in uncrossable borders that are also front lines of war.

Jihad wants to show me a piece of land that he thinks I should buy ("because you are one of us!"). It is the cheapest land in the village—a great bargain. Jihad said that the cheapest land in the South is in his village (which was all but flattened in 2006). Is it because of the endless threat of war? I told him that actually I would like to get a piece of land right there next to the minefields, adjacent to the border—it looks so pristine and wild!—and he said no, you shouldn't. So I asked why? He said because when there is war, those frontline residences are the ones commandeered first by the invaders, and you don't want that. So although he scoffs at the possibility of war, he is not actually ruling it out—and he makes plans accordingly.

NOMADOLOGY AND THE WAR MACHINE

Living on the border is a strange affair—not least when that border is also a front line. Things get even more complicated when that border, which is now closed, was open not so long ago, a semiporous boundary internal to an occupation that accommodated a kind of traffic subordinate to the power of the occupier. What are the effects on life of such a phenomenon as a militarized and mined crossable/uncrossable war border? Bundled up with the divisive and violent nature of bordering—especially that of enemy borders—is the contrast of a landscape that is seamless and whole: natural continuities flaunt the lethal barriers and impositions of political sovereignty and enmity. Traveling the border and living along it gives the body a sensation similar to that of coastal living: edge-ness (Wylie 2007), a change of substance along a defined limit, the un-goable, the unknown that nevertheless lies before the eyes, at the tip of the nose, within reach. A looking glass. An uncanny and yet dead-real set of affairs.

Making this all the more dense a place and difficult a phenomenon to grasp are the lived (and narrated) experiences of this landscape's cutting and rending, crossing (Yeh 2018) and traversing (Myrivili 2004), and the daily practices that defy or at least prosaically accommodate the border's violent and often deadly presence (De León 2015) and potential. As the landscape is recovered/reclaimed as a site of living and livelihood, new sources of everyday violence and danger emerge.

Limits, Life, Limbs, and Love

The *bedu* in this borderland inhabit an ambiguous place vis-à-vis the fixed and violent borderline and other neighboring communities, as they are a handful of Sunni in a politically Shi'i landscape. And at a moment where Shi'i and Sunni politics are at loggerheads they do not fare well. They are ignored by Shi'i politicians because their numbers are quite negligible in terms of votes, and there are no Sunni representatives in the area who bother to cultivate them as constituents. The *bedu* communities of the borderland look elsewhere for political leadership: the slain prime minister Rafiq Hariri looms large, as he was instrumental in getting many of the *bedu* Lebanese citizenship in 1994 (Hariri gained a large voting bloc in the cities of Saida and Beirut as a result). In the half-forgotten *bedu* villages one encounters posters of Yasser Arafat and Saddam Hussein—who are also Sunni political icons.

J. is a small hamlet that still exists on the Israeli side of the border, on a small hill, but it is today empty of dwellers. It is adjacent to (or rather continuous with) the Lebanese village of Dhaira (where on the day of liberation I witnessed the families reuniting), which is contiguous with Bustan to the east along the border. The inhabitants of both hamlets are *bedu*, and they are of one tribe, one family. The abandoned stone homes of J. are clearly visible from across the border, but J. is no longer a functioning village. It is a village of ghosts: it stands empty and silent among its proliferating cypress trees. Its former inhabitants are now all in the Israeli "interior," forced out of their village soon after the end of the occupation of

Lebanon when the Israeli state cut off water and electricity and forced the villagers to leave; the Israeli state was uncomfortable with nomadic Arab kinship extending across frontlines.

Unlike the Shi'a and Christian inhabitants of the borderland, the *bedu* have strong ties of kinship to Bedouin Israeli citizens. The inhabitants of Dhaira and Bustan still attend the funerals of their kinfolk in J., as the cemetery is flush with the borderline. When the villagers of Dhaira hear the mosque in J. announcing a burial, they head up the hill to participate in the funeral across the uncrossable border and pay their respects by lining up along the barbed-wire fence. Even now after the village has been emptied, its former inhabitants come back from whatever Israeli Bedouin development town they now inhabit to be buried there—in *their* place.

Im Alaa is a daughter of J. but now lives in Dhaira, Lebanon, with her husband and son in a tidy, well-kept house a stone's throw from the border. We are sitting in her beautiful and lovingly tended garden among a few young fruit trees and birds of paradise. The aerial that has been planted in the middle of J. among the low stone houses and trees towers (or glowers) nearby, just up the hill from where we sit. Her immediate family members are all Israeli citizens, and she would be one too, but it so happens that she is married to a man from Dhaira, which fell a few meters on the Lebanese side of the border when it was drawn through everyone's lives. Although Dhaira and J. are practically the same village, inhabited by one extended family, one tribe, they are now on either side of an uncrossable divide and included in the subjected citizenry and incarcerated territory of enemy nations. Im Alaa's body may be thought to allegorize this ripping and rending of the continuous spaces of her life and loves. It is because of her ties of kinship drawing her across this lethal political front that Im Alaa lost a limb to a mine ten years ago. As we sit in her tidy, colorful, and fragrant little garden she re-members.

> IM ALAA: That day I was at home, and my family is inside *juwwa* [in Israel]; there are some girls from Yareen [a nearby village], and around here, if they didn't work in Israel they would be expelled from the zone [by the SLA]. Either you go and work in Israel or else get out! I don't have any girls who work. . . . So there were some women who went to work in Israel; they were forced to. They came to me, and they said your father is sick in the hospital.

Those girls who work in there, they would come and tell me about my father, that his days were numbered. So one day, as God is my witness, here I was in the house and my neighbor came to me and said there is a funeral in J., which is where my father is from, and so what did I think? I thought my father had died! So I said I would go and call on an [SLA] officer and ask him about my father—if my father had died I would need to get a permit from him to stay a week in there. So in order to go and get a permit and go and see my father, I set out walking toward the village, and on my way along the borderline I saw a boy walking inside of Israel. He was walking down toward the interior. So I said I would call him to ask him about my father. I took one step toward him [toward the border fence], and I stepped on something that came under my foot and it made a sound. And I did not think of mines at all. I didn't think of anything! It felt like a tin can or something like that. The moment I removed my leg, and just as I was about to call out to the boy, the bomb exploded and I fell on the ground.

HER HUSBAND: The Israelis came and took her to the hospital. Here there were no roads [to take her to a hospital in Lebanon].

ME: When was this?

IM ALAA: Before the Liberation in a little.

HUSBAND: In February.

IM ALAA: Yes it was winter. The rain is what saved me. If it wasn't for the rain I wouldn't have gotten up again. It was cold and it started to rain and my blood started to pour, but the rain made the blood cool on my leg.

ME: So what happened?

IM ALAA: There is a goatherd a little to the west from here. Our house is here, and you know where the house of Im Khaled is? That is where I was, near the olives. My daughters were at their aunt's house down the road. I started to pull myself in that direction, and I kept thinking what would happen if I died here and none of my family knew where I was! God is my witness, I started to drag myself, and I was shouting, "Come to me O people, *ya 'Arab!* Pick me up!" They heard me and started shouting, and people came running with their children. People came running from here, and my family came running from Israel. My sister came to me and started calling me by someone else's name! I told her "I am your sister!" They came and they took me. They took me to a hospital inside [in Israel] and I slept there, and for four days I didn't know who I was.

Figure 23. Im Ali remembers to me how she lost her limb on a cold February morning.

Im Alaa's leg was amputated right below the knee, and in time she recovered. Soon after that her father did die. Then in May of that same year the Israeli occupation of Lebanon ended. She remained on this side of the border, and her two daughters who are married to Israeli citizens "inside" stayed on that side of the border. They remain just down the hill from her home but another world away across an uncrossable divide. She hasn't seen them since.

Im Alaa's limb is gone; it exists as a memory. Her village containing the remains of her kin stands silent and ghostly nearby. And her daughters, who live in the Israeli "interior," on the other side of a line upon the earth that is at once ephemeral and lethal, are absent objects of a motherly love that transcends the deadly violence of the borderline. Im Alaa's life and her loves have and do cross this border, but her physical body has been viciously split by it: a devastating and constant reminder of the deadly violence of man-made political limits and ends, however arbitrary. Her life was saved by the coldness of the earth in *shbat,* February, the same earth that she lives from today and that concealed the weapon that almost killed her.

The House at the End of the World

Im Khaled lives alone with her son Khaled. They live on the last handsbreadth *shibr* of Lebanese land on a bend in the border road in Dhaira, the largest of the cluster of *bedu* settlements on the edge of the former central sector of the occupation zone. Khaled was but a few months old when his father was shot dead by an Israeli sniper. This was in 1976, at the peak of Palestinian guerrilla activity in the borderland, when Sunni villages were especially caught up in the guerrilla war. Some of the local *bedu*—following the well-worn paths of generations—would guide guerrillas along hidden paths to infiltrate Israel/Palestine—and many had relatives living on the other side of the front in villages a stone's throw and another world away. Khaled's father, though, was doing nothing so dramatic. He was out under the cover of night on another mission, a very mundane one: to steal government electricity. He was climbing up an electricity pole just outside his home to hook a wire to the state line and extend it to his home—a common practice. "An Israeli, thinking he was a *fida'i* on a night mission, shot him dead," Im Khaled says. Soon after that the 1978 Israeli invasion smashed and emptied their village and neighboring *bedu* villages as suspected nests of Palestinian *fida'i* activity. She and many of her relatives were displaced and bided their time in Saida until they were able to return in the mid-1980s. Then she fixed up the house she lives in today with her son. She never remarried. Im Khaled and her son are members of a tribe most of whom today reside in Dhaira, and many of her relatives live nearby (she is related to Im Alaa who lost her leg to a mine; it is her olive grove that Im Alaa refers to in her story) and her older brother is today the head of Dhaira municipality. They too have relatives across the uncrossable border. Im Khaled has the round face, dancing eyes, and snub nose of many of the Bedouin/Arab inhabitants of Lebanon's borderland. She is dressed in a flowery bright red housedress and wraps her hair in a scarf that is knotted at the nape of her neck; she dons a straw hat outdoors. Her eyes crinkle behind wire glasses as she

Figure 24. Hills, valleys, terraces of tobacco tucked into the folds; the borderline and an Israeli outpost.

enthusiastically shows us around her house and immaculately tended garden.

Im Khaled is part of a women's cooperative network that was supported briefly by European funders and then left to wither. Like many development projects here, the cooperative survived as long as it was directly overseen by the funders and could not sustain itself for long after. Im Khaled complained about the lack of local cooperation among the women but also of a lack of marketable networks for the products that the women of the cooperative prepared in their home: jars of pickles, tomato paste, jams, honey, and other staples of a southern larder. She continues to make these preserves, though, and markets them through personal networks. She generates most of her cash through her tobacco and olives and honey and preserves. Her son helps her. Apart from that there is not much else for him to do around here.

At the back of Im Khaled's home is a lovingly tended garden planted with kitchen vegetables and fruit trees, a grape vine; a row of beehives, a pile of firewood, tomatoes drying on a piece of cloth in the sun; rainbow blooms of fragrant roses. Beyond her garden is her tobacco field and past that her olive grove. Flush with the olive grove is a swath of purple grasses:

the minefield. And past the minefield slinks the fenced-off border road where Israeli Humvees constantly patrol, trailing behind them clouds of dust that hang in the air long after they are gone. Im Khaled skirts the minefields to get to her olives. She walks the same path each time. To her this is nothing out of the ordinary. "I know where the mines are," she says. "I simply steer clear of them."

I stand there and gaze out at the razor-edge of Lebanon and what lies beyond. Here my feet are planted in a lovingly tended garden adjacent to an olive grove and minefield, borderline and front. After that the agricultural landscape resumes, but in an impersonal, industrial manner: a patchwork of geometric plots, irrigated furrows of crops, row upon row upon row of fruit trees. I can discern some large hangars in the distance. Above us only sky.

Conclusion

LIFE AS WAR

On August 4, 2020, at a little past 6:00 p.m., a massive explosion ripped through Beirut. One of the most powerful nonnuclear explosions in human history, the blast was caused by more than 2,750 tons of ammonium nitrate that had been unsafely stored in the city's port since 2013 and had caught fire. The ensuing detonation that billowed out in a powder-pink mushroom cloud and sent shockwaves through the city killed 210 people, injured 7,500, left 300,000 homeless, and caused $15 billion in damages. The "Beirut blast" (which has since become ground zero for the latest era of dystopian Lebanese unraveling) was an anthropogenic event recorded on a geological, atmospheric (Kundu et al. 2021), and planetary scale. It left scenes of apocalypse in its wake and upended the lives of many already reeling from the many-layered, many-pronged disasters continuously unfolding in Lebanon, such as the coronavirus pandemic, ongoing financial and economic collapse, civil unrest, and endless political deadlock (to name a few). The exact causes of the blast have yet to be determined, and those responsible (the corrupt and neglectful leadership of Lebanon writ large) have not been held accountable.

Ever since its inception, this small country of 6.8 million (including 1.5 million refugees)[1] has stumbled from one calamity to the next, one war to the next. Since the official end of the civil war in 1990 that formally brought a leadership of warlords to power, Lebanon has gone from post-war wunderkind to dystopian nightmare. The flashy petrodollar-fueled "rebuilding" of the country stalled in the wake of the 2005 assassination of its self-proclaimed champion, Prime Minister Rafiq Hariri, then ground to a jarring halt after the war in Syria began in 2011. In 2015, a garbage-disposal crisis resulting (like pretty much everything) from the audacious corruption and constant infighting of the political elites who run the state like their private business empires, or more accurately mafias, triggered protests that rallied around the cry "You stink!" (Nucho 2019; Ziad Abu Rish 2015). By the summer of 2019, the local currency that for more than twenty years had been pegged at 1,500 Lebanese pounds to the dollar began a precipitous slide, due to the central bank's mismanagement of Lebanon's massive national debt. As of this writing, the lira has lost 95 percent of its value. To protect their ransacked reserves, the banks (which belong to the millionaire politicians who plunder this country and are the cause of this disaster) have slapped on capital controls, denying people access to their own money. The possibility that the life savings of most are gone for good is devastatingly real. For an economy that is 85 percent dependent on imports, the shortage of hard currency is ruinous and impacts all sectors of society. Price inflation is out of control. Unemployment is skyrocketing, hunger is rife, and street protests (that began as the 2019 "October Revolution" and then fizzled out) erupt every now and again as the political class batten down the hatches in their gilded palaces in Lebanon or abroad in European capitals where they have safely stored their personal wealth. According to the World Bank, around 50 percent of the Lebanese population (refugees included) live below the poverty line; this number is ballooning. And of course throughout all of this there are chronic shortages of electricity, water, and other basic services, as the public sector is consistently mismanaged and persistently plundered. Anyone who can leave the country has.

Catastrophe upon catastrophe upon catastrophe. How do people live like this? This is the question on many people's lips these days (and one of the guiding questions of this book). Yet even within these disastrous conditions life goes on. The inhabitants of Lebanon (and many other places in the Global South) have been living in dysfunctional, predatory, impoverished, and often deadly systems for so long, they have no illusions about these systems' ability to care for them and expect both nothing and the worst from their governments. Because of this, catastrophes such as the Beirut blast and the coronavirus pandemic, entering an already crowded field of disaster, are faced up to not so much as existential shocks (as the pandemic was experienced across many more affluent and stable systems) but as yet more blasted layers of difficulty to navigate. And to stay alive, navigate them one must. A friend of mine who was not far from the epicenter of the blast and who had lived through the many calamities of the civil war, calmly navigated the explosion as he would a wartime disaster (and many people in the first instance assumed this blast was war-related): he moved away from windows as the first explosions were heard and took the stairs out of the building as glass shattered, ceilings collapsed, and shocked and injured people flailed about everywhere. He quickly and deftly made his way to a place of relative safety.

To get by as the world ends (Wimmen 2021), most rely on several alternate networks and practices to ameliorate the shortcomings of the available system and somewhat counter constant existential threats. Over time, people have devised ways of making-do, and some of these makeshift practices became ingrained as resistant ways of life: cultivating sustainable networks of protection and care (and subsistence, if possible), expecting the worst, hoping for the best, living the moment, and always being prepared. I call these life-making practices and relationships in deadly times and places resistant ecologies. They are homegrown, diverse, durable, and (as counterintuitive as it may sound) rooted in the difficulty of life and the realistic expectation that the world can end at any moment. Resistant ecologies are not immune to catastrophe (nothing is), but they are the everyday soil upon which life in difficult places is stubbornly grown. Resistant ecologies may grow in the weakness or absence of stable and reliant systems and assist survival when systems break down. They may also grow in the interstices of such systems and resist-by-living the wholesale consumption of life by exploitative or deadly processes and systems.

In Lebanon, war is no metaphor. Here, war is real and it is genealogical: inhabited as an ongoing way of life and a fight for survival in shockingly suboptimal conditions. Resisting, adapting, making-do: wars (like other disasters) make our worlds. They unmask a precarious ordinary always laced with mortal danger wherein we must carry on. Wars show us latent fault lines of our social worlds: the structural violence that constitutes the world is exposed, the inequalities that we normalize suddenly can no longer be ignored. Yet at the same time that our differences emerge, we realize a commonality (vulnerability, inevitable mortality, a will to live), and we recognize just how vitally interconnected and interdependent we are (with other humans, with other animals, with plants and kindred spirits, with this planet). Can such contrapuntal realizations be reconciled and generatively approached? There is political hope in such revelation. The challenge is to translate it into (resistant) action.

Anthropologists, especially those who work on war, on poverty, on disease, on violence, on the environment, and on disasters, are critically positioned to describe the ordinary, inhabited grounds of catastrophic worlds. Instead of the turning away from these disastrous realities (by understanding them as savage or broken other worlds) so as to dream up better alternatives, a careful ethnographic rendering of life in war and other disasters allows us to grasp brutal lived experiences as more than occasional, exotic, or other. These battered worlds are the here and now where life forges on. From this wretched earth, we can (we hope) plot a path to a better present. For too many on this planet, life is waged in the midst of catastrophic disaster. The focus must shift to the resistant hope that making life brings and the insistent demands for something better.

I was recently talking to Rabih, a dear friend, a fellow southerner with whom I was often in the field and who is from the same Lebanese generation as me (the "war child" generation). He was describing to me the contours of his life now amidst the concatenated and sometimes unbelievable social and economic catastrophes that have befallen Lebanon as a result of generations of audacious political mishandling. "All that we thought we believed in is gone," he said. "All we have left are those we love, and they are what we have to live for and fight for right now."

THE END OF THE WORLD IS NOTHING NEW

In this book, I have examined life in war with an eye to a larger set of questions preoccupying anthropologists around life on this doomed planet, where an inescapable trajectory towards imminent (climate) catastrophe has suddenly come to dominate our senses, our existential anxieties, our temporal horizons, our scholarship. But many on this planet—largely in the Global South—have long been contending with catastrophic conditions as matter of their daily lives. Here, lives are being made every day in worlds that are calamitously ending and have ended time and again. This book has presented bittersweet scenes of what it is to live in war and what life in war can tell us about life, resistance, and survival on a doomed planet.

An anthropology of war that holds close to the grounds of life attunes us to ecologies of practice, vitalizing relations actively cultivated by those living in unlivable worlds. These humble ecologies are eclipsed by narratives dominated by the agency of military actors that relegate the ordinary dwellers of such worlds to passive roles, such as that of victim. Warzones are deadly places, inhabited, navigated, domesticated by beings who must live with lethality and make resistant life in its midst. A bitter life, but a life nonetheless. What I have illuminated in this book is no green-tinged dreamland or utopia that knits together sweet twines of togetherness in places of perennial devastation. The resistant ecologies I have explored in this book are among the last recourses available to those who have extremely limited choices and exceedingly difficult lives. Survival in such worlds is crafted within overlapping violent processes along vitalizing but *also* destructive relations and practices that nevertheless shape the possibility of life in catastrophic quarters. In recognizing these ecologies, we also recognize the inability of politics, governance, ideologies, and analysis to account for, or more importantly, to care for, what ultimately enlivens and sustains.

Scholarly theory must take seriously the experience and wisdom of those on the front lines of living. They are living in this world with all of its difficulties and making it work because they have to somehow stay alive. We may not be able to extract a politics we can easily celebrate (or sell to humanitarian outfits and concerns) from the fraught entanglement of tobacco and its cultivators, or the deadly art of goat herding amidst explosive military waste, or the ambiguous affects and confusing solidarities generated by life lived in close quarters to one's political enemies, but that does not mean that we look elsewhere. Looking straight at these "gray zones" (Levi 1989) of life and survival, in the wreckage of nation-states,

extractive orders, and military hubris, helps us gain a more careful understanding of the contradictions of staying alive in a harsh and deadly world.

Focusing on vitalizing relationships in spaces of military-industrial
destruction brings to light new understandings around life on an ecologi-
cally and politically unstable planet and may help us shape more grounded
and effective struggles for better worlds. If we pay careful ethnographic
attention to the practical ways of surviving and the everyday lifeworlds of
ordinary people inhabiting worlds that appear exceptional and theoretical
to some (but are prosaic and painfully real to many others), this will
ground anthropological theory (and social struggle) in a charged and palpable political field that pushes against mythologizing and radically other-
ing tendencies in theoretical formulations around existential and political
struggles in zones of extraction and ruination and war. In closing, I want
to connect worlds devastated by war with other (more familiar) disastrous
worlds in this terrifying age of climactic upheaval, where extensive and
extended suffering is a blatant result of political chauvinism and impudent
neglect. At a time when we are all beginning to recognize the tenuousness
of our mastery of this planet, the precariousness of our technological
progress, the limits of extractive capitalist growth, and the impending
human-made "natural" disasters that will engulf us all, it is worthwhile to
stop and notice the durable safety nets being knit together in places where
catastrophe is not yet to come but forms the very grounds of being. What I
have shown through resistant ecologies in a landscape of war is that life
itself is often rooted in structures and processes that seek to violently
extinguish it.

Coda

A MARRIAGE IN GALILEE

It is early summer, the month of May, a pregnant season in the highlands of Jabal ʿAmil, also known as Galilee. We are here for the wedding of Ahmad, Jihad's eldest son, and everyone has gathered. Even Abu Jalil, who rarely comes to the village he does not love, is here. Bou Sahel made me promise, last time I came by, to bring Abu Jalil to him. He wants to reminisce with him about times gone forever. They are among the last of their generation in the village. Bou Sahel senses, with sadness, that an end is approaching.

That morning, amidst currents of intrigue and "putting the pot on the fire" (gossiping), many actual pots were put on the fire and a feast was concocted by the women: wife and daughters, sisters and aunts, cousins, neighbors, friends, me. The village table explodes with freshness and flavor: raw and grilled meats, cracked wheat and smoked barley, fresh herbs and vegetables, steaming bread.

In the lull between the preparations and the festivities, as the unmarried girls fret about their festive outfits, I slip off with Abu Jalil and his daughters Munya and Ghida to pay a visit to the home of Bou Sahel nearby. As everyone watches, the old men haltingly approach each other. Bou Sahel greets Abu Jalil with the pretense of nonrecognition. Everyone knows his straight-faced jokes, and soon the quivering anticipation

Figure 25. A wedding in Galilee.

dissolves into peals of laughter. Im Sahel rushes to offer us chocolate candies and caramels wrapped in gold paper. The two old men sit side by side under the eaves of the house alongside the road, the one who stayed rooted through rain and shine and the one who left as soon as he could and never returned. They talk about the almost century they have lived on this difficult and wretched, beautiful and bountiful, beloved earth. Bou Sahel is overcome with emotion and his eyes twinkle with tears. "My eyes are crying," he says. "I can't stop them! It's because I am old now." We soothe him and say: "May God keep you! May God lengthen your life!" Soon we take our leave to return to the wedding. This was the last time I saw his dear face. Bou Sahel died in the spring.

The whole village (and some of the nearby village) assembles as twilight embraces us with its shimmering colors. The asphalt courtyard at the front of Jihad's house, usually cluttered with parked cars and plastic tables and chairs and other random junk, has been transformed into an open-air reception and dance floor. A podium festooned with puffs of pastel tulle has been mounted at one end to showcase the young couple celebrated today, the hallowed hills of Palestine rise purple pink as seamless backdrop. The bride arrives dolled up like a bonbon, holding a bouquet of flowers aloft, a smile on her young face, and the women received her with ululations and spontaneous dances. The younger brother of the groom and his friends go up to the roof of the house and pepper the sky with Kalashnikov rounds (they are all in the Resistance). The familiar staccato stokes everyone's excitement and joy.

Jihad is proud and generous and struts around the festivities in his suit, a smile on his kind face, a perpetual cigarette hanging off his lip, his big belly. He is happy I am there. We take many pictures in different configurations in front of the house. A formidable *dabke* circle forms, expressing different chains of relationships, friendships, rivalries, attractions. The youngsters at the head of the chain break it down with extraordinary saltos, squats, and twirls and the crowd effervesces with shouts, whoops, and whistles amidst the invigorating patter of the hand drums, the querulous quarter tones of the flute, and *zajal*, inspired improv poetry shouted over the sound system. This circle of light illuminates this celebration, this *sahra*, embraced by the summer, which is pleasant and cool here in the highlands of South Lebanon, Galilee.

The following evening we are sitting around drinking tea and going over the still bubbling excitement and various slights, intrigues, and victories of the wedding. An incessant buzzing that I gradually become more aware of textures the humid night air as we converse, and I lift my face in its direction, squinting into the dark night that is illuminated by the glorious moon. Layla, one of the daughters of the household sees my quizzical expression and bursts out laughing: "Oh it's just the Im Kamel [local nickname for the Israeli MK drone] taking pictures of us. Smile!"[1]

Notes

INTRODUCTION

1. Palestine dwells at the heart of this book, as it sits at the heart of most stories and struggles defining what we know as the "Middle East" today. The histories, politics, pasts, and presents of Lebanon and Palestine are inextricably entwined, and these histories, as narrated from the vise of national categories, are hopelessly incomplete. The continuous landscape of Galilee and the tangles of stories and lives across the land show the folly of these false containers.

2. The war that began in 1975 and formally ended in 1990 is commonly referred to as the Lebanese Civil War, but this can be misleading. The "civil" war encompassed many wars between many factions in Lebanon (including Palestinian and Syrian) that were fed and fueled by the Cold War contest and included two Israeli invasions and Israeli and Syrian occupations. I refer to it as the Lebanese civil war in this book for reasons of convention while acknowledging how this naming is inadequate and often problematic.

3. South Lebanon, or *janub lubnan*, refers to the province stretching south of the Awwali River and bounded on the west by the Mediterranean Sea. South Lebanon encompasses the ancient port cities of Saida (Sidon) and Sur (Tyre) and extends to Ras al Naqura on the coastal border with Israel/historical Palestine. Turning inland from the Mediterranean Sea, the borderline unfurls for 70 km through the Western Bekaa to Mount Hermon (Jabal al Sheikh) on the Lebanese-Syrian-Israeli border. The highlands of South Lebanon are historically

known as Jabal 'Amil, the historical heartland of Lebanese Shi'ism, and northern Galilee. But in this book when I refer to the South, *al-janub,* unless indicated otherwise, I am referring to the 10-kilometer-wide stretch of Lebanese borderland encompassing more than 150 small towns and villages occupied by Israel from 1978–2000. This area is also referred to as "the border strip," *al shareet al hududi,* or simply "the strip." I also use the term "occupation zone," referring to what that the Israelis insisted throughout the occupation was their "security zone."

4. W. J. T. Mitchell in *Landscape and Power* (2002) suggests that landscape should be a verb.

5. Ziad Rahbani, composer, playwright, and political commentator, is the son of the Lebanese singer Fairouz and composer Assi Rahbani. A communist, he rose to prominence during the Lebanese civil war, when he composed songs and staged musical plays satirizing the social and political conditions.

6. Marcel Khalife is a Lebanese musician and communist whose compositions and ballads addressed political issues relating to Palestine, South Lebanon, the plight of the peasantry and proletariat, war, and occupation.

7. Resistant ecologies have underwritten continued survival across the rest of Lebanon since the apocalyptic meltdown of the Lebanese economy that began in October 2019 (see World Bank 2021). Resistance through staying alive is a widespread orientation among Lebanese citizens toward the ongoing necropolitics of the corrupt and self-serving Lebanese political class.

8. "Life in Marx's analysis of capital, is similarly a 'standing fight' against the process of abstraction that is constitutive of the category 'labor.' It is as if the process of abstraction and ongoing appropriation of the worker's body in the capitalist mode of production perpetually threatens to effect a dismemberment of the unity of the 'living body'" (Chakrabarty 2008, 60–61).

9. This observation was also echoed by Sahel, Khawla's brother, who told me: "So people here, my dear, they wake up at 5:00 a.m. to tend to their plants and land, be it tobacco or wheat or grain or olives or figs and grapes—they go out *'ala al sarwa,* which means early morning, as our neighbors the *bedu* say. During the occupation though, it was impossible to go outside at 5:00 a.m., because of the Israelis. So the farmers would wait until sunrise, and then they would go out. But that is destructive, because you can't work under the summer sun! This was the state of things until 2000, and after that things go better, and people would be able to get up and go out in the night and in the day and any time they wanted, and they were able to live in this comfort and luxury."

10. *Rizq* refers to livelihood and to the agriculture that sustains it. In counterpoint to tobacco, the "profane" cash crop, fruit trees like olives are considered a blessing from God. *Al-razzaq,* the livelihood-giver, is one of God's ninety-nine

names. Fruit trees are referred to as *rizq*, livelihood, which is invariably linked to divine provenance, *al-rizq min Allah*.

11. Metulla is an Israeli settlement on the erased Palestinian village of Mtulleh, right on the borderline abutting the Lebanese town of Kfar Kila in the Eastern Sector of the border zone where the famous cross-border Fatima Gate is located.

12. The analytical grasp on war, militarization, and their wreckage is opened up to the relational, lived tendrils of ecological thinking in the work of Kristina Lyons (2020), Bettina Stoetzer (2018), and others. In the introduction to the recent forum entitled "Ecologies of War" that I and others contributed to, Bridget Guarasci and Eleana Kim write (2022): "*Ecologies of War,* extends ethnographic attention beyond 'war itself' to include forms of war that are often unrecognized as such—in everyday experiences, material effects, and affective resonances of violence that have penetrated and contaminated the environments and ecologies of places where perpetual wars of US empire, never-ending wars, and peaceless-ness of political enmity continue."

13. Empire is an intimate matter for all of us, as I explored with my sisters in an article we wrote entitled "Piece of US: the Intimate as Imperial Archive" (M. Khayyat et al. 2018).

14. Viet Thanh Nguyen, whose biting commentary on the US-centered narra-tives of American empire and the lives obscured by them, drives this point home in his latest novel, *The Committed:* "Whether the thesis or the antithesis was communism or anticommunism, the point was that they composed the polar opposites of what the West unironically called the Cold War, as fought between the USA and the USSR. But the synthesis was the recognition that this war had been extremely hot for us Asians, and Africans, and Latin Americans" (2022, 62).

15. Lubkemann (2008), who worked in the same "warscape" as Nordstrom, disagrees with her equating war with violence and her description of war as "the world unmade." Instead of "focusing on the violent contest for political power" or "framing war as a violent condition," he finds it more fruitful to think in terms of continuities rather than ruptures, and hence his ethnography follows the unbroken threads of peoples' ongoing lives, examining war as a "social condi-tion" (14). War then becomes about "everyday social life and the process of its realization" (ibid.).

16. During the Second World War, the French resistance, the Maquisards, named themselves for this hardy scrubland that assisted and enabled their fight against the Nazis (Pearson 2008).

17. This cadaster was begun after the establishment of the British and French protectorates in 1923 but was suspended after the establishment of the state of Israel, as the borderland became a warzone.

CHAPTER 1. A BRIEF HISTORY OF WAR IN SOUTH LEBANON

1. The Israeli Army is officially named the IDF, which stands for Israel Defense Forces. This is an ideological naming of a military force that construes all its acts of violence and aggression as defensive by nature and intent. I do not agree with this naming and prefer to refer to it as the Israeli Army.

2. What's in a name? A lot. The state of Israel today occupies the land of historic Palestine. To many (to me), the land recognized as Israel today is also Palestine. It is important to understand that the state of Israel occupies more than the Occupied Territories of the West Bank and Gaza. This is much more than a theoretical point. It is a historical reality that has shaped the lives of millions of people for generations. There are some who consider the naming of Israel to be a political concession, preferring terminology such as "occupied Palestine" or "the Zionist entity." I believe that it is possible to recognize the ongoing presence of Palestine while naming the state that exists there now. So in this book I refer to the *state* of Israel that occupies the land of Palestine as "Israel" and to the *land* that the state of Israel now occupies as "Palestine." Sometimes I write Palestine/Israel.

3. Like the Crusader-built Beaufort Castle near Nabatiyyeh.

4. *Fida'i* means "the one who will sacrifice theirself." The intention of the freedom fighters was to free Palestine or to die trying.

5. In "South Lebanon its History and Politics," Sharif (1978) writes: "The Palestinian presence led to a better political awareness among the masses of the South. It made the Palestinian problem and the danger of the state of Israel a living issue. It awakened the national and social consciousness of the people and made the South a more fertile land for political activities compared to other parts of Lebanon. The Palestinians themselves with their suffering were important raw material for rebellion and unrest and were fast to answer the call of the revolution after 1967."

6. The Palestinian cause spurred transnational solidarities from the United States to Japan in a way not seen since. Alex Lubin (2014), in his *Geographies of Liberation: The Making of an Afro-Arab Political Imaginary*, details the powerful African American–Arab solidarities that burgeoned in this moment.

7. A *maybar* is a long flat needle used to thread green tobacco leaves on twine for drying.

8. Following district boundaries and sectarian communities, these sectors structured the Israeli occupation and are still referenced as an orienting framework today. From Sharif (1978, 16):

> 1. The eastern sector, called Arkoub, is formed of rugged mountains overlooking Israeli settlements. Here the Palestinian Revolution was given complete freedom; the Lebanese Army withdrew completely, leaving even the strategic defense of the area against Israeli raids in the hands of the Palestinian resistance.

2. The central sector, less hilly than the east, extends to the edge of the coastal plain. Here the Lebanese Army was to undertake the strategic defense against Israel while the Palestinian armed presence, equipped with light weapons, was restricted to certain locations and limited to supply and early warning functions.

3. The western sector, or the coastal plain, was kept under complete Lebanese Army control; no Palestinian armed presence outside the Palestinian camps was allowed. The Fedayeen were to use this sector in emergencies only.

9. Timur Göksel half-jokingly said to me that compared to the Hizbullah fighters of today, the Palestinian guerrillas took much less care to blend into the landscape or cover their traces, and when the Israelis invaded all that were missing were neon signs pointing out their positions and locations.

10. "The disinherited" or "dispossessed," *al mahrumeen*, was the epithet that the mobilizing Shi'a used as their political rallying cry.

11. For example, in 1969 Sadr instigated the formation of the Higher Shia Islamic Council, which would articulate Shi'i demands in Lebanese governmental matters; up until this point Shi'a religious representation in the state had been subsumed under the Sunni council.

12. Twenty thousand civilians were killed during the 1982 Israeli invasion that included the siege of Beirut and the Sabra and Shatila massacres.

13. Maquis is a Mediterranean shrubland consisting of dense evergreen shrubs such as oak, sage, juniper, olive, and myrtle. Maquis is by definition natural, but its presence is mostly the result of the destruction of forest by recurrent burning that prevents saplings from maturing. Maquis tends to grow in arid, rocky areas where only drought-resistant plants can survive.

14. "Although it was not widely appreciated at the time, many believe that the U.S. military lost the Vietnam War because of how routinely it misunderstood the importance of village life, as both a wellspring of identity and insurgency. The village and the land that it occupied were sacred to many Vietnamese people, connecting them to their ancestors in an undying spiritual constant. Moreover, the village was the principal source of NLF power: Due to its dispersed and decentralized organization across hamlets big and small, the NLF was nearly impossible to erase. This meant that the average Vietnamese peasant played a delicate balancing act between Saigon and NLF cadres" (Shaw 2016, 9).

15. Hizbullah is more than a military force in South Lebanon (see Norton 2014; Saad-Ghorayeb 2002; Blanford 2011; Daher and Randolph 2019). It is an organization with a long history and presence. It emerged as a political group during the 1982 Israeli invasion and subsequent occupation of Lebanon, growing out of the Shi'a "movement of the dispossessed" that was formed during the 1970s by Musa Sadr. Hizbullah came to spearhead the military resistance against the Israeli occupation in South Lebanon and continued to grow in military prowess, political and social prominence, leading up to the 2000 liberation of the borderland and beyond. Since the 1990s it has participated in Lebanese politics.

16. In war terms, the period between 2000 and 2006 was the quietest that this border has seen practically since its inception. Norton (2006) dubbed it an "interregnum," as it does in retrospect (post 2006) seem like a kind of interlude or a waiting/preparing for the next round. During this time the tentative border separating the longtime enemy nations, the Blue Line, was defined by UNFIL (by July 2000).

17. I covered these elections as a journalist.

18. I attended this conference as a journalist.

19. "Hizballah spent the years leading up to the 2006 war improving on the favorable topography of southern Lebanon to better resist an invading army from the south. As one Israeli general put it, Hizbullah has spent the years from 2000 until 2006 thinking about the coming war in *tactical* terms. That is, Hizbullah thought about its defense of southern Lebanon with an eye toward how the IDF would fight and what weapons, personnel, fortifications, and tactics would be needed to stop the IDF or at the very least slow its progress" (Exum 2006, 3).

20. A saying in Arabic describing surprising vanishing.

21. Often, farming income is combined with remittances from family members living in the cities or abroad.

22. This book focuses upon those who still inhabit the towns, villages, and hamlets of the borderland, although the much bigger story of migration has been addressed by Munzir Jabir (1999) in his encyclopedic tome on the occupied border strip.

CHAPTER 2. BATTLE/FIELD

1. Not all of the borderland's villages were equally impacted; some were flattened and some were spared. This has much to do with geography and demography: in general, Shi'i villages were the ones directly targeted, invaded, and destroyed, although the inhabitants of the entire borderland (and beyond), regardless of geography and demography, were under constant bombardment for the thirty-four days of the conflict.

2. A journalist who visited Bint Jbeil in the immediate wake of the conflict wrote: "I got the same response from almost everyone we interviewed. 'Normal' seemed to be the consensus, but the clear signs of destruction, the fear of unexploded bombs and an uncertain future indicated a place that was anything but normal." Kevin Sites, "Revisiting Bint Jbail," http://hotzone.yahoo.com/b/hotzone/blogs23989.

3. In reference to the visit of then Iranian President Mahmud Ahmedinejad to Columbia University in 2007.

4. This village has major land disputes with Israel. The villagers claim that Israel has swallowed up acres of their legally owned land.

5. This was a period when many spy networks were being uncovered, and like all things in Lebanon such "discoveries" had a political motive and played into the political game at the center. As usual, the lives of those at the margins were harvested for whatever use they could be put but otherwise neglected; the story of the margins in Lebanon is a story of political exploitation and perpetual neglect. The overemphasis on the political center (Beirut) is part of what I am trying to address and redress in this book, where I would like to turn my full attention to the neglected *life* in the borderland. South Lebanon, relative to other margins, manifests an even more powerful discrepancy between political use and actual disregard. It is simultaneously both a powerful symbol of national mobilization and resistance and a place of profound state neglect.

6. Nazan Ustundag (2010) echoes these methodological dilemmas in her moving piece on Turkish Kurdistan, "A Landscape of Violence": "In this absence of words and stories, which is at once an overwhelming abundance of the untold, the untellable, a void too full, one trains her ear to the landscape itself."

7. This is what Das (2007) calls the "frozen slide quality of narrations or 'non-narrations' of the violence of the Partition."

8. Advice given to me in my first year in graduate school at the University of Chicago by Michel-Rolph Trouillot. I also followed the advice of Michael Taussig upon my move to Columbia: to pay attention to that which constitutes the main livelihood of villagers in South Lebanon—farming.

10. Hizbullah, "the Party of God," is also commonly known as "al Hizb," simply, "the Party."

11. The *qura al saba'*, or Seven Villages, are a cluster of Shi'a (and Maronite) villages that fell within the borders of British Mandate Palestine. The inhabitants of these villages almost all left and came to live in Lebanon when Israel was created. As they shared sectarian identity (and family connections) with villagers just across the border, many married Lebanese and eventually got Lebanese papers, although they still hold land deeds for their homes and fields that are now in Israel.

12. Uncannily enough this particular phase of the 1982 Israeli of Lebanon invasion is portrayed in the animated feature *Waltz with Bashir*.

13. It is important to point out that the lines of allegiance to the occupation by no means only followed sectarian lines. It is generally true that the Israelis favored the Christian populations of the borderland and cultivated them to build up an occupation administration and proxy militia (SLA). But it is equally true that many Christians refused this occupation, suffered death or imprisonment and interrogation, as it is also true that Shi'a (and Sunni and Druze) were recruited as stalwart local allies and foot soldiers. In some of the Shi'a villages that I worked, the homes of infamous "collaborators" remain as landmarks (often scoffed at for their ostentatiousness) even as their occupants have fled over the

border to Israel and will never return. Also, generally speaking, it was the Shi'a, the most populous constituency in South Lebanon, who made up the rank and file of SLA foot soldiers. This was a very big factor in the exodus of the youth from the South—to escape service in the SLA—and families paid accordingly.

14. I have long mused at the wild contrast between impersonal global wars and the intimate snugness of local context—the contrast plays out a little like the theater of the absurd. The quaint domesticity of such global power struggles has always struck me, growing up in a warzone and reading stories Lebanon, the context of my life, in newspapers printed in New York and Washington, DC; I was reminded of this as I encountered the southern border-strip. What is played out in soaring tones and black and white in the global media is usually a more practically muddled, emotionally charged shade of gray in local terms.

15. We have an impressive collection of paraphernalia from this day: papers, IDs, license plates, empty weapon boxes, posters of Antoine Lahd, IDF fatigues, helmets, Israeli-made candy, chips and soda packages . . .

16. Although the Israelis are well known for eating land to their strategic advantage by taking refuge in elevations along the Lebanon-Israel border, their territory begins where the high elevations of Jabal 'Amil begin to melt into the low hills of Galilee. Although their border is located atop as many ridges as they could manage, for the most part they occupy the lower ground. This is clear when traveling this border, and it is one of their long-held excuses for maintaining the occupation.

CHAPTER 3. THE BITTER CROP

1. Indeed this is one of the long and ongoing justifications for the tobacco-farming subsidy in Lebanon: to keep poor villagers from continuing to migrate to the already overcrowded coastal cities.

2. Many multispecies ethnographies have flocked to the wilder end of the nonhuman spectrum to access the "outside" of power and human social worlds. Some (Swanson et al. 2018; Besky and Blanchette 2019), like me, have turned to domesticated beings to examine further the natural-cultural entanglement of humans with other life-forms in the making and propagating of shared worlds nevertheless dominated by human hubris. Such multispecies ethnographies do not allow the observer an easy foothold in utopian critiques of the Anthropocene.

3. The significance of tobacco as a cross-sectarian rallying point must be appreciated. So much did tobacco crystallize cross-sectarian class consciousness that it was taken up as a sectarian rallying cry by Musa al-Sadr as *qadiyat al qadaya*, the issue of issues, as he mobilized the downtrodden Shi'a into the sec-

tarian-based *harakat al mahrumin*, movement of the dispossessed, in the early 1970s (Ajami 1987).

4. This era is portrayed in the 2017 documentary by Mary Jirmanus Saba entitled *A Feeling Greater than Love.*

5. Tobacco is the only crop that is regulated by a monopoly in Lebanon. Its primacy to the state as a capitalist commodity is clear by its regulation by the Ministry of Finance. Funnily enough, it is not recognized as an agricultural crop, and the Ministry of Agriculture provides no support to tobacco farmers, whose life is tobacco and who live from tobacco and who are left to make the most of this strange configuration.

6. Asma Issa Bazzi (2008) writes:

In 1968, the issuing of licenses was discontinued and replaced with special permits for extra production on a yearly basis to help farmers. Ministry of Finance Decision No. 10412/1, dated September 27th 1994, gave the Régie Libanaise des Tabacs et Tombacs . . . the exclusive right to import and export tobacco leaves and products and to produce tobacco products. Regie Memorandum . . . #35 in 1997 with the approval of the Minister of Finance restricted the areas of tobacco production to (i) 15 dunum (1 du = 1000 m^2) or 1.5 hectare maximum for licensed farmers with 100 Kg/du as a ceiling for maximum production of tobacco leaf variety "Saada 6"; and, (ii) 4 du maximum for farmers with special permits in the South with a maximum ceiling of 100 Kg/du. Regie Memo #35 restricted the issuing of tobacco production permits to farmers who actually plant tobacco. It further specified that farmers' permits are restricted to one village and that only one family member can apply for a special permit.

7. The old lords of the South find themselves powerless in South Lebanon today, "unable to even step one foot into their old villages," said Timur Göksel, who for twenty-five years was the UNFIL spokesman in South Lebanon. "They got out with the invasion and the occupation, and their abandoned dependents had to find a way to survive on their own somehow, and they did." Göksel was describing the realities that the *fallaheen* who stayed on the land had to contend with when the rural landscape upon which they had subsisted for years under the yoke and "protection" of their lords transformed into a battleground beneath their very feet, and in the absence of their masters. Something was broken and something new grew in its place: according to Göksel, a remarkable social revolution was catalyzed during these years of exception and extremity in South Lebanon.

8. Because of war and labor migration, tobacco is almost entirely worked by women (and children) who remain in the village while men work (or war) elsewhere. Tobacco cultivation thus must also be understood as a relationship of love and care that grounds life in a difficult corner, giving it both purpose and meaning. Furthermore, tobacco work sheds light on an underrecognized role that women play in resistance. In South Lebanon, women assist on-the-ground resistance in times of active warfare, when villages transform into battlegrounds and

homes become strategic nodes of supply and shelter. Although it is insufficiently recognized, women have always actively participated in resistance, such as with the partisans during the Second World War in Nazi-occupied Europe and in the Algerian war of independence (Fanon 2007).

9. Tobacco work is the main source of cash for those inhabiting the rural margins, but it is not the only one, as extended families are distributed across the country and the globe and provide relatives back in the village with supplementary income when needed. Migration (Jabir 1999) has been the main survival strategy of Lebanon's border villagers, as told by how sparsely inhabited the borderland is today. While recognizing migration's importance to those continuing to inhabit South Lebanon's battlefields, I have a different focus: those who stay. As Bou Sahel told me about his village, which compared to many villages in South Lebanon is rather well-inhabited, because it has not been so terribly violated, relatively speaking (I was often reminded that it has no strategic value in terms of either geography or demography, and that is a blessing): "Many people left the strip. Look at the registers of our village. It has about four thousand people. Do you know how many live here permanently? Two hundred and fifty. Many people secured jobs [abroad], and here there is nothing but tobacco. What are my sons or the sons of my neighbors going to come to the village to do? At the present time Bint Jbeil has eighty thousand registered inhabitants. Do you know how many actually reside there now? Three thousand only." This is a reality and a pattern that repeats itself across the borderland.

10. In his blog "Land and People" Rami Zurayk, professor of landscape design and ecosystem management at the American University of Beirut writes:

> Tobacco is a very labor-intensive crop, requiring 610 workdays per hectare per year. For comparison cereals require 25 days per hectare per year, and irrigated vegetables cultivation 242 days per hectare per year. The gross income of the average 4 dunums plantation in the South was $3,210 per year in 1999, five times greater than that for wheat (another dryland crop). . . . While tobacco is important for the livelihoods of farmers from all over Lebanon, it is especially crucial for the Southerners. A survey dating from 1999 indicated that tobacco provides 25% to 85% and sometimes 100% of the total income of farmers.

11. Tobacco farming increased after the liberation of the South in 2000. It currently contributes to the livelihoods of twenty-four thousand farmers. Most tobacco farmers farm fulltime and depend on tobacco for their livelihood. Lebanon is one of five countries worldwide that farm more than 1 percent of their agricultural land with tobacco (Hamade 2014).

12. Interesting wording, because it implies giving up, handing over goods already owned by the monopoly and not a sale transaction.

13. *Khabeer*, expert, is the term for employees of the Régie who assess the quality of and price the tobacco that is brought to the warehouses for sale. They are figures of local authority, for their assessment determines the value and price

of the commodity. Like everyone in the Lebanese system, they can be bought off. But Abu Fawzi was a rare bird; he was known to be not corrupt and thus (counterintuitively!) was considered a nuisance by the villagers, because he meticulously "searched" their tobacco and priced the leaves accurately.

14. This was narrated to me anecdotally, and the source swore he was speaking the truth. And although I did pursue the question of what happens to the tobacco after it is sold to get more definitive substantiation of this shocking assertion, what I was told mostly corresponded to the "correct" narrative. Farmers claimed their tobacco was the best in the world. The Régie did too. It must be repeated here how hard it was to get a straight story about tobacco.

15. In his blog Rami Zurayk describes the very practical ways in which tobacco makes resistant and steadfast:

> Tobacco farming increased by 24% after the liberation of the South in 2000, especially in the cazas of Bint Jbeil, Marjeyoun and Sour. Tobacco cultivation has been vital in the livelihood rebuilding process that followed liberation, both for those who were in the resistance and for those who were in the pro-Israeli South Lebanon Army. Moreover, a number of farmers from villages on the border used to work in the Israeli settlements and had to stop their activities after the liberation. Tobacco offered a post-war alternative and an opportunity to re-adapt to working in Lebanon.
>
> In the South tobacco is called "the crop of steadfastness." Had it not been for tobacco and its subsidies, the South would have witnessed more intensive migration and emigration, and Israel would have easily reinvaded Lebanon in July 2006. Tobacco subsidy may have been a central factor in determining the outcome of the war.

16. Tobacco is the only "subsidized" crop in Lebanon and the only monopoly.

CHAPTER 4. HOW TO LIVE (AND DIE) IN AN EXPLOSIVE LANDSCAPE

1. Michel de Certeau (1984) writes, "The goal is not to make clearer how the violence of order is transmuted into a disciplinary technology, but rather to bring to light the clandestine forms taken by the dispersed, tactical, makeshift creativity of groups or individuals already caught in the nets of 'discipline'. Pushed to their ideal limits, these procedures and ruses of consumers compose the networks of an antidiscipline" (xv).

2. Cluster bombs were first developed during the Second World War. They are dropped from aircraft in large cannisters, which open up mid-air to saturate a large area with submunitions or "bomblets." Many of these explosives fail to detonate in the air and remain on the ground as unpredictable explosives.

3. After the July War, an international movement against such weapons gained steam, and a global treaty banning cluster munitions came into force in 2010 that required signatories to stop the use, production, stockpiling, and

transfer of the weapons. More than one hundred parties have signed on, but Israel, China, the US, and Russia have not: they manufacture, sell, and stockpile most of the world's cluster munitions.

4. It is evident that Israel is targeting *life* in Lebanon—and by extension Hizbullah and the war-formation it generates and sustains. Yet here we tread a treacherously fine line: Israel insists it sees only military formations, whereas the life within which these formations are inextricably tangled becomes at best secondary, irrelevant, invisible and at worst justifiably targeted, eradicable, destroyable. "Unpacking rhetorical slippages that try to isolate Hizbullah from its civilian constituencies through phrasings like 'hides behind civilians' or 'Hizbullah stronghold' may seem beside the point in the face of the devastation wrought in Lebanon. But it is precisely such slippages that work to justify civilian deaths and infrastructural destruction. This is one area where anthropological work matters," argues Lara Deeb (2006). "Playing devil's advocate, my point that Hizbullah and civilians are not easily separable may seem to legitimate Israeli strikes against civilians because 'the water is as hostile as the fish swimming in it.' The obvious problem with this logic is that draining the pond is tantamount to ethnic cleansing. To remove Hizbullah from Lebanon would require "removal" of a civilian population, precisely what Israel seems to have been undertaking in this attack" (ibid.).

5. In a similar vein, and as observed by Brennon Jones in a *New York Times* article entitled "Southern Lebanon's Deadly Crop" (October 12, 2006):

> In Vietnam, where I was a journalist and social worker in the early 1970s, I saw farmers forced off their land by American and South Vietnamese bombing and corralled into refugee camps to keep them from returning. Cluster bombs were a weapon of choice in cleansing the countryside of its rural communities, in an effort to better target the Communist soldiers who moved among them.
>
> But many of these rural Vietnamese, denied income or work in the refugee camps, were desperate to return to their land and to farming, the only livelihood they had ever known. They broke out of the barbed-wire encampments and rushed for home, only to be maimed and killed by the cluster bomblets that littered their land.
>
> History is now repeating itself in the cruelest of ways in southern Lebanon. It's the farmers, once again, who are bearing the greatest physical and economic toll from unexploded cluster bomb submunitions.

CHAPTER 5. *MASKUN*, OR NATURE'S RESISTANCE

1. I search for hidden landscape portals to flee the hegemonic script of singular ideologies and political containers, similarly to Navaro (2017) in another borderland:

> I have been doing fieldwork in a city in southern Turkey one hour's drive from Aleppo, on the other side of the border, during one of history's most cataclysmic wars. In this radical shifting of grounds, I have studied affect not in the mass politi-

cal gatherings, either pro- or anti-government, or in any other such emergent social form reflecting or reacting to the Syrian war, but in interstices—in the gaps, creaks, and crevices not entirely smothered by the bombastic politics at play nor flattened by the conflicting governmentalities in the region. What has been most curious to observe and experience in Antakya at this height of political tension—and during the incitements to divide along sectarian lines—is the social life that has endured in its mundanity, against all odds, reproducing bonds of reciprocity and affection across the local communities and engendering new ones with Syrian refugees. (211)

2. Mleeta is not the first time that Hizbullah puts its recent history on display; it has been doing it for years. I will never forget the exhibit staged in Hamra in West Beirut in 1986 celebrating (and claiming authorship of) the Israeli withdrawal from the southern half of Lebanon. My father was a hot-blooded (southern) nationalist at the time, passionately proud of the defeat of Israel at the hands of the Lebanese resistance and Israel's recent withdrawal from Saida, our hometown, and he took us to see the show. I was ten years old, my siblings much younger; my mother, a Saudi Arabian, was skeptical of such "Islamic" things. I remember gazing with fascinated horror at the images of Israeli atrocities, events that had barely just happened and that were constitutive of the atmosphere I was growing up in, yet still not clearly enunciated in my perception, as my mother sought—only partly successfully—to shield us from the worst this war was generating. The exhibit took place in the dank and dusty showroom of the Lebanese Ministry of Tourism in Hamra and was probably the first foray of this surly and dour—and generally feared, at the time—Islamic movement into the Lebanese public sphere. Hizbullah then was a hardline Islamist faction among many warring Lebanese factions and had yet to reinvent itself as heroically Lebanese. But here was one of its first attempts. Bearded men lurked at the sidelines as my father herded us in to view an exhibit whose centerpiece was the actual bloodstained clothes of Ragheb Harb, a leader of the resistance before it became known as Hizbullah and who was assassinated by an Israeli commando on the doorstep of his home in Jibsheet, South Lebanon, on February 16, 1984, a mere two years before. One of Harb's first acts of defiance was refusing to shake the extended hand of an occupying Israeli officer, saying "You are occupiers, I do not shake hands with you and I do not sit with you, get out of my country." At the time, southerners, and the Shi'a in particular, were perceived by the Israelis as meek local peons and willing allies in their war against the Palestinians. Harb's stance powerfully indicated otherwise. As we left the exhibit, my father grasped the hand of the stern-faced organizer of the show and spoke heated words of emotional compassion and political allegiance as we looked on, slightly stunned. I couldn't get the bloodied clothes and the dusty shoes out of my mind. The blood and the dust—out of place materials that conveyed at once the mystical and the mortal aspects of Hizbullah's project.

3. And also provocatively. Most of the southern suburbs were flattened in 2006, with the explicit aim of assassinating Nasrallah, who never ceased to address his people throughout the war. He has gone underground since and only

appears in person briefly on significant occasions, more commonly making addresses via video link.

4. According to Navaro-Yashin (2009), *ganimet*, loot, is the term used by Turkish Cypriots in reference to the abandoned and appropriated property and objects of Greek Cypriots after the partition of Cyprus in 1974.

5. This infamous tank-column debacle was previously showcased as a sound and light show in the 2007 "Spider's Nest," *beit al 'ankabut*, exhibition, a well-attended installation (which I visited) on the 2006 war staged in the victorious rubble of the southern suburbs *al-dahiyeh;* it was an experimental and temporary forerunner of this much more elaborate and sophisticated permanent exhibit.

6. This reminded me of a trip I took as a journalist in 1999, the year before the liberation, that was organized by Hizbullah to show the media their boys, *shabab,* "in action" on the field of battle. It was somewhere in these areas but when it was still an active front line. It was a thrilling trip, as we left our cars at a designated meeting point and were driven to the front in vans with blacked-out windows. We tumbled out into a wild area of terraces and olive trees and deafening crickets. Our hosts presented to us their arts of warfare in Powerpoint underneath camouflage netting under the trees and showed us their field operations setting and allowed us to pose for a souvenir photographs underneath a "real" Katyusha rocket launcher in the back of a pickup truck (with real guerrilla *mujahid!*). As the day ran into afternoon we heard the buzzing of Israeli jets in the sky above our heads. This indicated to our hosts that it was time for us to go. Show and tell was over. Real war was at hand. We were quickly packed back into the vans and driven to our cars.

7. Such as the Crusader fortress Beaufort Castle that was successively used by Palestinian armed groups and the Israeli occupiers. Today it has been taken over and entirely renovated by Hizbullah as another Resistance tourist landmark.

8. Toufoul Abou Hodeib (2015) writes:

> A Jewish prophet who appears in the Old Testament and is "commonly known as Nabi Sujud, both by Jews, who visited during the fourth week of Lag ba-Omer, and by Muslims, who also venerated the place, visited regularly, and prayed in the building that stood beside it . . . . The shrine was an occasion for an interreligious encounter as well as a meeting place for members of the Jewish faith converging from different countries in the region. Moreover, the act of pilgrimage, particularly the passing through Sidon, and the site itself constituted a place for intersectarian encounters at a time of increasing hardening of national identities along religious lines in Palestine. The caretaker of the maqam [shrine] was a Shi'i man from the village of Sujud nearby. He held the keys, the responsibility having been handed down to him through several generations. The three-day stay of the Jewish pilgrims at the shrine concluded with a feast (hilulah) and a bonfire, at which local Christians and Muslims joined the Jewish pilgrims, offering their own sacrifices. (387–88)

9. Across South Lebanon linger heterogeneous beliefs and practices, fading forms of cultural memory that collect in places (Basso, 1996). Often these places

are sacred spots where good spirits continue to dwell. These sometimes take the shape of "inhabited" *maskun* places, trees or hilltops identified by villagers as spaces imbued with sacred, mythological or magical qualities (Thubron 2008). More often these sacred spots are shrines that are (or were) tended to by the diverse religious communities inhabiting the borderland: Shi'a, Sunni, Christian, Druze, and Jewish. Some of the places that collect memory in South Lebanon are Roman or Crusader structures or fortifications that have fallen into ruin; the latter have been reused by the many militaries that have passed through since.

10. *The Hills of Adonis: A Quest in Lebanon* is a travelogue penned by Colin Thubron (2008) about his journey on foot through Lebanon in 1968. In a lyrical account both familiar and strange, Thubron tells of the many enchanted natural shrines dotting the landscape:

> Shrines like these grow from half the crags and knolls of Lebanon, rude-walled and white-domed under trees descendent from the pagan groves. Every village has its saint's tomb, or *weli*. Sometimes they belong to mad or holy men who actually lived, but more often villagers know nothing of their origin. 'A great prophet is buried there', they say, or 'a famous lady who died long ago', or sometimes, embarrassed by the absence of any grave, they declare that a holy man or woman passed that way and so the place is blessed. . . . The shrines are sought out by every sect . . . who shun each other's mosques or churches [but nonetheless] murmur prayers together before the unknown spirits on the hilltops, and tie strips of sick relatives' clothing to the bars of the windows or on the holy tree as talisman for health, and sometimes give a small gift or offer henna as libation. (69–70)

11. Another example. for the confrontations it has sparked in the postliberation era, is 'Abbad hill, which straddles the borderline near the Lebanese village of 'Adaiseh and is a point of pilgrimage for both Muslims and Jews who respectively believe that a holy man—a Sufi saint/a Jewish sage—is interred there.

12. "The grunts' unease was heightened by the ability of the North Vietnamese Army and the Viet Cong to disappear into the earth itself, into networks of tunnels which in some cases dated back to the wars against the Japanese and the French but which had since been extended and elaborated, and which deepened the American conviction that the Vietnamese were not only at home in the jungle but at one with its trickster nature. They would disappear 'like will o' the wisps,' wrote Franklin Cox, 'like ghosts into a different dimension, slipping into the friendly concealment of the green, lush, wet Asian environment, as elusive to hold as mercury in the fingers of a five-year-old child.' Like most Americans, Cox believed that quicksilver ability to disappear and reappear was innate to the Vietnamese. 'You had to live there to know how to employ the tunnel systems,' he explained. 'It was his [the guerrilla's] home and he knew every foot of each rice paddy, every spider-hole position he could climb into and cover with natural camouflage and shoot from after the Marines walked past . . . and every entrance into the elaborate tunnel honeycomb beneath his hamlets'" (Gregory 2016, 32).

CHAPTER 6. THE GRAY ZONE

1. Driving along the border, I often unintentionally tune in to Israeli radio. The sound of cheery and casual FM radio chit-chat in Hebrew chimes uncannily with the militarized, multiple, and mutilated landscape of the borderland, high-lighting the closeness and farness, the divisions and disjunctures, of the political and the physical terrains.

2. Jihad al-Bina' is a building and contracting company owned by Hizbullah.

3. Since the 2006 war the Lebanese Army has deployed along the border.

4. Avivim.

5. The coastal Israeli town closest to the Lebanese border.

6. Emrys Peters article "Aspects of Rank and Status among Muslims in a Leb-anese Village" (1977),based upon fieldwork in a village in South Lebanon in 1952–53, is a gem of British structural-functionalist anthropology. Peters subse-quently revised his argument in an article following fieldwork a few years later to accommodate socioeconomic mobility and flows within and without the village, which in the first work was considered—characteristically for this school of thought—self-contained.

7. During the occupation, Israel implemented what they called a "good fence" policy, whereby inhabitants of the occupation were allowed to work menial jobs in Israel. This was framed as an act of friendship and generosity but was a source of captive and cheap labor.

CONCLUSION

1. Lebanon has the highest per capita refugee population in the world. Every fourth person in Lebanon is a refugee; most are Syrians from the civil war next door and Palestinians, both from the war in Syria and from the 1948 disposses-sion of Palestine. Many refugees are crowded into camps in the major coastal cit-ies and in the interior, but some have found ways of weaving themselves into the local social fabric through relations of kinship or labor. Lebanon also has hun-dreds of thousands of multiply-vulnerable migrant laborers from Africa and South and Southeast Asia.

CODA

1. According to the manufacturer's website (https://www.iai.co.il/p/searcher-mk-iii): "Searcher Mk III is a multi-mission tactical unmanned aerial system (UAS) used for surveillance, reconnaissance, target acquisition, artillery adjust-

ment and damage assessment. The Searcher Mk III Unmanned Aerial System (UAS) is a compact system designed for use in military, law enforcement, and homeland security missions. The Searcher Mk III enables high-quality real-time intelligence gathering and transmission while operating at a distance from the mission region."

Bibliography

Abou Hodeib, Toufoul. 2015. "Sanctity across the Border: Pilgrimage Routes and State Control in Mandate Lebanon and Palestine." In *The Routledge Handbook of the History of the Middle East Mandates,* edited by Cyrus Schayegh and Andrew Arsan, 383–94. New York: Routledge.

Abu el-Haj, Nadia. 2022. *Combat Trauma.* New York: Verso.

Abukhalil, As'ad. 2001. "Cataloging Israel's Impact on South Lebanon." *Journal of Palestine Studies* 30 (4): 88–92.

Abu-Lughod, Lila. 1990. "The Romance of Resistance: Tracing Transformations of Power through Bedouin Women." *American Ethnologist* 17 (1): 41–55.

———. 2016. *Veiled Sentiments: Honor and Poetry in a Bedouin Society.* Oakland: Univ. of California Press.

Abu Rish, Ziad. 2015. "Garbage Politics." *Middle East Report,* no. 277:35–40.

Achcar, Gilbert, and Michel Warschawski. 2007. *The 33-Day War: Israel's War on Hezbollah in Lebanon and Its Consequences.* Boulder, CO: Paradigm.

Aciksoz, Salih Can. 2019. *Sacrificial Limbs: Masculinity, Disability, and Political Violence in Turkey.* Oakland: Univ. of California Press.

Ajami, Fouad. 1987. *The Vanished Imam: Musa al Sadr and the Shia of Lebanon.* Ithaca, NY: Cornell Univ. Press.

Albera, Dionigi, and Maria Couroucli, eds. 2012. *Sharing Sacred Spaces in the Mediterranean: Christians, Muslims, and Jews at Shrines and Sanctuaries.* Bloomington: Indiana Univ. Press.

Al-Dewachi, Omar. 2017. *Ungovernable Life: Mandatory Medicine and Statecraft in Iraq*. Stanford, CA: Stanford Univ. Press.

Al-Harithy, Howayda, ed. 2010. *Lessons in Post-War Reconstruction: Case Studies from Lebanon in the Aftermath of the 2006 War*. New York: Routledge.

Al-Hout, Bayan Nuwayhed. 2004. *Sabra and Shatia: September 1982*. London: Pluto Press.

Allen, Diana. 2013. *Refugees of the Revolution: Experiences of Palestinian Exile*. Stanford, CA: Stanford Univ. Press.

Allen, Lori. 2008. "Getting by the Occupation: How Violence Became Normal During the Second Intifada." *Cultural Anthropology* 23 (3): 453–87.

Altorki, Soraya, and Camilia Fawzi El-Solh, eds. 1988. *Arab Women in the Field: Studying Your Own Society*. Syracuse, NY: Syracuse Univ. Press.

Anidjar, Gil. 2003. *The Jew, the Arab: A History of the Enemy*. Cultural Memory in the Present. Stanford, CA: Stanford Univ. Press.

AP (Associated Press Wire Service). 2011. "Israel Releases Army Map Showing Nearly 1,000 Purported Hezbollah Underground Military Sites."

———. 2019. "Israel Destroys Last Hezbollah Tunnel from Lebanon." June 3.

Appadurai, Arjun. 1998. "Dead Certainty: Ethnic Violence in the Era of Globalization." *Public Culture* 10 (2): 225–47.

———. 2021. "Beyond Domination: The Future and Past of Decolonization." *The Nation*, March 9 2021.

Archambault, Julie Soleil. 2016. "Taking Love Seriously in Human-Plant Relations in Mozambique: Toward an Anthropology of Affective Encounters." *Cultural Anthropology* 31 (2): 244–71.

Aretxaga, Begoña. 1997. *Shattering Silence: Women, Nationalism, and Political Subjectivity in Northern Ireland*. Princeton, NJ: Princeton Univ. Press.

Arsan, Andrew. 2018. *Lebanon: A Country in Fragments*. London: Hurst.

Asad, Talal. 2003. "Redeeming the 'Human' through Human Rights." In *Formations of the Secular: Christianity, Islam, Modernity*, 127–58. Stanford, CA: Stanford Univ. Press.

Barad, Karen Michelle. 2007. *Meeting the Universe Halfway: Quantum Physics and the Entanglement of Matter and Meaning*. Durham, NC: Duke Univ. Press.

Basso, Keith. 1996. *Wisdom Sits in Places: Landscape and Language among the Western Apache*. Albuquerque: Univ. of New Mexico Press.

Bataille, Georges. 1985. *Visions of Excess: Selected Writings, 1927–1939*. Minneapolis: Univ. of Minnesota Press.

Bazzi, Asma Issa. 2008. "The Impact of Raw Tobacco Subsidies on the Rural Economy and Environment in Lebanon: Opportunities and Challenges to Income Diversification in the Caza of Bint Jbeil." MS thesis, American Univ. of Beirut.

Bearman, Eliezer. 2010. "Meeting the Hybrid Threat: The Israel Defense Forces Innovations against Hybrid Enemies, 2000–2009." MA thesis, Georgetown Univ.

Bechara, Souha, and Gabe Levine. 2003. *Resistance: My Life for Lebanon*. New York: Soft Skull.

Bellacasa, María Puig de la. 2012. "'Nothing Comes without Its World': Thinking with Care." *Sociological Review* 60 (2): 197–216. https://doi.org/10.1111/j.1467-954X.2012.02070.x.

Bernal, Victoria. 1994. "Peasants, Capitalism, and (Ir)Rationality." *American Ethnologist* 21 (4): 792–810. https://doi.org/10.1525/ae.1994.21.4.02a00070.

Besky, Sarah, and Alex Blanchette, eds. 2019. *How Nature Works: Rethinking Labor on a Troubled Planet*. Albuquerque: Univ. of New Mexico Press.

Beydoun, Ahmad. 1992. "The South Lebanon Border Zone: A Local Perspective." *Journal of Palestine Studies* 21 (3): 35–53.

———. 1993. *Le Liban: Itinéraires dans une Guerre Incivile*. Paris: CERMOC.

Biehl, João Guilherme, and Peter Andrew Locke, eds. 2017. *Unfinished: The Anthropology of Becoming*. Durham, NC: Duke Univ. Press.

Blanford, Nicholas. 2007. "A Rare Trip through Hizbullah's Secret Tunnel Network." *Christian Science Monitor*, May 11.

———. 2011. *Warriors of God: Inside Hezbollah's Thirty-Year Struggle against Israel*. New York: Random House.

Blaser, Mario. 2016. "Is Another Cosmopolitics Possible?" *Cultural Anthropology* 31 (4): 545–70.

Bond, David. 2021. "Contamination in Theory and Protest." *American Ethnologist* 48 (4): 386–403.

———. 2022. *Negative Ecologies: Fossil Fuels and the Discovery of the Environment*. Oakland: Univ. of California Press.

Bonneuil, Christophe, and Jean-Baptiste Fressoz. 2017. *The Shock of the Anthropocene: The Earth, History and Us*. Translated by David Fernbach. New York: Verso.

Bou Akar, Hiba. 2018. *For the War yet to Come: Planning Beirut's Frontiers*. Stanford, CA: Stanford Univ. Press.

Bowman, Glenn. 1986. "Unholy Struggle on Holy Ground: Conflict and Interpretation in Jerusalem." *Anthropology Today* 2 (3): 14–17.

———. 1993. "Nationalizing the Sacred: Shrines and Shifting Identities in the Israeli-Occupied Territories." *Man* 28 (3): 431–60.

———. 2013a. "Popular Palestinian Practices around Holy Places and Those Who Oppose Them: An Historical Introduction." *Religion Compass* 7 (3): 69–78.

———. 2013b. "A Weeping on the Road to Bethlehem: Contestation over the Uses of Rachel's Tomb." *Religion Compass* 7 (3): 79–92.

Brun, Brigadier General Itai. 2010. "'While You're Busy Making Other Plans'—The 'Other RMA.'" *Journal of Strategic Studies* 33 (4): 535–65. https://doi.org/10.1080/01402390.2010.489708.

Bulushi, Samar al-, Sahana Ghosh, and Madiha Tahir. 2020. "American Anthropology, Decolonization, and the Politics of Location." *American Anthropologist* 122 (3).

Butler, Judith. 2009. *Frames of War: When Is Life Grievable?* London: Verso.

Buttimer, Anne, and David Seamon. 2016. *The Human Experience of Space and Place.* New York: Routledge.

Callon, Michel, and John Law. 1997. "Agency and the Hybrid *Collectif*." In *Mathematics, Science, and Postclassical Theory*, edited by Barbara Herrnstein Smith and Arkady Plotnitsky, 95–117. Durham, NC: Duke Univ. Press. https://doi.org/10.1215/9780822382720-006.

Cammet, Melanie. 2014. *Compassionate Communalism: Welfare and Sectarianism in Lebanon.* Ithaca, NY: Cornell Univ. Press.

Carmel, Yohay, and Zev Naveh. 2003. "The Evolution of the Cultural Mediterranean Landscape in Israel as Affected by Fire, Grazing, and Human Activities." In *Evolutionary Theory and Processes: Modern Horizons, Papers in Honor of Eviatar Nevo.* Netherlands: Kluwer Academic.

Casey, Edward S. 1996. "How to Get from Space to Place in a Fairly Short Stretch of Time: Phenomenological Prolegomena." In *Senses of Place*, edited by Steven Feld and Keith Basso. Santa Fe, NM: School of American Research.

———. 2001. "Body, Self and Landscape: A Geophilosophical Inquiry into the Place-World." In *Textures of Place: Exploring Humanist Geographies.* Minneapolis: Univ. of Minnesota Press.

———. 2002. *Representing Place: Landscape Painting and Maps.* Minneapolis: Univ. of Minnesota Press.

———. 2005. *Earth-Mapping: Artists Reshaping Landscape.* Minneapolis: Univ. of Minnesota Press.

Chaaban, Jad, Nadia Naamani, and Nisreen Salti. 2010. "The Economics of Tobacco in Lebanon: An Estimation of the Social Costs of Tobacco Consumption." Beirut: AUB Tobacco Control Research Group.

Chakrabarty, Dipesh. 2008. *Provincializing Europe: Postcolonial Thought and Historical Difference.* Reissue, with a new preface by the author. Princeton Studies in Culture, Power, History. Princeton, NJ: Princeton Univ. Press.

Chomsky, Noam. 1984. "Terror in South Lebanon." *Journal of Palestine Studies* 13 (4): 175–77.

Choy, Tim. 2009. "A New Form of Collaboration in Cultural Anthropology: Matsutake Worlds." *American Ethnologist* 36(2): 380–403.

Clausewitz, Carl von. 1989. *On War.* New York: Knopf.

Connell, Raewyn. 2019. "Canons and Colonies: The Global Trajectory of Sociology." *Estudos Históricos* (Rio de Janeiro) 32 (67): 349–67. https://doi.org/10.1590/s2178-14942019000200002.

Cooper, Frederick, and Ann Laura Stoler, eds. 1997. *Tensions of Empire: Colonial Cultures in a Bourgeois World*. Berkeley: Univ. of California Press.

Cosgrove, Denis E. 1998. *Social Formation and Symbolic Landscape*. Madison: Univ. of Wisconsin Press.

Daher, Aurélie, and H. W. Randolph. 2019. *Hezbollah: Mobilisation and Power*. New York: Oxford Univ. Press.

Das, Veena. 2007. *Life and Words: Violence and the Descent into the Ordinary*. Berkeley: Univ. of California Press.

Das, Veena, and Deborah Poole. 2004. *Anthropology in the Margins of the State*. Santa Fe, NM: School of American Research Press.

Das, Veena, Arthur Kleinman, Pamela Reynolds, and Mamphela Ramphele, eds. 2000. *Violence and Subjectivity*. Berkeley: Univ. of California Press.

De Cadena, Marisol. 2015. *Earth Beings: Ecologies of Practice across Andean Worlds*. Durham, NC: Duke Univ. Press.

de Certeau, Michel. 2013. *The Practice of Everyday Life*. Berkeley: Univ. of California Press.

Deeb, Lara. 2006. "'Hizbullah Strongholds' and Civilian Life." *Anthropology News*, October 2006.

Deeb, Lara, and Mona Harb. 2013. *Leisurely Islam: Negotiating Geography and Morality in Shi'ite South Beirut*. Princeton Studies in Muslim Politics. Princeton, NJ: Princeton Univ. Press.

de Goede, Marcel. 2009. "The Israeli Actions during the Second Lebanon War: A Case Study into Strategic Culture." *NL-Arms*, 197–223.

De León, Jason. 2015. *The Land of Open Graves: Living and Dying on the Migrant Trail*. California Series in Public Anthropology 36. Oakland: Univ. of California Press.

Deleuze, Gilles, and Felix Guattari. 1987. *A Thousand Plateaus: Capitalism and Schizophrenia*. Minneapolis: Univ. of Minnesota Press.

De Sousa Santos, Boaventura. 2018. *The End of the Cognitive Empire: The Coming of Age of Epistemologies of the South*. Durham, NC: Duke Univ. Press.

Exum, Andrew. 2006. "Hizballah at War: A Military Assessment." Washington, DC: Washington Institute for Near East Policy.

Fanon, Frantz. 2007. *A Dying Colonialism*. Translated by Haakon Chevalier. New York: Grove.

FAO. 2006. "Damage and Early Recovery Needs Assessment of Agriculture, Fisheries and Forestry." Special Emergency Programmes Service Emergency Operations and Rehabilitation Division, Food and Agriculture Organization of the United Nations, Rome.

Farhat, Albert, and Hanna Saleh. 1978. *The Sun Rises from the South: The Israeli Aggression against South Lebanon: Facts and Testimony.* Beirut: Dar Al-Farabi.

Farmer, Paul. 1996. "On Suffering and Structural Violence: A View from Below." *Daedalus* 125 (1): 261–83.

———. 2004. "An Anthropology of Structural Violence." *Current Anthropology* 45 (3): 305–25. https://doi.org/10.1086/382250.

Fassin, Didier. 2009. "Another Politics of Life Is Possible." *Theory, Culture & Society* 26 (5): 44–60. https://doi.org/10.1177/0263276409106349.

———. 2012. *Humanitarian Reason: A Moral History of the Present Times.* Berkeley: Univ. of California Press.

Fawaz, Mona. 2009. "Hezbollah as Urban Planner? Questions to and from Planning Theory." *Planning Theory* 8 (4): 323–34.

Federici, Silvia. 2012. *Revolution at Point Zero: Housework, Reproduction, and Feminist Struggle.* Oakland, CA: PM Press.

Feldman, Allen. 1991. *Formations of Violence: The Narrative of the Body and Political Terror in Northern Ireland.* Chicago: Univ. of Chicago Press.

Ferme, Mariane C. 2001. *The Underneath of Things: Violence, History and the Everyday in Sierra Leone.* Berkeley: Univ. of California Press.

Fisk, Robert. 2002. *Pity the Nation: The Abduction of Lebanon.* New American ed. New York: Nation Books.

Folman, Ari, dir. 2008. *Waltz with Bashir.* Film. Israel: Bridgit Folman Film Gang.

Friedman, Jeffrey A., and Stephen D. Biddle. 2011. *The 2006 Lebanon Campaign and the Future of Warfare: Implications for Army and Defence Policy.* Carlisle, PA: US Army War College Press.

Gan, Elaine, and International Association for Environmental Philosophy. 2017. "An Unintended Race: Miracle Rice and the Green Revolution." *Environmental Philosophy* 14 (1): 61–81. https://doi.org/10.5840/envirophil20174648.

Geertz, Clifford. 1963. *Agricultural Involution: The Process of Ecological Change in Indonesia.* Berkeley: Univ. of California Press.

Genet, Jean. 2003. *Prisoner of Love.* New York: New York Review Books.

Gilsenan, Michael. 1996. *Lords of the Lebanese Marches: Violence and Narrative in an Arab Society.* London: Tauris.

Gooch, Pernille. 2008. "Feet Following Hooves." In *Ways of Walking: Ethnography and Practice on Foot,* edited by Tim Ingold and Jo Lee Vergunst. Farnham, UK: Ashgate.

Gordillo, Gastón R. 2014. *Rubble: The Afterlife of Destruction.* Durham, NC: Duke Univ. Press.

———. 2018. "Terrain as Insurgent Weapon: An Affective Geometry of Warfare in the Mountains of Afghanistan." *Political Geography* 64 (May): 53–62. https://doi.org/10.1016/j.polgeo.2018.03.001.

Gourevitch, Philip. 2004. *We Wish to Inform You That Tomorrow We Will Be Killed with Our Families: Stories from Rwanda.* New York: Picador.

Govindrajan, Radhika. 2018. *Animal Intimacies: Interspecies Relatedness in India's Central Himalayas.* Animal Lives. Chicago: Univ. of Chicago Press.

Gray, John. 1999. "Open Spaces and Dwelling Places: Being at Home on Hill Farms in the Scottish Borders." *American Ethnologist* 26 (2): 440–60.

Gregory, Derek. 1998. *Geographical Imaginations.* Reprint. Cambridge: Blackwell.

———. 2016. "The Natures of War: The Natures of War." *Antipode* 48 (1): 3–56. https://doi.org/10.1111/anti.12173.

Grossman, David. 2010. *To the End of the Land.* Translated by Jessica Cohen. New York: Knopf.

Grove, Jairus Victor. 2019. *Savage Ecology: War and Geopolitics at the End of the World.* Durham, NC: Duke Univ. Press.

Guarasci, Bridget, and Eleana Kim. 2022. "Introduction: Ecologies of War." *Fieldsights,* January 25. https://culanth.org/fieldsights/introduction-ecologies-of-war.

Guevara, Che. 2013. *Guerrilla Warfare.* CreateSpace Independent Publishing Platform.

Haaretz. 2018. "Israel Prepares to Destroy Hezbollah Tunnels inside Lebanon." December 4.

Hage, Ghassan. 2015. *Alter-Politics: Critical Politics and the Radical Imagination.* Melbourne: Melbourne Univ. Press.

Hamade, Kanj. 2014. "Tobacco Leaf Farming in Lebanon: Why Marginalized Farmers Need a Better Option." In *Tobacco Control and Tobacco Farming: Separating Myth from Reality,* edited by Wardie Leppan and Daniel Buckles. London: Anthem Press.

Hanf, Theodor. 1994. *Coexistence in Wartime Lebanon: Decline of a State and Rise of a Nation.* London: I. B. Tauris.

Haraway, Donna Jeanne. 2016. *Staying with the Trouble: Making Kin in the Chthulucene.* Experimental Futures: Technological Lives, Scientific Arts, Anthropological Voices. Durham, NC: Duke Univ. Press.

Harb, Mona, and Lara Deeb. 2011. "Culture as History and Landscape: Hizballah's Efforts to Shape an Islamic Milieu in Lebanon." *Arab Studies Journal* 19 (1): 10–41.

Harrison, Faye Venetia, and Association of Black Anthropologists, eds. 1997. *Decolonizing Anthropology: Moving Further toward an Anthropology of Liberation.* 2nd ed. Arlington, VA: Association of Black Anthropologists, American Anthropological Association.

Haugbolle, Sune. 2012. *War and Memory in Lebanon.* Cambridge: Cambridge Univ. Press.

Henig, David. 2012. "'This Is Our Little Hajj': Muslim Holy Sites and Reappro-
    priation of the Sacred Landscape in Contemporary Bosnia." *American
    Ethnologist* 39 (4): 751–65. https://doi.org/10.1111/j.1548-1425.2012.01393.x.
———. 2019. "Living on the Frontline: Indeterminacy, Value, and Military Waste
    in Postwar Bosnia-Herzegovina." *Anthropological Quarterly* 92 (1): 85–110.
Hermez, Sami Samir. 2017. *War Is Coming: Between Past and Future Violence
    in Lebanon.* Ethnography of Political Violence. Philadelphia: Univ. of
    Pennsylvania Press.
Hirsch, Eric, and Michael O'Hanlon, eds. 1995. *The Anthropology of Land-
    scape: Perspectives on Place and Space.* Oxford Studies in Social and
    Cultural Anthropology. New York: Oxford Univ. Press.
Hirst, David. 1999. "South Lebanon: The War That Never Ends?" *Journal of
    Palestine Studies* 28 (3): 5–18.
———. 2011. *Beware of Small States: Lebanon, Battleground of the Middle East.*
    New York: Nation Books.
Ho Chi Minh and Walden Bello. 2007. *Down with Colonialism!* London: Verso.
Hof, Fredric. 1985. *Galilee Divided: The Israel-Lebanon Frontier, 1916–1984.*
    New York: Routledge.
Hoffman, Daniel. 2011. "Violence, Just in Time: War and Work in Contempo-
    rary West Africa." *Cultural Anthropology* 26 (1): 34–57. https://doi.org/10
    .1111/j.1548-1360.2010.01079.x.
Hoffman, Frank G. 2007. *Conflict in the 21st Century: The Rise of Hybrid Wars.*
    Arlington, VA: Potomac Institute for Policy Studies.
———. 2009. "Hybrid Threats: Reconceptualizing the Evolving Character
    Modern Conflict." Institute for National Strategic Studies, National Defense
    Univ. Strategic Forum no. 24.
HRW (Human Rights Watch). 2007. *Why They Died: Civilian Casualties in
    Lebanon During the 2006 War.* https://www.hrw.org/report/2007/09/05
    /why-they-died/civilian-casualties-lebanon-during-2006-war.
———. 2008. *Flooding South Lebanon Israel's Use of Cluster Munitions in
    Lebanon in July and August 2006.* https://www.hrw.org/report/2008
    /02/16/flooding-south-lebanon/israels-use-cluster-munitions-lebanon-july-
    and-august-2006.
Huyssen, Andreas. 2003. *Presents Past: Urban Palimpsests and the Politics of
    Memory.* Stanford, CA: Stanford Univ. Press.
Ingold, Tim. 1993. "The Temporality of the Landscape." *World Archaeology* 25
    (2): 152–74.
Ingold, Tim, and Jo Lee Vergunst. 2008. *Ways of Walking: Ethnography and
    Practice on Foot.* Farnham, UK: Ashgate.
IWFCL. 2002. "Child Labor on Tobacco Plantations: A Rapid Assessment."
    International Labor Organization International Programme on the Elimina-
    tion of Child Labor.

Jabir, Munzir. 1999. *Al-Sharit al-Lubnani al-Muhtall : Masalik al-Ihtilal, Masarat al-Muwajahah, Masair al-Ahali* [The occupied Lebanese border strip: Paths of occupation, lines of confrontation, the fate of the population]. Beirut: Institute for Palestine Studies.

Jirmanus Saba, Mary, dir. 2017. *A Feeling Greater Than Love.* Film.

Johnson, Penny. 2019. *Companions in Conflict: Animals in Occupied Palestine.* London: Melville House.

Jones, Brennon. 2006. "Southern Lebanon's Deadly Crop." *New York Times,* October 12.

Jones, Owain, and Paul Cloke. 2002. *Tree Cultures: The Place of Trees and Trees in Their Place.* Oxford: Berg.

Joseph, Suad, ed. 2000. *Gender and Citizenship in the Middle East.* Contemporary Issues in the Middle East. Syracuse, NY: Syracuse Univ. Press.

———. 2008. "Pensée 2: Sectarianism as Imagined Sociological Concept and as Imagined Social Formation." *International Journal of Middle East Studies* 40 (4): 553–54. https://doi.org/10.1017/S0020743808081464.

———. 2011. "Political Familism in Lebanon." *Annals of the American Academy of Political and Social Science* 636 (1): 150–63. https://doi.org/10.1177 /0002716211398434.

Kadmon, Ronen, and Ruthie Harari-Kremer. 1999. "Landscape-Scale Regeneration Dynamics of Disturbed Mediterranean Maquis." *Journal of Vegetation Science* 10 (3): 393–402.

Kaldor, Mary. 1999. *New and Old Wars: Organized Violence in a Global Era.* Cambridge, UK: Polity Press.

Kassir, Samir. 1985. "The Resistance Front in South Lebanon." *MERIP Reports,* no. 133:23–24.

Khalidi, Walid. 1983. *Conflict and Violence in Lebanon.* Cambridge, MA: Harvard Univ. Press.

Khalili, Laleh. 2009. *Heroes and Martyrs of Palestine: The Politics of National Commemoration.* Cambridge: Cambridge Univ. Press.

———. 2012. *Time in the Shadows: Confinement in Counterinsurgencies.* Stanford, CA: Stanford Univ. Press.

———. 2020. *Sinews of War and Trade: Shipping and Capitalism in the Arabian Peninsula.* New York: Verso.

Khayat, Tristan. 2004. "Overview of Land Use and Land Property Issues in Liberated Southern Lebanon." UNDP.

Khayyat, Munira. 2006. "One Week of War: Every Decision is a Gamble." *Electronic Infifada,* July 23. https://electronicintifada.net/content/one-week-war-every-decision-gamble/6210.

———. 2020. "On Living Through Plagues and Wars in Lebanon." *Anthropology News,* May/June. https://doi.org/10.1111/AN.1436.

———. 2022. "Resistant Ecology, Bitter Life." *Fieldsights*, January 25. https://culanth.org/fieldsights/resistant-ecology-bitter-life.

Khayyat, Munira, Yasmine Khayyat, and Rola Khayyat. 2018. "Pieces of Us: The Intimate as Imperial Archive." *Journal of Middle East Women's Studies* 14 (3). https://doi.org/10.1215/15525864-7025385.

Khayyat, Yasmine. 2023. *War Remains: Ruination and Resistance in Lebanon.* Syracuse, NY: Syracuse Univ. Press.

Khleifi, Michel, and Eyal Sivan, dir. 2003. *Route 181: Fragments of a Journey to Palestine.* Film. Israel and Paris: Momento!

Khoury, Elias. 1985. "Sidon, 'Ain al-Hilweh and the Villages Are Only the Beginning." *Al-Safir,* February 18.

Kim, Eleana J. 2014. "The Flight of Cranes: Militarized Nature at the North Korea–South Korea Border." *RCC Perspectives,* no. 3:65–70.

———. 2016. "Toward an Anthropology of Landmines: Rogue Infrastructure and Military Waste in the Korean DMZ." *Cultural Anthropology* 31 (2): 162–87. https://doi.org/10.14506/ca31.2.02.

Kleinman, Arthur. 2000. "The Violences of Everyday Life: The Multiple Forms and Dynamics of Social Violence." In *Violence and Subjectivity,* edited by Veena Das, Arthur Kleinman, Pamela Reynolds, and Mamphela Ramphele, 226–41. Berkeley: Univ. of California Press.

Kohn, Eduardo. 2013. *How Forests Think: Toward an Anthropology beyond the Human.* Berkeley: Univ. of California Press.

Korf, Benedikt, Michelle Engeler, and Tobias Hagmann. 2010. "The Geography of Warscape." *Third World Quarterly* 31 (3): 385–99. https://doi.org/10.1080/01436597.2010.488466.

Kubovich, Yaniv, Noa Landau, and Jack Khoury. 2018. "Israel Prepares to Destroy Hezbollah Tunnels Inside Lebanon." *Haaretz,* December 4.

Kundu, Bhaskar, Batakrushna Senapati, Ai Matsushita, and Kosuke Heki. 2021. "Atmospheric Wave Energy of the 2020 August 4 Explosion in Beirut, Lebanon, from Ionospheric Disturbances." *Scientific Reports* 11 (1): 2793. https://doi.org/10.1038/s41598-021-82355-5.

Laffin, John. 1985. *The War of Desperation: Lebanon 1982–85.* London: Osprey.

Lan, David. 1985. *Guns and Rain: Guerrillas and Spirit Mediums in Zimbabwe.* Berkeley: Univ. of California Press.

Langwick, Stacey Ann. 2018. "A Politics of Habitability: Plants, Healing, and Sovereignty in a Toxic World." *Cultural Anthropology* 33 (3): 415–43. https://doi.org/10.14506/ca33.3.06.

Leenders, Reinoud. 2012. *Spoils of Truce: Corruption and State-Building in Postwar Lebanon.* Ithaca, NY: Cornell Univ. Press.

Levi, Primo. 1989. *The Drowned and the Saved.* New York: Vintage International.

Lubin, Alex. 2014. *Geographies of Liberation: The Making of an Afro-Arab Political Imaginary.* Chapel Hill: Univ. of North Carolina Press.

Lubkemann, Stephen C. 2008. *Culture in Chaos: An Anthropology of the Social Condition in War.* Chicago: Univ. of Chicago Press.

Lutz, Catherine. 2001. *Homefront: A Military City and the American Twentieth Century.* Boston: Beacon.

Lyons, Kristina M. 2016. "Decomposition as Life Politics: Soils, Selva, and Small Farmers under the Gun of the U.S.-Colombia War on Drugs." *Cultural Anthropology* 31 (1): 56–81. https://doi.org/10.14506/ca31.1.04.

———. 2020. *Vital Decomposition: Soil Practitioners and Life Politics.* Durham, NC: Duke Univ. Press.

Maček, Ivana. 2005. "Sarajevan Soldier Story: Perceptions of War and Morality in Bosnia." In *No Peace No War: An Anthropology of Contemporary Armed Conflicts.* Athens: Ohio Univ. Press.

———. 2011. *Sarajevo under Siege: Anthropology in Wartime.* Ethnography of Political Violence. Philadelphia: Univ. of Pennsylvania Press.

MacLeish, Kenneth T. 2013. *Making War at Fort Hood: Life and Uncertainty in a Military Community.* Princeton, NJ: Princeton Univ. Press.

Mahmood, Saba. 2001. "Rehearsed Spontaneity and the Conventionality of Ritual: Disciplines of Salat." *American Ethnologist* 28 (4).

Makdisi, Karim. 2011. "Constructing Security Council Resolution 1701 for Lebanon in the Shadow of the 'War on Terror.'" *International Peacekeeping* 18 (1): 4–20. https://doi.org/10.1080/13533312.2011.527502.

Makdisi, Saree. 1997. "Laying Claim to Beirut: Urban Narrative and Spatial Identity in the Age of Solidere." *Critical Inquiry* 23 (3). https://doi.org/10.1086/448848.

Makdisi, Ussama Samir. 2000. *The Culture of Sectarianism: Community, History, and Violence in Nineteenth-Century Ottoman Lebanon.* Berkeley: Univ. of California Press.

Makhzoumi, Jala. 1997. "The Changing Role of Rural Landscapes: Olive and Carob Multi-use Tree Plantations in the Semi-Arid Mediterranean." *Landscape and Urban Planning,* no. 37:115–22.

———. 2008. "Interrogating the *Hakura* tradition: Lebanese Village Gardens as Product and Production." *Traditional Dwellings and Settlements Review* 20 (1): 20–21.

———. 2009. "Unfolding Landscape in a Lebanese Village: Rural Heritage in a Globalising World." *International Journal of Heritage Studies* 15 (4): 317–37. https://doi.org/10.1080/13527250902933793.

———. 2016. "From Urban Beautification to a Holistic Approach: The Discourses of 'Landscape' in the Arab Middle East." *Landscape Research* 41 (4): 461–70. https://doi.org/10.1080/01426397.2016.1156068.

Malkinson, D. 2011. "Effects of Repeated Fires on the Structure, Composition, and Dynamics of Mediterranean Maquis: Short- and Long-Term Perspectives." *Ecosystems,* no. 14:478–88.

Mao Tse Tung and Samuel B. Griffiths. 2000. *On Guerrilla Warfare.* Champaign: Univ. of Illinois Press.

Marcus, Rafael D. 2018. *Israel's Long War with Hezbollah: Military Innovation and Adaptation Under Fire.* Washington, DC: Georgetown Univ. Press.

Marder, Michael. 2013. *Plant-Thinking: A Philosophy of Vegetal Life.* New York: Columbia Univ. Press.

Mathews, Andrew S. 2018. "Landscapes and Throughscapes in Italian Forest Worlds: Thinking Dramatically about the Anthropocene." *Cultural Anthropology* 33 (3): 386–414. https://doi.org/10.14506/ca33.3.05.

Matless, David. 1998. *Landscape and Englishness.* Picturing History. London: Reaktion.

Matthews, Matt M. 2006. "We Were Caught Unprepared: The 2006 Hezbollah-Israeli War." The Long War Series Occasional Paper 26. Kansas: Combined Arms Center.

Mbembe, Achille. 2002. "African Modes of Self-Writing." *Public Culture* 14 (1): 239–73.

———. 2020. *Out of the Dark Night: Essays on Decolonization.* New York: Columbia Univ. Press.

Melhem, Ahmad. 2015. "Inside the West Bank's Homemade Cigarette Industry." *Al-Monitor,* March 19. https://www.al-monitor.com/originals/2015/03/palestinians-consumers-al-arabi-tobacco-smoke.html.

Meneley, Anne. 2014. "Resistance Is Fertile." *Gastronomica,* no. 14:69–78.

———. 2020. "The Olive and Imaginaries of the Mediterranean." *History and Anthropology* 31 (1): 66–83.

Mignolo, Walter D. 2018. *On Decoloniality: Concepts, Analytics, Praxis.* Durham, NC: Duke Univ. Press.

Mitchell, Tim. 1991. *Colonizing Egypt.* Cambridge: Cambridge Univ. Press.

Mitchell, W. J. T., ed. 2002. *Landscape and Power.* 2nd ed. Chicago: Univ. of Chicago Press.

Mowles, Chris. 1986. "The Israeli Occupation of South Lebanon." *Third World Quarterly* 8 (4): 1351–66.

Mundy, Martha, and Richard Saumarez Smith. 2007. *Governing Property, Making the Modern State: Law, Administration and Production in Ottoman Syria.* Library of Ottoman Studies 9. London: I. B. Tauris.

Myers, Natasha. 2017. "From the Anthropocene to the Planthroposcene: Designing Gardens for Plant/People Involution." *History and Anthropology* 28 (3): 297–301. https://doi.org/10.1080/02757206.2017.1289934.

Myrivili, Eleni. 2004. "The Liquid Border: Subjectivity at the Limits of the Nation-State in Southeast Europe." PhD Dissertation, Columbia Univ., New York.

Nash, Catherine. 1996. "Reclaiming Vision: Looking at Landscape and the Body." *Gender, Place and Culture* 3 (2): 149–70. https://doi.org/10.1080/09663699650021864.

Nash, Thomas. 2006. "Foreseeable Harm: The Use and Impact of Cluster Munitions in Lebanon: 2006." London: Landmine Action.

Nasrallah, Fida. 1992. *The Question of South Lebanon*. Oxford: Centre for Lebanese Studies.

Nassib, Salim, and Caroline Tisdall. 1983. *Beirut: Frontline Story*. Trenton, NJ: Africa World Press.

Navaro, Yael. 2017. "Diversifying Affect." *Cultural Anthropology* 32 (2): 209–14. https://doi.org/10.14506/ca32.2.05.

Navaro-Yashin, Yael. 2009. "Affective Spaces, Melancholic Objects: Ruination and the Production of Anthropological Knowledge." *Journal of the Royal Anthropological Institute* 15 (1): 1–18.

———. 2012. *The Make-Believe Space: Affective Geography in a Postwar Polity*. Durham, NC: Duke Univ. Press.

Navaro-Yashin, Yael, Zerrin Özlem Biner, Alice von Bieberstein, and Seda Altuğ, eds. 2021. *Reverberations: Violence across Time and Space*. Ethnography of Political Violence. Philadelphia: Univ. of Pennsylvania Press.

Nguyen, Viet Thanh. 2022. *The Committed*. New York: Grove.

Nixon, Rob. 2007. "Of Land Mines and Cluster Bombs." *Cultural Critique*, no. 67:160–74.

———. 2013. *Slow Violence and the Environmentalism of the Poor*. Cambridge, MA: Harvard Univ. Press.

Nkrumah, Kwame. 2015. *Handbook of Revolutionary Warfare*. London: Panaf Books.

Nordstrom, Carolyn. 1997. *A Different Kind of War Story*. Philadelphia: Univ. of Pennsylvania Press.

Norton, Augustus Richard. 1987. *Amal and the Shi'a: Struggle for the Soul of Lebanon*. Austin: Univ. of Texas Press.

———. 2000. "Hizballah and the Israeli Withdrawal from Southern Lebanon." *Journal of Palestine Studies* 30 (1): 22–35.

———. 2006. "Hizballah through the Fog of the Lebanon War." *Journal of Palestine Studies* 36 (1): 54–70. https://doi.org/10.1525/jps.2006.36.1.54.

———. 2014. *Hezbollah: A Short History*. New paperback ed. Princeton Studies in Muslim Politics. Princeton, NJ: Princeton Univ. Press.

Nucho, Joanne Randa. 2016. *Everyday Sectarianism in Urban Lebanon: Infrastructures, Public Services, and Power*. Princeton Studies in Culture and Technology. Princeton, NJ: Princeton Univ. Press.

———. 2019. "Garbage Infrastructure, Sanitation, and New Meanings of Citizenship in Lebanon." *Postmodern Culture* 30 (1). https://doi.org/10.1353/pmc.2019.0018.

Olwig, Kenneth R. 2005. "Liminality, Seasonality and Landscape." *Landscape Research* 30 (2): 259–71. https://doi.org/10.1080/01426390500044473.

———. 2008. "Performing on the Landscape versus Doing Landscape: Perambulatory Practice, Sight and the Sense of Belonging." In *Ways of Walking: Ethnography and Practice on Foot*. Farnham, UK: Ashgate.

O'Shea, Brendan. 2004. "Lebanon's Blue line: A New International Border or Just Another Cease-Fire Zone?" *Studies in Conflict and Terrorism*, no. 27:19-30.

Palestine Economic Policy Research Institute. 2016. "The Economic and Social Impact of the Expansion in Tobacco Cultivation in Palestine." Ramallah: Palestine Economic Policy Research Institute.

Pandolfo, Stefania. 1997. *Impasse of the Angels: Scenes from a Moroccan Space of Memory*. Chicago: Univ. of Chicago Press.

Pearson, Chris. 2008. *Scarred Landscapes: War and Nature in Vichy France*. New York: Palgrave Macmillan.

——— 2012. "Researching Militarized Landscapes: A Literature Review on War and the Militarization of the Environment." *Landscape Research* 37 (1): 115–33. https://doi.org/10.1080/01426397.2011.570974.

Peteet, Julie M. 2005. Landscape of Hope and Despair: Palestinian Refugee Camps. Philadelphia: Univ. of Pennsylvania Press.

Peters, Emrys. 1977. "Aspects of Rank and Status Among Muslims in a Lebanese Village." In *Mediterranean Countrymen*, edited by Julian Pitt-Rivers. Westport, CT: Greenwood.

Picard, Elizabeth. 1996. *Lebanon: A Shattered Country: Myths and Realities of the Wars in Lebanon*. New York: Holmes & Meier.

Povinelli, Elizabeth A. 2012. "The Will to Be Otherwise/The Effort of Endurance." *South Atlantic Quarterly* 111 (3): 453–75. https://doi.org/10.1215/00382876-1596236.

———. 2016. *Geontologies: A Requiem to Late Liberalism*. Durham, NC: Duke Univ. Press.

Qassem, Naim. 2012. *Hizbullah: The Story from Within*. London: Saqi.

Rabinovitch, Itamar. 1985. *The War for Lebanon: 1970–1985*. Ithaca, NY: Cornell Univ. Press.

Raffles, Hugh. 2002. *In Amazonia: A Natural History*. Princeton, NJ: Princeton Univ. Press.

Randall, Jonathan. 1983. *Tragedy of Lebanon: Christian Warlords, Israeli Adventurers and American Bunglers*. Charlottesville, VA: Just World Publishing.

Reisman, Emily. 2021. "Plants, Pathogens, and the Politics of Care: *Xylella fastidiosa* and the Intra-active Breakdown of Mallorca's Almond Ecology." *Cultural Anthropology* 36 (3). https://doi.org/10.14506/ca36.3.07.

Richards, Paul, and Bernhard Helander, eds. 2005. *No Peace, No War: An Anthropology of Contemporary Armed Conflicts*. Athens: Ohio Univ. Press.

Rival, Laura, ed. 1998. *The Social Life of Trees: Anthropological Perspectives on Tree Symbolism*. London: Routledge.

Rodman, Margaret. 1992. "Empowering Place: Multilocality and Multivocality." *American Anthropologist* 94 (3): 640–56.

Rose, Mitch. 2002. "Landscape and Labyrinths." *Geoforum* 33 (4): 455–67.

Saad-Ghorayeb, Amal. 2002. *Hizbullah: Politics and Religion*. Critical Studies on Islam. London: Pluto Press.

———. 2003. "Factors Conducive to the Politicization of the Lebanese Shi'a and the Emergence of Hizbullah." *Journal of Islamic Studies* 14 (3): 273–307.

Said, Edward W. 1979. *Orientalism*. New York: Vintage.

———. 1989. "Representing the Colonized: Anthropology's Interlocutors." *Critical Inquiry* 15 (2): 205–25.

Salibi, Kamal S. 1989. *A House of Many Mansions: The History of Lebanon Reconsidered*. Berkeley: Univ. of California Press.

Santner, Eric L. 2006. *On Creaturely Life: Rilke, Benjamin, Sebald*. Chicago: Univ. of Chicago Press.

Save the Children. 2005. "Rapid Livelihoods Assessment in Southern Lebanon." https://reliefweb.int/sites/reliefweb.int/files/resources/1E50549602173FAC C12571DF0036A5BD-sc-lbn-29aug.pdf.

Sawalha, Aseel. 2010. *Reconstructing Beirut: Memory and Space in a Postwar Arab City*. Austin: Univ. of Texas Press.

Sayigh, Rosemary. 1979. *Palestinians: From Peasants to Revolutionaries, A People's History*. London: Zed Press.

———. 1993. *Too Many Enemies: The Palestinian Experience in Lebanon*. London: Zed Books.

Scheper-Hughes, Nancy, and Philippe Bourgois, eds. 2007. *Violence in War and Peace: An Anthology*. Blackwell Readers in Anthropology. Malden, MA: Blackwell.

———. 2009. *Death without Weeping: The Violence of Everyday Life in Brazil*. Berkeley: Univ. of California Press.

Schiff, Ina, and Ze'ev Yaari. 1985. *Israel's Lebanon War*. London: Allen and Unwin.

Scott, James C. 1990. *Domination and the Arts of Resistance: Hidden Transcripts*. New Haven, CT: Yale Univ. Press.

———. 2000. *Weapons of the Weak: Everyday Forms of Peasant Resistance*. New Haven, CT: Yale Univ. Press.

Sebald, W. G., and Anthea Bell. 2004. *On the Natural History of Destruction*. New York: Modern Library.

Sharif, Hasa. 1978. "South Lebanon: Its History and Geopolitics." In *South Lebanon*, edited by Elaine Hagopian and Samih Farsoun. Detroit: Association of Arab-American University Graduates.

Shaw, Ian G. R. 2016. "Scorched Atmospheres: The Violent Geographies of the Vietnam War and the Rise of Drone Warfare." *Annals of the American Association of Geographers* 106 (3): 688–704. https://doi.org/10.1080/0004 5608.2015.1115333.

Shuttleworth, Kate. 2015. "Palestinian Tobacco Is the West Bank's 'New Cash Crop.'" *National News*, September 1. https://www.thenationalnews.com/ world/palestinian-tobacco-is-the-west-bank-s-new-cash-crop-1.128350.

Simpson, Audra. 2007. "On Ethnographic Refusal: Indigeneity, Voice and Colonial Citizenship." *Junctures*, December 2007.

———. 2017. "The Ruse of Consent and the Anatomy of 'Refusal': Cases from Indigenous North America and Australia." *Postcolonial Studies* 20 (1): 18–33. https://doi.org/10.1080/13688790.2017.1334283.

Sloterdijk, Peter. 2009. *Terror from the Air*. Semiotext(e) Foreign Agents Series. Cambridge, MA: Semiotext(e).

Stamatopoulou-Robbins, Sophia. 2020. *Waste Siege: The Life of Infrastructure in Palestine*. Stanford Studies in Middle Eastern and Islamic Societies and Cultures. Stanford, CA: Stanford Univ. Press.

Stengers, Isabelle. 2005. "Introductory Notes on an Ecology of Practices." *Cultural Studies Review* 11 (1): 183–96.

Stewart, Kathleen. 2007. *Ordinary Affects*. Durham, NC: Duke Univ. Press.

Stoetzer, Bettina. 2018. "Ruderal Ecologies: Rethinking Nature, Migration, and the Urban Landscape in Berlin." *Cultural Anthropology* 33 (2): 295–323. https://doi.org/10.14506/ca33.2.09.

Stone, Nomi. 2018. "Imperial Mimesis: Enacting and Policing Empathy in US Military Training." *American Ethnologist* 45 (4): 533–45.

Swanson, Heather Anne, Marianne E. Lien, and Gro Ween, eds. 2018. *Domestication Gone Wild: Politics and Practices of Multispecies Relations*. Durham, NC: Duke Univ. Press.

Taneja, Anand Vivek. 2018. *Jinnealogy: Time, Islam, and Ecological Thought in the Medieval Ruins of Delhi*. South Asia in Motion. Stanford, CA: Stanford Univ. Press.

Taussig, Michael T. 1992. *The Nervous System*. New York: Routledge.

———. 2003. *Law in a Lawless Land: Diary of a Limpieza in Colombia*. New York: New Press.

———. 2004. *Shamanism, Colonialism, and the Wild Man: A Study in Terror and Healing*. Chicago: Univ. of Chicago Press.

———. 2006. Walter Benjamin's Grave. Chicago: Univ. of Chicago Press.

Tesdell, Omar, Yusra Othman, and Sahar Alkhoury. 2019. "Rainfed Agroeco-system Resilience in the Palestinian West Bank 1918-2017. *Agroecology and Sustainable Food Systems* 43 (1): 21-39.

Thubron, Colin. 2008. *The Hills of Adonis: A Quest in Lebanon.* London: Vintage.

Traboulsi, Fawaz. 2012. *A History of Modern Lebanon.* 2nd ed. London: Pluto Press.

Tomaselli, Rugero. 1977. "The Degradation of the Mediterranean Maquis." *Ambio* 6 (6): 356–62.

Touhouliotis, Vasiliki. 2018. "Weak Seed and a Poisoned Land Slow Violence and the Toxic Infrastructures of War in South Lebanon." *Environmental Humanities* 10 (1): 86–106.

Trouillot, Michel-Rolph. 1991. "Anthropology and the Savage Slot: The Poetics and Politics of Otherness." In *Recapturing Anthropology: Working in the Present,* edited by Richard G. Fox. Santa Fe, NM: School of American Research.

———. 2001. *Silencing the Past: Power and the Production of History.* Boston: Beacon Press.

Tsing, Anna Lowenhaupt. 2005. *Friction: An Ethnography of Global Connection.* Princeton, NJ: Princeton Univ. Press.

———. 2015. *The Mushroom at the End of the World: On the Possibility of Life in Capitalist Ruins.* Princeton, NJ: Princeton Univ. Press.

Tsing, Anna Lowenhaupt, Andrew S. Mathews, and Nils Bubandt. 2019. "Patchy Anthropocene: Landscape Structure, Multispecies History, and the Retooling of Anthropology: An Introduction to Supplement 20." *Current Anthropology* 60 (S20): S186–97. https://doi.org/10.1086/703391.

Tuan, Yi-Fu. 2011. *Space and Place: The Perspective of Experience.* Minneapolis: Univ. of Minnesota Press.

Tuhiwai Smith, Linda. 2012. *Decolonizing Methodologies: Research and Indigenous People.* London: Zed Books.

Turner, Victor. 1995. *The Ritual Process: Structure and Anti-structure.* London: Routledge.

Ustundag, Nazan. 2010. "A Landscape of Violence." In *Anywhere but Now: Landscapes of Belonging in the Eastern Mediterranean,* edited by Samar Kanafani, Munira Khayyat, and Rasha Salti. Beirut: Heinrich Böll Foundation.

van Creveld, Martin. 2002. *The Sword and the Olive: A Critical History of the Israeli Defense Forces.* New York: Public Affairs.

Viveiros de Castro, Eduardo. 2016. *The Relative Native: Essays on Indigenous Conceptual Worlds.* Special Collections in Ethnographic Theory. Chicago: HAU.

Weiss, Max. 2010. *In the Shadow of Sectarianism: Law, Shiism and the Making of Modern Lebanon.* Cambridge, MA: Harvard Univ Press.

Weizman, Eyal. 2007. *Hollow Land: Israel's Architecture of Occupation*. New York: Verso.

Wimmen, Heiko. 2013. "Citizens of Void: Power-Sharing and Civic Political Action in Lebanon." In *Democratic Transition in the Middle East*, edited by Larbi Sadiki, Heiko Wimmen and Layla al-Zubaidi. London: Routledge.

———. 2021. "Lebanon: A Journey to the End of the State." International Crisis Group. https://www.crisisgroup.org/middle-east-north-africa /east-mediterranean-mena/lebanon/lebanon-journey-end-state.

Wood, James. 2017. "The Other Side of Silence: Rereading W. G. Sebald." *New Yorker*, June 5.

Woodward, Rachel. 2005. "From Military Geography to Militarism's Geographies: Disciplinary Engagements with the Geographies of Militarism and Military Activities." *Progress in Human Geography* 29 (6): 718–40. https:// doi.org/10.1191/0309132505ph579oa.

Wool, Zoë Hamilton. 2015. *After War: The Weight of Life at Walter Reed*. Critical Global Health. Durham, NC: Duke Univ. Press.

World Bank. 2021. "Lebanon Sinking into One of the Most Severe Global Crises Episodes amidst Deliberate Inaction." Press release, June 1. https://www .worldbank.org/en/news/press-release/2021/05/01/lebanon-sinking-into- one-of-the-most-severe-global-crises-episodes.

Wylie, John. 2007. *Landscape: Key Ideas in Geography*. New York: Routledge.

Yeh, Rihan. 2018. *Passing: Two Publics in a Mexican Border City*. Chicago: Univ. of Chicago Press.

Yermiya, Dov. 1983. *My War Diary: Lebanon June 5–July 1982*. Boston: South End Press.

Yildirim, Umut. 2021. "Spaced-Out States: Decolonizing Trauma in a War-Torn Middle Eastern City. *Current Anthropology*. 62 (6): 717–40.

Zani, Leah. 2019. *Bomb Children: Life in the Former Battlefields of Laos*. Durham, NC: Duke Univ. Press.

Žižek, Slavoj, Kenneth Reinhard, and Eric L. Santner. 2013. *The Neighbor: Three Inquiries in Political Theology*. Trios. Chicago: Univ. of Chicago Press.

Zurayk, Rami. *Land and People: A Source on Food and Farming and Rural Society*. Blog. https://landandpeople.blogspot.com.

Index

Founded in 1893,
UNIVERSITY OF CALIFORNIA PRESS
publishes bold, progressive books and journals
on topics in the arts, humanities, social sciences,
and natural sciences—with a focus on social
justice issues—that inspire thought and action
among readers worldwide.

The UC PRESS FOUNDATION
raises funds to uphold the press's vital role
as an independent, nonprofit publisher, and
receives philanthropic support from a wide
range of individuals and institutions—and from
committed readers like you. To learn more, visit
ucpress.edu/supportus.

Milton Keynes UK
Ingram Content Group UK Ltd.
UKHW010118200124
436347UK00005B/368